The

ALSO BY CHARLES N. BILLINGTON
AND FROM MCFARLAND

Comiskey Park's Last World Series:
A History of the 1959 Chicago White Sox (2019)

The 1963 Chicago Bears

*George Halas and the Road
to the NFL Championship*

CHARLES N. BILLINGTON

McFarland & Company, Inc., Publishers
Jefferson, North Carolina

ISBN (print) 978-1-4766-9043-8
ISBN (ebook) 978-1-4766-5095-1

LIBRARY OF CONGRESS AND BRITISH LIBRARY
CATALOGUING DATA ARE AVAILABLE

Library of Congress Control Number 2023050231

Front cover: Chicago Bears fullback Rick Casares (35) finds an opening
against the Green Bay Packers on November 17, 1963,
in a game at Wrigley Field (Vernon J. Biever)

Printed in the United States of America

*McFarland & Company, Inc., Publishers
Box 611, Jefferson, North Carolina 28640
www.mcfarlandpub.com*

Acknowledgments

I am grateful to many for their help and encouragement with this book. I suppose the best individuals to start with would be my coaches and teammates more than 50 years ago at North Park Academy. Thanks to the discipline, guidance and teachings of coaches like Dan McCarrell, Ted Hedstrand, Jim Matson, and Don Young, my experiences in and memories of the Academy's very successful football program have stayed with me to this day.

I am thankful for the encouragement from many of my teammates from those days to take on this project. Others to whom I am grateful, who remember what I have written about with fondness, include Edwin Benn, Noel Barker, Stephen Cole, Jim Doss, Jim Kapsa, the late Dick Loescher, Stephen Norman, Shelly Parker, Al Pavezza, Dr. Joseph Ptasinski (Weber High School Chicago Football champions, 1964), and Phil Schubitz.

Most of the work putting this book together took place during the Covid pandemic, which limited research opportunities. Individuals like Ronnie Bull, Rick Kogan, Don Nelson, and Jon Kendle at the Pro Football Hall of Fame were invaluable resources, as were institutions like the Evanston Public Library, Glencoe Public Library, and Skokie Public Library. Also, this book, like my writing on the 1959 Chicago White Sox, would not have been possible without the invaluable guidance and assistance of Gary Mitchem at McFarland.

Nobody can think about, let alone complete, a book without the consultation, encouragement, patience, and tolerance of their family. I especially want to extend my gratitude to my wife Cynthia, son Matthew, daughter Sarah Norman, and son-in-law Matthew Norman.

Again, my sincere thanks to all.

Table of Contents

Preface

I think my neighborhood gang first got into football in 1956. Chicago was the only city with two teams in both Major League Baseball and the National Football League at that time. The fortunes of the Cubs and Sox that year, in stark contrast to the Bears' and Cardinals' successful start to their season, got us interested in following football. The Cubs were 29 games out of first place by Labor Day and ended the season once again dead last, at 60–94. The Sox were 11 games behind the Yankees by Labor Day and finished the season 12 games off the pace, behind Cleveland and New York, albeit with an admirable record of 85–69. While the baseball and football seasons overlapped, the incredible start Chicago's football teams had put the Cubs and Sox that much further in the rearview mirror. The Cardinals won five of their first six games and would finish the year at 7–5. The Bears won seven of their first eight, finished 9–2–1, and won the Western Division title. It wasn't just our little gang of guys suddenly following football—the whole city was. This was the best start on Comiskey Park's and Wrigley Field's gridirons since 1948.

I remember that fall that Fred's Finer Foods, the little grocer near Pratt and Cicero avenues, suddenly quit carrying Topps baseball cards earlier than usual and instead stocked up on football cards. We young collectors had our fill of Walt Moryn, Bob Rush, Ernie Banks, Minnie Miñoso, Nellie Fox, and Billy Pierce cards, so we eagerly plopped down our five cents—sometimes every day—to get a package of the football cards. How cool it was to be introduced to a whole new genre of sports heroes. The cards of local stars like Rick Casares, Bobby Watkins, Ed Brown, Night Train Lane, and Ollie Matson opened up a whole new fascinating world. Nobody in baseball had a nickname like Night Train Lane (although Puddin' Head Jones came close). Nobody looked as fearsome on a baseball card as Casares or Matson, but, then again, nobody looked at Kansas City's Spook Jacobs' card in dim light either. Of course, every package came with one card that seemingly was in every pack you would buy, no matter where it was purchased. In baseball that year it seemed to be Charlie Silvera; in

1

football, Art Donovan. So all around the neighborhood there were more Silvera and Donovan cards clothes-pinned to the front wheels of the Huffys, Monarchs, and Schwinns than any other professional athletes.

It was not enough to just collect the cards; we had to play our own version of football as well. This was a bit more complicated than pick-up baseball. Two guys, a bat, a rubber ball, and a concrete wall might be all you needed for baseball. Three guys, two newspapers, and a ball to play running bases. More guys than that, you could start thinking about a makeshift baseball game. We did not figure out football the same way. The ball was difficult for latency-aged hands to throw, so catch with a football back then was not as gratifying as with a baseball. Organizing teams to establish who would play what position, the boundaries, and some semblance of rules required more bodies than were usually available, not to mention such planning was impossible for our young minds. So, like kids all over the world, we made up our own game.

The lad that brought the ball would throw it in the air, up for grabs, and anyone could catch it. The person who caught it was then the runner. He would announce who he was—"Crazy Legs Hirsch," maybe "Hopalong Cassady," or maybe Rick Casares or Ollie Matson—then start running, while everyone else would tackle him. Once he was down, we all got up, the ball was tossed in the air, someone would catch it, announce who he was, and proceed to get smeared. This was great fun, until the rare occasions when it wasn't. Someone would get put down too roughly, not appreciate being on the bottom of a pile, or get painfully bumped on the nose, and if the perpetrator didn't acknowledge some level of sorrow, there might be more pushing, maybe eventually some punches. But such instances were soon forgotten, and the game continued. Parents ended the contest with calls for dinnertime; later in the autumn, the five o'clock darkness brought things to a close. Another cause of the game's ending was "You kids are ruining my lawn"; such a call was a 1950s version of the two-minute warning, since our primitive football exploits were much harder on the turf than any baseball activity was.

The Bears continued to play well and went to the championship game in Yankee Stadium to play the Giants. I had an aunt and uncle who had just moved into a new home, and my family's custom was to visit some relatives every Sunday afternoon. My uncle had the game on his black-and-white RCA. When I asked him the score and he rather disgustingly said, "47–7, I'm gonna turn it off," I couldn't believe it; the other team must be from outer space to be beating our heroes by 40 points! It was a hard way to learn that the Bears weren't invincible.

Not invincible, but always fun to watch, especially in Wrigley Field. The very idea of going to the Cubs' park in the cold weather was an event in itself, but to sit that close to the field for a pro football game left a deep impression. As a youngster I remember being there when the Bears dismantled Red Hickey's shotgun offense; trying to keep warm on a snowy November Sunday with Jack Quinlan narrating "Rick Casares Day" before the kickoff; going to a game for the first time with just my buddies by taking the United Motor Coach to the corner of Irving Park and Clark streets to sit in the cheapest seats available, five stories up, underneath the center-field scoreboard; and watching one of the most brutal contests of the pre–Super Bowl era when the Bears' suffocating defense beat the Lions, 3–0. Seeing two losses in the disappointing 1964 season was a huge letdown, but the significance of the experience was still the same. All totaled, the seven Bears games I was lucky enough to attend at Wrigley Field over the years are unforgettable memories, and I have heard the same sentiments from so many others.

In high school I was lucky enough to be a part of one of the most successful high school football programs in the Chicago area, coached by Dan McCarrell, at North Park Academy. We were a proud bunch on September 19, 1965, when the *Chicago Tribune* pointed out that our 15 consecutive victories was the longest winning streak in Chicagoland, and the *Chicago Sun-Times* ranked us 18th in their high school poll for the entire area. My experiences playing quarterback on those teams, which I did as a sophomore on a frosh soph team and as a senior on the varsity team, have stayed with me to this day. The psychological and emotional effects of playing competitive football—being able to concentrate under the duress of potential harm, ignoring the intimidations of the opponents across the line, having but a few seconds to make the right decisions, struggling with your sensorium after a hit—leave profound impressions on young men's minds that do not seem to be forgotten when they age. For some reason the failures on the gridiron are more ruefully remembered than the triumphs.

Our athletic ego ideals at the time were the Bears, who reached their post-war zenith in the early 1960s, with their 1963 championship the climax. I think playing the game at our scholastic level back then gave us a keener appreciation of how good those teams were. The size, strength, and skills demonstrated in the NFL, measured against our own experiences attempting the same endeavors, were rather awe-inspiring. As a try-hard high school quarterback, I could not understand how anyone could have the arm strength of a Rudy Bukich, the keen understanding of the game of a Bill Wade, or the cool, clear-headed approach of the ever-consistent Bart Starr.

The mission of this book is to help the reader remember, and gain a better understanding of, this unique year in NFL history. Younger Bears followers have no appreciation for how influential the Bears franchise was

in this critical NFL era. They think of George Halas as a founding pio-
neer, which he was, but they know little about how autocratic and narrow his thinking could be, or how, tragically, in his later years, the game
went well past him. They have read about Vince Lombardi's "greatness"
but not about what drove him to excel or how much his quest for greatness eventually cost him. Lastly, they have been fed and believe the myth
that the Bears have had poor quarterbacking ever since Sid Luckman hung
his spikes up some 70 years ago, when Bear quarterbacks that followed—
Johnny Lujack, Ed Brown, Bill Wade, Rudy Bukich—had seasons in which
they were the premier field generals in professional football. The 1963 Chicago Bears left a profound impact on a city badly in need of champions.

Introduction

Chicago, Illinois, Sunday, December 29, 1963, 3:10 Central Standard Time, temperature +4, wind 11 mph, wind chill -11. A crowd of more than 45,000 football fans at Wrigley Field are chilled to the bone. Their beloved Chicago Bears are clinging to a 14–10 lead over the hated New York Giants. The sun, blindingly bright all day, has fallen further into the southwestern sky, leaving 70 yards of frozen field in shadow. With only 10 seconds left in the game, the Giants have a fourth down on the Bears' 38-yard line. The worry at this late stage of the game among the Bear faithful makes the weather seem even worse. Just one minute earlier the Giants were 84 yards away, but some daring and desperate wizardry by a bloodied but not yet bowed Y.A. Tittle resulted in pass completions to Aaron Thomas, Hugh McElhenney, and Frank Gifford, which now have everyone in the stadium standing, apprehensively, for the most important 10 seconds the Bears have experienced in 17 years.

Some of the Giants have paid a high price for their efforts. Tough Tom Scott, sitting glumly with his arm in a sling, suffered a broken forearm in the first quarter. Halfback Phil King, no stranger to bitter physical contact with the Bears, has a badly wrenched knee and one ankle twice the size of the other. The official word was that King got hurt on a running play, but many remember his history with the Bears' surly Ed O'Bradovich in the Giants-Bears game the year before. Suffice it to say that on that fateful running play a score was settled. The Chicagoans' treatment of Giants guard Bookie Bolin put the entire New York medical staff on high alert when he was blindsided so hard that he was knocked out cold, rumored to have swallowed his tongue. No Giant, however, had suffered as much at this point as the one taking the snap from center and dropping back one last desperate time—Y.A. Tittle. He had been subjected all afternoon to a merciless beating in near-zero temperatures by relentless Bear defenders. Tittle's left leg was mummified in tape from hip to ankle. He did not feel the two torn ligaments in his knee because of the flood of cortisone and Novocain he received at halftime. Tittle had endured seven direct, brutal hits by Doug Atkins, who

5

toyed with massive Giants offensive tackle Roosevelt Brown all through the game, and Larry Morris, who would be named the game's Most Valuable Player. But at this point in time the pain and intimidation did not matter to Tittle as much as his legacy. Having lost the last two championship games to the Green Bay Packers, Tittle was on a mission to prove he could win the big game. He had known all season that this might be his last chance at an NFL championship, and now it all hinged on this final play. He grimly realized that the next 10 seconds might have more bearing on the rest of his life than all the other moments of his previous 15 years in pro football.

The old bald warrior took the snap from his center Greg Larson and dropped back seven yards, looking to his right. On his blind side the charging Atkins was met by Brown, and the huge Tennessean drove the massive Giant tackle back three yards with a bull rush. Atkins' fury forced Brown to the ground. He pirouetted around him and extended his left arm its full 40 inches as he reached for Tittle's head. In the middle of the Bears' line Johnny Johnson, who had been all over the field on this day, and middle linebacker Bill George ran a stunt with George shooting the gap between Larson and left guard Darrell Dess, while Johnson looped behind George a split second later. Larson, completely unfazed by the stunt, simply dropped back three yards to protect Tittle deeper in the pocket. Dess made quick work of George with a brutal forearm blow to the head, instantly knocking the future Hall of Famer on his back.

On the far-right side of the line, Giant tackle Jack Stroud and the Bears' ill-tempered young firebrand Ed O'Bradovich shared the last steps of their day-long, violent pas-de-deux. The quicker, younger Bear easily pushed Stroud to the inside, but just as he started his sprint toward Tittle the old warrior wound up for his last pass.

The desperate heave headed for the east corner of the south end zone, where Tittle hoped Aaron Thomas would be, but since he had to hurry this last desperate throw Thomas was barely past the 10-yard line when the ball descended into the end zone. The Bears' pass defense, which confounded Tittle all game, knew exactly what was coming. Four Bears—J.C. Caroline, Bennie McRae, Davey Whitsell, and Richie Petitbon—were waiting in the end zone. Petitbon looked up, palms up and elbows together, and gathered the last pass in, as easily as infielders had been handling pop-ups in the same exact spot in the storied stadium on much warmer days for 47 years. The Bears jubilantly celebrated their fifth interception of the game, while 40 yards north of their celebration Tittle despairingly fell to his knees in defeat.

The fate of two helmets told the tale. Tittle, crushed by his failure, tearfully slammed his into the frozen turf. O'Bradovich, ecstatic with his team's accomplishment, jubilantly threw his into the stands. For the first time in 20 years, Wrigley Field crowned a champion.

1

January

He Who Gambles Lives in Shambles

By the end of December 1962 the Chicago Bears had put the pro football world on notice that the next time the leaves started falling they would be a force to be reckoned with. They had an offense that occasionally scored points at will and a defense that was often impenetrable. Offensively the Bears featured a sturdy line: Billy Wade, an intelligent, patient quarterback who had the NFL's highest passer rating in 1961 and third highest in 1962; four speedy receivers, Charley Bivins, Angelo Coia, Billy Martin, and Johnny Morris; the swiftest scat back in the league, Willie Galimore; two bruising fullbacks, the peerless Rick Casares and rugged Joe Marconi; and the two most recent NFL Rookies of the Year, Mike Ditka and Ronnie Bull. Thanks to this excellent cast and an assemblage of capable backups, the Bears could be very dangerous when they had the ball.

Defensively the team was led by Doug Atkins, the most feared player in the NFL. Atkins, capable of high-jumping his 6'8" height, was thought of as unstoppable—when the mood struck him. His opposite number on the other end of the line was the brash young Ed O'Bradovich, whose chippy, truculent style of play quickly became a perfect fit for the Bears' take-no-prisoners defensive demeanor. Defensive tackles Fred Williams and Earl Leggett ably anchored the middle of the line. Behind them was one of the greatest trios of linebackers in NFL history, captain Joe Fortunato, Bill George, and Larry Morris. A quartet of ball hawks, as swift as they were confident, backed up in the secondary: Bennie McRae, Richie Petitbon, Roosevelt Taylor, and Davey Whitsell. Joining this group in George Allen's innovative nickel-back situations was one of the most versatile athletes in Bears history, the veteran J.C. Caroline.

After splitting their first four games in the 1962 season, the Monsters of the Midway won five of their last six contests. They snatched victory from the jaws of defeat with something that had been missing in several seasons of the previous decade, a consistent and intelligently run offense. The team traveled to Baltimore in early November, and Wade's cool-headed play calling and pin-point passing accuracy, coupled with a Bear defense that had blood in its eye, decimated a proud Colts team on their home field, 57–0. Back in Chicago the following week the Bears had the mighty New York Giants right where they wanted them when they reverted to their patented roughhousing and an unnecessary roughness penalty led to a game-winning Giant field goal. Ending the season in Chicago on a chilly mid–December Sunday, the Bears put on one of the greatest defensive exhibitions ever seen in Wrigley Field, beating the Detroit Lions, the "team that beat Green Bay," 3–0. Things looked bright for this team if they could ever conquer their peerless rivals 207 miles to the north, Vince Lombardi's Packers. The 1962 Chicago Bears, with their fifth-ranked defense and fourth-ranked offense, was the most balanced squad Chicago had seen since their division championship in 1956.

The happy post-season vibes came to an abrupt end, however, after New Year's Day. On January 4, 1963, all the Chicago papers carried a story about a gambling investigation the NFL initiated at owner/coach Halas' request.[1] The Papa Bear was concerned about gambling and point-shaving rumors and asked commissioner Pete Rozelle to look into the situation. Two days later Chicago's dailies used even more ink reporting the questioning and lie detector tests given to Rick Casares, the Bears' biggest offensive star of the 1950s and one of the most popular sports figures in the city.[2] The big fullback from Florida was asked a series of pointed questions about his associates, financial situation, friends, and recreational interests.[3] What nobody knew at the time was how big the investigation already was, and how different parts of it simply mirrored the relationship between gambling and pro football that existed since the league's inception four decades before.

The link between betting and professional football since the earliest days was well known and undeniable. The NFL worked hard, however, to keep gambling out of the public spotlight. Over the years the league became comfortable with a huge double standard; gambling was profuse and widespread among the team owners but swiftly addressed and strictly forbidden for the players. The background of many of the NFL's founders bears this out.

Timothy Mara, founder of the New York football Giants, was an established bookmaker at New York racetracks. He started out as a runner for one of Arnold Rothstein's associates, Tony "Chicago" O'Brien, and at one point handled bets totaling $30,000 a day. Legend has it that another gambler gave Mara a marker for the Giants franchise, and when he could not redeem it, Mara owned the team.[4]

Arthur Rooney was a gambler involved in local politics. In 1927 he won $275,000 at Saratoga Springs, New York, and took less than one-tenth of his winnings to pay a franchise fee of $2500 to the NFL to establish a team in Pittsburgh. At the time Rooney anticipated a change in Pittsburgh's blue laws that banned Sunday sports activities. In 1935 Rooney hired Joe Bach as his head coach to repay a gambling debt.[5]

Charles Bidwill was a wealthy Chicago horseracing magnate and minority owner of the Chicago Bears. He sold his interests in the Bears in 1933 after he purchased the cross-town Chicago Cardinals for $50,000. One of Bidwell's associates at the Hawthorne Race Track was Eddie O'Hare.[6] O'Hare was also associated with Al Capone and was implicated in Capone's imprisonment for tax evasion as one of the government's chief informants. A year after Capone was released from Alcatraz O'Hare paid for this association with his life, shot to death while driving his LaSalle coupe at 2613 West Ogden in Chicago's near West Side.[7]

Bert Bell was born into wealth and heavily involved in horseracing when he bought the Frankfort Yellow Jackets in 1933, moved them to his native Philadelphia, and christened them the Eagles.[8] The following year professional gambler and automobile dealer George "Dick" Richards bought the Portsmouth (Ohio) Spartans, moved them to Detroit, and changed the name to the Lions.[9]

Cleveland Browns founder Mickey McBride also owned the Continental Press Wire Service, which emerged after World War II as the most prominent bookmaking service in the country.[10] In 1951 the U.S. Senate Special Committee to Investigate Crime in Interstate Commerce—commonly referred to as the Kefauver Committee—named the Continental Wire Service "public enemy number one." He sold the Browns in 1953 to an investment group that included Saul Silberman, owner of the Tropical Park Track in Miami and two Cleveland area tracks, the Randall Racing Park and the Thistledown Racecourse. Silberman boasted that he bet about two million dollars a year.[11] Silberman's group sold the Browns to a syndicate headed by Arthur Modell in 1961. One of Modell's partners was Morris "Mushy" Wexler, another target of the Kefauver Committee, which referred to Wexler as one of the nation's "leading hoodlums." One of Wexler's holdings was the Empire News Service, a telegraph operation that bookies routinely used for illicit horseracing tips and personnel layoffs in college and pro football.[12]

Bert Bell became the NFL commissioner in 1946, and six years later he convinced Carroll Rosenbloom to take ownership of the Baltimore Colts. Rosenbloom made a fortune during World War II when his family's clothing business got a lucrative government contract to make military uniforms. Rosenbloom was initially reluctant to get involved in pro football, but his hesitancy disappeared when Bell promised him that the NFL would always underwrite any losses that the Colts might incur. Rosenbloom's interests in betting, bookmaking, and casino development were very well known, and he had close ties to Louis Chesler, a business associate and a fellow gambler.[13] Chesler was also a confidant of and consultant to the mob boss Meyer Lansky.[14] Chesler's activities in Caribbean gambling and vice was so widespread that in May 1963 he was investigated by the FBI as part of the Kennedy assassination probe.[15]

In 1958 Rosenbloom and Chesler took over Havana's Hotel Nacional and all its casino operations, entrusting it, along with $200,000 in seed money, to Michael McLaney, a professional gambler. At about the same time Fidel Castro was rising to power, and when McLaney fled the island in fear for his life, he left Rosenbloom and Chesler's funds behind. In a bizarre turn of events McLaney sued Rosenbloom for $4.2 million in a Miami federal court. The testimony in the case revealed a long history of Rosenbloom making bets both on and against his Colts, from 1953 up through the famous 1958 World Championship game against the New York Giants.[16] Rosenbloom was even implicated in the final play selection in overtime at the end of the historic Giants-Colts 1958 championship contest.[17] During the trial federal judge Joseph P. Lieb dismissed McLaney's suit and, incredibly, ordered the records sealed. He claimed that if the depositions became public they would humiliate and embarrass Roosenbloom.[18]

With the number of owners openly involved in gambling from the onset of the NFL, gambling was obviously something the league had to at least minimally *appear* to control very tightly to maintain any level of credibility. With owners so heavily involved in gambling the only way the NFL could maintain this credibility was to exercise extremely tight control over the activities of the coaches, players, and other on-field personnel. Since players obviously influenced the outcome of games more than owners, a double standard evolved, with gambling being a draconian no-no for players and at the same time the raison d'être for some of the owners.

As the NFL commissioner, Bell never thought he could eradicate gambling. He told the *Saturday Evening Post* writer W.C. Heinz, "I don't care if people bet, because people are going to bet, I just want to be sure they stay away from our ballplayers and don't spread rumors."[19] He habitually looked the other way with the owners while he worried about influences and pressures that could be applied directly to the individuals on the field. In spite of Bell's desires, the dark shadows cast by players and gamblers were illuminated by an inquisitive press on several occasions.

During the 1943 NFL season the *Washington Evening Star* writer Walter McCallum wrote about Washington Redskins quarterback Sammy Baugh being involved with gamblers linked to point-shaving schemes.[20]

In December 1946 the biggest gambling scandal in the NFL history up to that time occurred on the eve of the championship game between the New York Giants and the visiting Chicago Bears. At the time Bert Bell had been commissioner for only 10 months, and he was suddenly facing a crisis of major proportions.

On the eve of the championship game, Saturday, December 14, the wire services consistently sent out wildly swinging point spreads, and word got out that Giants quarterback Frankie Filchock and fullback Merle Hapes were interrogated at length, in New York City mayor William O'Dwyer's home, no less, regarding bribes they were offered to throw the game to the Bears' favor. Both players faced lengthy questioning from Commissioner Bell, Giants owner Timothy Mara, Mayor O'Dwyer, and New York City police chief Arthur Wallander. The results of this interrogation would set the tone for how the NFL would handle the gambling threat for many years to come.[21]

The Filchock-Hapes affair revealed that on Tuesday, December 10, 1946, five days before the championship game, one Alvin Paris, a Manhattan novelty store owner, offered both Filchock and Hapes $2,500 each and the profits from a $1,000 bet on the Bears to win if they would "lay down" in the game to ensure a Chicago victory.[22] After vehemently denying the offer even existed, Filchock was cleared of any suspicions and allowed to play. Hapes was not so lucky. Instead of denying the offer, Hapes admitted he was approached but did not report it. Nervous and thinking that full disclosure would help his predicament, Hapes raised additional suspicions when he admitted that he hoped Paris would hire him for off-season employment in the aforementioned novelty shop. Hapes did not play in the Giants' loss to the Bears.[23]

Four months later in April 1947 both players were suspended indefinitely by the NFL. Filchock played three years for the Hamilton Tigers in the Canadian Football League and one game with the Baltimore Colts after his suspension was lifted in 1950. Hapes never played another down of professional football, a stiff consequence for a chance to spend an off-season selling magic tricks and Chinese handcuffs.[24]

For about a dozen years following the Filchock-Hapes affair the NFL effectively kept gambling allegations and rumors involving players out of the public eye while maintaining a hear-no-evil, see-no-evil attitude toward betting by the owners. During his tenure as commissioner Bert Bell frequently received reports directly from bookmakers concerning unusual changes in betting lines.[25] The absence of publicity, however, did not mean that illicit activities involving players were non-existent. In his autobiography *Golden Boy* Paul Hornung points out that Hall of Fame quarterback Bobby Layne was involved in a successful point-shaving scheme in the College All-Star game in front of 70,000 at Chicago's Soldier Field on August 15, 1958. Layne uncharacteristically threw six interceptions and the huge crowd witnessed a rare All-Star win as the Lions lost to the collegians, 35–19.[26] The turn of events in a Chicago Bear-San Francisco 49er matchup in October 1960 was so suspicious it made national news.[27]

During the October 16 contest at Wrigley Field, Rick Casares uncharacteristically fumbled twice, once with dire results. The following week, when the Bears played the Rams in Los Angeles, Casares was offside when quarterback Ed Brown tried to sneak over from the one-yard line. Several plays after this penalty, with the Bears back at the one, Brown called a running play for Casares to dive over the goal line. He ran the wrong way on a play he and Brown had executed hundreds of times in previous games and practices. The very surprised Brown was smothered by Rams defenders before he could score.[28] The 0–4–1 Rams ended up tying the 3–1–1 Bears, 24 to 24. George Halas benched Casares in favor of little-used fullback John Adams three days later.[29]

During the 1962 NFL season there were additional reports of unusual odds changes and suspicious point spread fluctuations involving the Green Bay Packers. On October 7 they beat the Detroit Lions 9–7 and the following week easily routed the Minnesota Vikings 48–21. Nobody questioned the Packers' superiority over these two opponents. However, the Lions contest was much closer than expected and the Viking game surprised the experts by being a blowout. The red flags were raised when one betting establishment won a great deal of money, wagering correctly on the outcome and nature of both games.[30]

These developments and information that George Halas received through his extensive grapevine led to his decision in early January 1963 to ask Commissioner Rozelle to intervene. On January 6 Casares talked about his interrogation.[31] He said he voluntarily took the two lie detector tests and the first one was soon after the October 23, 1960, Bears-Rams tie game. He mentioned that the following year, with rumors of collusion and association with known gamblers swirling around him, he agreed to take a second test, on October 10, 1961. This test was administered by the Keely Laboratory near Grand and Michigan avenues in downtown Chicago. Albert H. Johnson, one of the 16 former FBI agents employed by the NFL, administered the interrogation. Content covered included his association with two well-known gambling individuals, his own gambling, and his financial difficulties.[32]

Casares admitted having a 25 percent stake in a bowling alley in Buffalo Grove, Illinois, an Eisenhower-era suburb northwest of Chicago in an area earmarked for future growth as the suburban beltway expanded with a big assist from the newly-opened Illinois Tollway between Chicago and

Milwaukee.[33] The establishment was almost a half million dollars in debt: $200,000 to the Brunswick Corporation for equipment and $275,000 to William R. Rose & Associates, a Joliet, Illinois, corporation that financed bowling alley construction. At the time Casares was one of the higher paid players in the NFL at $20,000 per year, but his share of the bowling alley debt was almost six times that. He also admitted to gambling in Las Vegas and losing $1,500, but then he curiously added that he "didn't bet any of his NFL salary," as if that would make any difference.[34] Lastly the popular Chicago Bear spoke freely about his fondness of and friendship with two individuals well known in Chicago gambling circles, Abe Samuels and Ray Edward, aka "Zsa Zsa Yitcovich."

Abe Samuels was a high-roller who once admitted to the *Chicago American* that he bet $190,000 a year on pro football games.[35] He was a good friend of Paul Hornung and had been involved with Hornung as far back as Hornung's playing days at Notre Dame.[36] Aside from his gambling interests Samuels owned a lumber yard and a business machine manufacturing concern and he was a minority investor in the Tropicana Gambling Casino in Las Vegas. To the great chagrin of George Halas, the *Chicago American* also revealed that during the offseason over a 12-year period Samuels employed Bears assistant coach Phil Handler as a lumber salesman.[37] A stunned and embarrassed Halas said nothing about this for almost a week. Finally, on January 11, Halas tried to minimize the fallout from the situation, saying that the company had been around for 50 years and that Samuels held a minority interest, but the damage was done.[38]

Samuels also mentioned that he and a four-person betting syndicate used to place sizable wagers with a covert Terre Haute, Indiana, gambling establishment that was broken up by federal agents in 1958. He avoided prosecution by testifying for the government against the principals of the Terre Haute establishment, who were sentenced to time in a federal penitentiary. Samuels lived at 1550 North Lake Shore Drive, a newly constructed, tony high rise at the end of Chicago's Gold Coast neighborhood bordering the LaSalle Drive Parkway and North Avenue Beach, close to Chicago's dining, gambling, nightlife, and red-light hot spots.[39]

Zsa Zsa Yitcovich, a short, balding 58-year-old, was linked to the mobster Albert "Obbie" Frabotta, a shake-down artist who frequented establishments in Chicago's Old Town neighborhood and was considered the boss of organized gambling north of Madison Street.[40]

Interviewed by the *Chicago Sun-Times*' Pulitzer Prize–winning crime reporter Art Petacque, Yitcovich admitted that his real name was Ray Edward and that he got the nickname "Zsa Zsa" from his unique manner of heckling opposing players from the bleachers at Wrigley Field. He vowed to Petacque that he was only a small-time gambler and that the closest he ever came to bookmaking was when he worked as an $80 per week clerk at the Gym Club, an establishment at 221 North LaSalle in the Chicago Loop near the financial district. The Gym Club was the betting headquarters for well-heeled white collar Chicago gamblers that took wagers on sports events other than just horse racing. It closed in 1950 after the Kefauver Senate Committee Investigation.

Zsa Zsa proudly admitted to knowing Casares and two other Bears, pass receiver Harlon Hill and quarterback Ed Brown, both of whom left the Bears in 1961. The interview revealed that Yitcovich was a passing acquaintance of them at best and a groupie at worst. He would encounter them and then pal around at neighborhood taverns around the Diversey-Pine Grove area, not far from their living quarters at the nearby Embassy Hotel.[41]

There were two establishments that drew particular interest during this gambling and corruption investigation, the Talk of the Town in Chicago and the Sahara North Motel in suburban Schiller Park, Illinois. The Talk of the Town was a strip-tease theater at 1159 North Clark Street, a few blocks west of the Gold Coast. It was managed by 47-year-old Dominick "Hunk" Galliano with help from crime syndicate muscleman Leonard "Needles" Gianola. The Sahara North was owned by Manny Skar and was located in the middle of an area bordering Chicago's newer O'Hare Airport, an area that was quickly establishing itself as a center of illicit nightlife and vice in the greater Chicago area.[42] Yitcovich denied any involvement in either establishment.[43]

The following day Casares was dismayed that his lie detector tests were publicized in the local papers, and he agreed to be interviewed by the trusted Chicago sports commentator Jack Brickhouse on WGN television and radio. His teammate Bill George cut short a hunting trip to be with him and provide moral support. Casares said, "I definitely feel I have been betrayed. I took two lie detector tests in strict confidence as a favor to the NFL. It was league business. I am amazed there could be so much total speculation over them. I have been in the company of unsavory characters, and I know many of these people, consciously and unconsciously [sic].

"But as I told Bert Bell I have nothing to be concerned about, so I am not worried."[44]

Bears defensive tackle Earl Leggett mentioned that the Bears might have come under fire for eating at the same restaurant as mob boss Tony Accardo. He pointed out Bears center Mike Pyle was at the restaurant and shook hands with Accardo, who just happened to be his brother Palmer Pyle's father-in-law.[45] However, it was evident that Bear players did not need to engage in such far-flung explanations; the NFL was not just looking at Casares. Two other players and a team owner were also under league scrutiny: Green Bay's Paul Hornung, Detroit's Alex Karras, and Baltimore Colts owner Carroll Rosenbloom. At the same time, the McClellan Committee in Washington disclosed its months-long interest in the San Francisco 49ers. This climate lent itself to casting a shadow on many sporting events that in reality were above any suspicion.

Widely respected sports columnist Al Munroe referenced the Rose Bowl between USC and point spread was four points. He used this to illustrate the NFL's frustration with any hints of scandal and suggested that George Halas should look back four decades ago to see what happened to White Sox owner Charles Comiskey because of his paranoia about individuals on his payroll.[46]

Suspicions about the Detroit Lions soon followed. The *Detroit News* said the FBI was questioning a man who was a partner in the Lindell Bar with star Lions defensive tackle Alex Karras. The questioning involved the entire team and gambling, and as a result of this the team's front office wanted Karras to divest himself of any interest in the establishment.[47] In Los Angeles Paul Hornung was being hounded by the press. Suspicious reporters wanted to know if he had taken lie detector tests, since Abe Samuels mentioned that he had been friends with Hornung for more than 10 years. Baltimore owner Carroll Rosenbloom, no stranger to the gambling tables or the underworld, also found himself under the NFL's microscope. Illicit activities by owners, which the NFL successfully kept under wraps and out of the public eye all these many years, were now rearing their ugly heads, casting a dark shadow of the integrity of the entire league.

The Rosenbloom issues presented vexing problems for Rozelle that were not going to conveniently disappear. Desperate for a stable franchise in Baltimore, Bert Bell virtually guaranteed Rosenbloom that he would never lose money if he took over the Colts as a civic duty, with the implication that the NFL would underwrite the operation if needed.[48] Rozelle's very existence as commissioner may not have ever occurred if he hadn't been sponsored and vigorously promoted by Rosenbloom during the league's selection process. Yet there were at least four affidavits filed in federal court stating that not only did Rosenbloom routinely bet on NFL games but also that on at least one occasion he bet against his own team, ordering that key players be removed from the Colts' roster in a meaningless game against San Francisco.[49]

Ironically the 49ers were implicated at this same time. The *San Francisco Examiner* and several other West Coast papers had front page stories about an investigation into whether three players on the team associated with gamblers had arranged to shave points. The game in question was the 1962 season opener, played in San Francisco, against the Chicago Bears. As the contest began the 49ers were favored by six points, yet the Bears sacked 49er quarterback John Brodie seven times and intercepted him twice for a lop-sided 30–14 Chicago victory. Senator John McClelland confirmed that an investigator on his staff was in San Francisco investigating but said little else about it. Predictably, the 49ers organization was outraged about the accusation. Head coach Red Hickey said, "I haven't been contacted by anyone else in the 49er organization. There is nothing to lead me to believe the 49ers are under investigation. I have complete faith in my players. These boys are high-class men. There isn't one who would risk ruining his life for anything like this. Nearly all are married and have families."[50]

Two key members of the offense, Brodie and All-Pro offensive tackle Bob St. Clair, added their own choice words. St. Clair, without commenting on how his offensive line managed to give up seven sacks in one game, said, "It's impossible to shave points in a pro football game. Anyone who played realizes how ridiculous this is. This isn't a one-man deal like boxing. The quarterback, the guy who handles the ball is the only man who'd have a chance, and it would be so obvious to the coaches and everyone else that he'd be out of the game fast."[51] Brodie was much more guarded in his response to the accusation. It was unclear if he had heard what St. Clair had said before he uttered his own comments: "No one has asked me anything. I haven't heard about any investigation. I try to mind my own store and it's clean."[52]

Also at this time the most revered individual in the sport offered his thoughts on the fomenting crisis. Nationally syndicated columnist Red Smith interviewed Vince Lombardi for his thoughts on the entire situation. Lombardi offered that he had a visit the other day from two FBI men. "They told me they are keeping a closer watch on pro sports than ever before. The Attorney General reads every report that comes in on pro sports and you all know what that means. You have all had this explained before, but I will explain it again. There are hundreds of thousands of dollars bet on pro football. ... [E]veryone is being watched. They gave me the names of two restaurants in Chicago that are owned by hoodlums. ... I've already told you what places are off-limits in Green Bay. If you are found in one of those places you won't be fined. You'll be off our ball club and out of pro football."[53]

To reinforce his rigidity in governing the conduct of his players, Lombardi went on to point out that on Saturday nights team members are expected to be in by 11:00 p.m. and that they face a $500 fine for being out after curfew at any time. Lombardi also instituted a fine of $10 per minute for being late for a practice or a meeting and a mandatory $150 fine for getting caught standing up in a bar or tavern. He said nothing about the suspicions NFL officials had about Hornung or any of his other players.[54]

News out of Detroit on January 9, 1963, was more serious than anything that previously uncovered. Police commissioner George Edwards reported that his officers had observed Detroit Lions players in the company of "known hoodlums" and said he notified the Lions 10 days earlier regarding several players' associations with notorious gamblers.[55] The gamblers were Vito and Anthony Gialcone, veterans of the Detroit underworld, whose roots went back to the days of Detroit's notorious Purple Gang and the Livacoli Squad. Two venues were mentioned as the meeting sites for underworld figures and Lions players, the Grecian Gardens and the Lindell A.C. (for "Athletic Club") Cocktail Lounge.[56] While the NFL was sensitive about initiating a witch hunt based on guilt by association, the media coverage regarding ethics and vice in professional football was becoming a public relations nightmare, and one Lions star in particular was about to make it even worse.[57] The Lindell Lounge was about to become the most famous drinking establishment in the United States since one of its managing partners was Alex Karras.[58]

Karras, one of the biggest athletic heroes in Detroit history, grew up in Gary, Indiana. He was the son of a physician who was an unselfish advocate for healthcare, often not charging patients and their families for his medical services.[59] Karras himself was articulate, engaging, very intelligent, and a great athlete. He starred at all sports in high school, where, legend has it, he was romantically involved with his English teacher.[60] Upon graduation he received a full scholarship to play football at the University of Iowa, where he was a consensus All-American and won the Outland Trophy, awarded annually to the best lineman in college football. The Lions took him in the first round of the 1958 NFL draft. He started eight of the Lions' 12 games his first year and admitted to betting on six of them.[61] In 1962 he bet $100 on his own team to beat Green Bay and another $100 on the Packers to defeat the New York Giants in the championship contest. He won both bets.[62]

Karras' partners at the Lindell were Jim and John Butsicaris, two individuals with FBI files linking them to gamblers and bookmakers.[63] Lions general manager Edwin Anderson exerted pressure on Karras to sell his interest in the bar, saying that he did not like the idea of a player owning part of a bar where he might run into undesirable individuals. Karras, knowing his value to the team, shot back that he would not give up his $45,000 investment in the tavern without a fight. Butsicaris told the *Detroit News* that FBI agents visited him at the Lindell earlier in the month and nonchalantly stated "they wanted to talk about the Lions and wanted to talk about gambling."[64] The brazen, candid information given so freely took the NFL establishment aback.

Karras' next move went even further. The following week he appeared on CBS television's *David Brinkley's Journal* and coolly told Brinkley, while on camera with a nationwide audience in full view, that he routinely bet on many NFL games.[65] An incensed Rozelle summoned him and Lions coach George Wilson to a conference at NFL headquarters in New York City scheduled for January 17. Seething that Karras could be so nonchalant about such damaging behavior, Rozelle had heard enough.[66] Nothing came of Rozelle's discussion with Wilson, but he confronted Karras about his flagrant violation of established gambling policies and told him not to leave town. The next day Rozelle interviewed Karras again, this time with his teammate, the linebacker Wayne Walker. When Rozelle was through with them he issued no statement and declared that both players were "unavailable for comment."[67]

There was *some* good news in the Bears camp during January. The *Chicago Tribune* reported that Halas' son Mugs, the Bears' team treasurer, became engaged to marry Therese Leona Martin of Decatur, Illinois.[68] And on January 28 the Bears signed their third pick in the December 3, 1962, rookie draft: lineman Steve Barnett from Oregon. Barnett was second team Associated Press All-American and first team AFCA All-American, playing both sides of the ball and averaging 40 minutes per game. Oregon coach Len Casanova said Barnett was the best blocker he ever coached; the Bears projected him as an offensive tackle behind Herman Lee.[69]

Another issue dear to Halas' heart was also a source of very good news. He could look back toward the end of 1962 and realize that, thanks largely to the foresight and modern thinking of the NFL's young commissioner, he was able to practically meet the entire team's payroll without selling a ticket. The television contract Rozelle arranged with national television networks for the 1962 season was $4.65 million, and the contract stipulated the same amount through 1964.[70] This meant that each of the 14 NFL teams received a little over $330,000 per annum for national broadcasting rights, excluding whatever additional revenue they might receive through outlets like radio or closed circuit/theater television. This windfall was a huge increase in television revenue. Prior to this time the Green Bay Packers had the smallest television contract, $75,000, and the New York Giants had the largest, $175,000.[71] The new agreement meant the team with the most lucrative TV broadcasting agreement saw TV revenue increase almost 90 percent and the team with the smallest more than 300 percent. Suddenly the "old guard," veteran owners like Halas, Mara, and Rooney—who were initially very skeptical about having such a young, inexperienced commissioner—were feeling much better about it. Halas could only wonder at his good fortune contentedly, thinking that just nine seasons ago the sales of the game programs was the only thing that year that kept him out of the red.[72]

Commissioner Pete Rozelle closed out the month with a private summit with NFL executives about the gambling crisis. It was a closed door, no press coverage affair limited to one representative from each NFL team. The purpose was to get each team on board with the league office's handling of the situation and ensure that no comments, discussion, or rumors would be made to the press or the public.[73]

2

February and March

*Rozelle Takes His Time
and Papa Bear's Youth Movement*

During February 1963 the gambling investigations continued at an intense pace but very little was revealed to the press or the public. The McClellan Committee released a statement early in the month mentioning how difficult it was to uproot information but that their work would continue. The FBI reported similar difficulties separating fact from fiction. The NFL headquarters had even less to disclose. Rozelle did not announce the final results of the league's investigation and gave no indication when he would do so.[1] The NFL's silence on the issues left Paul Hornung and Alex Karras to experience the most anxious month of their lives with their livelihood in doubt and powerless to plan any part of their future.[2]

Halas himself had nothing more to say about it and was perfectly content to let others do the legwork to settle the whole gambling mess; he was more concerned with on-field issues. The source of his dismay was the great success of the Green Bay Packers. While not dissatisfied with his legion's 9–5 record in 1962, it ate him up to realize that two of those losses were to Green Bay, and in those games his men were outscored 87–14. It hurt when he realized the last time he defeated Vince Lombardi was two and a half years ago, September 25, 1960, and that the Bears won on a measly field goal, 9–6.

Noticing the team's improvement in the last two months of the season, winning five of their last six games with the only loss by two points to a division champion New York Giants team—in a game in which Bill Wade outplayed Y.A. Tittle and the Bears outgained the Giants—he decided to put more responsibility on the young man who played such a big part in this success. Doing so, however, also meant snubbing a trusted associate and close friend of more than 25 years.

Halas called a press conference February 12 and announced the promotion of 41-year-old George Allen to the position of chief defensive coach, replacing Bear legend Clark Shaughnessy.[3] Allen actually functioned in this role the last three games of the season after Shaughnessy left the team unannounced November 29 and officially resigned December 3, 1962. Shaughnessy and Allen were at odds over several issues, particularly pass defense philosophy. Since Halas favored Allen's zone defense schemes over Shaughnessy's stubborn man-to-man or nothing approach, it was out with the old and in with the new.

"Only 13 touchdown passes were completed against us this year, compared to 28 in 1961," Halas told the press. "We also had the lowest percentage of completions in the league—only 46.8—and our defensive backs led the league in returning interceptions, running them back 468 yards."[4]

Shaughnessy's downfall was his inability to adjust to modern thinking about how to stifle an opponent's passing game. Allen's pass defense schemes included more than just the defensive backs trying to keep up with fleet receivers. He designed schemes where defensive ends sometimes took responsibility in the flat, linebackers dropped back into designated areas of the field, and defensive backs patrolled specific areas, playing for the ball, instead of directly covering just one receiver. The scheme resembled the hugely successful defensive tactics of the Giants and the Packers, the participants in the two most recent NFL championship games and two opponents the Bears were 1–6 against since the beginning of 1960. Allen, responsible for the Bears' success in the recent NFL drafts, was also named by Halas to head up all the scouting and player personnel matters.[5]

George Allen was a bright, ambitious individual and very much a self-made man. He was born in the affluent Grosse Pointe Woods district of Detroit but not born into wealth; his father was a privately employed chauffeur.[6] In high school he distinguished himself with his athletic accomplishments, lettering in football, track, and basketball. After graduation in 1940 he attended Michigan's Alma College, spent time at Marquette University in a naval training program, and got his bachelor of science in education at what was to become Eastern Michigan University. After getting a master's degree in physical education from the University of Michigan in 1947 he took the head coaching position at Morningside College in Sioux City, Iowa, in 1948. In three seasons at Morningside Allen's record was an admirable 16–11–2.[7]

The following year, on the strength of his efforts at Morningside, Allen was hired to head the football program at Whittier College in Whittier, California. Allen coached football and baseball at Whittier, compiling a record of 33–22–5 over six seasons. By 1956 he had nine seasons of college head coaching experience with very close to a .600 winning percentage, which drew the attention of Los Angeles Rams head coach Sid Gillman.

Gillman hired Allen for the 1957 season but fired him fired him after the last game, and Allen was out of football by December 1957.

To make ends meet Allen opened a car wash in Los Angeles which failed.[8] He took a sales job with Voit Sporting Goods, knowing that his travels would be good exposure in the football world, and met Bears assistant coach Chuck Mather during training camp at St. Joseph College in Rensselaer, Indiana, in 1958. The purpose of his visit was to sell the Bears weighted footballs, but Allen made a point of telling Mather that as an ex-Rams assistant coach he would love to talk George Halas. Not only did Halas nix the idea of weighted balls but he also refused to talk to him. When Allen got back to California he thanked Mather for his efforts and told him how lucky he was to still be involved in pro football.[9]

The 1958 NFL season started and as luck would have it the Bears had four games in one month against the Rams and the 49ers. Mather reminded Halas that since Allen was only a year removed from the Rams' coaching circle he could be a big help to the Bears. Halas reluctantly agreed, brought Allen in, and was very impressed with his work. His scouting report on the Rams was so thorough that the Bears won, getting a key interception off an audible that Allen informed them about.[10] Halas, appreciative but scared of what Rozelle's office would say about the Allen chicanery, told him that that was enough and sent him back to California. Mather would not give up, however, and worked on the owner/coach on Allen's behalf some more.

Just before that season started Frank Korch, a Halas employee since 1933, died on the airplane flying the team home from an exhibition game played in Dallas against the Detroit Lions. Korch was a jack-of-all-trades kind of guy for Halas, and among his many duties was coordinating the scouting reports and preparing the team for the annual draft. By mid-season there was still no talk of a replacement for Korch, and Mather brought up Allen's name again.

He reminded Halas that Allen, in his current sales position, probably knew a lot about the talented college players and could benefit the team with personnel matters. Halas finally relented, flew Allen back to Chicago at the team's expense, and hired him.[11]

For the first few years Allen lived at the YMCA Apartments at Dearborn and Chicago avenues in Chicago's Water Tower district off Michigan Avenue.[12] His family stayed in California during that period, joining him later, and the Allens eventually settled in northern suburban Deerfield, Illinois. Initially Halas only entrusted him with developing schemes and evaluating player personnel, not allowing him to do any coaching. Allen streamlined the defenses, which created strife between him and Shaughnessy.[13] Allen's achievements in player procurement and scouting, however, proved to the entire franchise that his was a very bright young football mind making huge contributions. He remembered Bill Wade from his Rams days and convinced Halas to stop playing musical chairs with the "three B's" (Blanda, Brown, and Bratkowski) and have the proven Wade put some stability in the quarterback position. Allen got Joe Marconi, Larry Morris, and Davey Whitsell from other teams. In 1960 he drafted three collegians who instantly played important roles: Charley Bivins, Angelo Coia, and Bo Farrington. The following year he drafted Ditka, Mike Pyle, Bill Brown, and two he could not sign but who went on to have huge careers in the rival AFL, Ernie Ladd and Keith Lincoln. In 1962 Ronnie Bull, Jim Cadile, Bennie McRae, and Ed O'Bradovich—who was chosen in the seventh round—were Allen's selections. Allen's picking Ditka and Bull made him only the third NFL executive in history to have drafted consecutive Rookies of the Year.[14]

Allen also proved to be very forward-thinking and open minded about integration. Halas had a strict preference for his roster's racial makeup: no more than seven Black players.[15] In 1961 defensive back Roosevelt Taylor was a free agent signee whom Allen scouted at Grambling. He was on the bubble to make the roster, and Halas much preferred Bobby Bethune, a white defensive back from Mississippi State. While it was clear Taylor was the superior athlete, Halas did not want to change his self-imposed racial mix. Allen much preferred Taylor and told him on the sly to pull out all the stops in the last exhibition game. Taylor flashed his speed all over the field, including a long runback on a punt return, and Halas had no choice but to keep him, quota or not.[16]

Of course, handling the Bears' personnel matters also meant that occasionally Allen would be required to get caught up in Halas' dirty work. Mike Ditka bitterly reminisced about his contract signing experiences after he was drafted in 1961. The contract wars between the NFL and the upstart AFL were just beginning to warm up at that time, and Houston Oilers owner Bud Adams offered Ditka a whopping $50,000 for two years. Halas ordered Allen to sign him but offered Ditka half of that annual amount for only one year—$12,500. Allen misled Ditka by telling him that the sum was the biggest offer the Bears made since the days of Red Grange.[17]

Promoting George Allen meant that Halas would part with a trusted advisor and friend of almost 30 years, Clark Shaughnessy. Shaughnessy was a football legend who attained national prominence in 1932, perhaps gaining that recognition as much for who he replaced as what he had accomplished. A native of St. Cloud, Minnesota, Shaughnessy was a gridiron star at the University of Minnesota, where he briefly coached after graduation. After that he traveled south and coached at Tulane, and then he took the head coaching position at Loyola University of the South. He stayed at Loyola for 10 years, earning a princely $17,500 per annum.[18]

Shaughnessy was thrust into the spotlight when Robert Maynard Hutchins of the University of Chicago thought that coaching legend Amos Alonzo Stagg, at age 70, was too old to effectively run the program.[19] He hired Shaughnessy to take his place. Shaughnessy was given a tenured position as a physical education professor at $7,500 per year. Hutchins did not reveal that over a period of years he planned to raise the facility's academic standards and de-emphasize athletics. After Heisman Trophy winner Jay Berwanger graduated in 1935 Shaughnessy did not have much to work with, and by 1939 Hutchins had ended football at the University of Chicago entirely.[20]

While at the University of Chicago Shaughnessy struck up a friendship with Halas. They both became intrigued with Ralph Jones' T formation offense, and in 1937 Halas started paying Shaughnessy $2,000 a year to be a "consultant," doing scouting reports and offensive schemes.[21] After the football program ended in Hyde Park Shaughnessy could have stayed on in his physical education post but instead took the head football coaching position at Stanford.

At Stanford Shaughnessy totally committed to the T formation offense. He liked to study infantry strategies and apply the same tactics to his gridiron schemes. To his later regret he became a big admirer of the tactics of German general Heinz Guderian, who spearheaded the invasion of Poland and soon after marched through France.[22] All the while he kept in contact with Halas, working up new concepts, evaluating players, and sharing strategies. The two of them, along with Jones, wrote a widely distributed manuscript which became familiar to coaches through the land, *The Modern "T" Formation with Man-in-Motion*.[23] Fearing Stanford might follow the University of Chicago's lead and drop football after World War II, Shaughnessy left Stanford for Maryland, but he left before the war's end to coach at Pittsburgh and be an advisor to the Washington Redskins.[24] Dissatisfied with this decision he returned to Maryland, leaving in 1948 to join the Los Angeles Rams.

The same issues that led to Shaughnessy's departure from the Bears first surfaced in Los Angeles. While the Rams won the Western Division championship in 1949 there were grumblings that Shaughnessy experimented too much and that his playbook contained too much material for the players to comprehend and execute.[25] He left the Rams and in 1951 became a "technical advisor" to Halas, working full-time for the Bears. The only problem was the Bears already had a legendary defensive coordinator, who was very miffed at Shaughnessy's appearance—Hunk Anderson.

Like Shaughnessy, Anderson was a football legend whose association with Halas went back decades. He was one of the original Chicago Bears in the 1920s. When Knute Rockne died in the Kansas airplane crash, Anderson became head coach at Notre Dame. During World War II, when Halas was serving in the U.S. Army, Anderson very successfully coached the Bears.

The situation between the two football legends led to divisiveness within the franchise. Business manager Rudy Custer claimed that Shaughnessy was much smarter than all of Halas' other assistants, which led to a great deal of jealousy.[26] Linebacker Bill George credited Shaughnessy with developing the middle linebacker position and shaping him into a premiere middle linebacker. Shaughnessy's scouting brought Harlon Hill, arguably the most impactful pass catcher in Bear history, from tiny Florence State Teachers College to NFL greatness.[27]

Others in the organization felt differently. Anderson amassed a 23–11–2 record as an NFL head coach, led the Bears to an undefeated season in 1942, and won the NFL championship in 1943. Shaughnessy's perseverative obsession with football schemes led to an unwieldly five-inch playbook by the mid–1950s.[28] Some felt his exaggerated reputation revealed itself in the 1956 NFL title game, when the Giants toyed with the Bear defense in a 47-7 wipeout. George Connor, the Bears' Hall of Fame lineman from the post–World War II era, thought Shaughnessy was a fraud, taking credit for others' work.[29] He cited an important contest against the 49ers on October 22, 1961, as a perfect example.

On that date head coach Red Hickey brought a team into Wrigley Field that was 4–1 and had outscored its opponents 157–27 in the four victories. Hickey had perfected the shotgun offense, and with John Brodie, R.C. Owens, and Monty Stickles, opponents could not figure out a way to stop them. George Connor and Bill George analyzed what few weak links the 49ers offense had and focused on them, one of the key tactics being the harassing of 49ers center Frank Morze. The result was an easy Bear victory, for which Shaughnessy took all the credit, irritating Connor and George no end.[30] Knowledge of Shaughnessy's flaws was widespread. *Chicago Sun-Times* reporter Bill Gleason recalled that Vince Lombardi said "Shaughnessy's defenses are so complicated and confusing that they are impossible to execute, even if they are understood."[31]

Also, during Shaughnessy's final period of coaching the defense, he was extremely possessive of his personnel and sometimes forbid them from even talking to Halas. The old coach had finally had enough and started relying on trusted ex-Bear Jim Dooley and Allen to work out more effective, up-to-date defensive schemes. Shaughnessy saw the handwriting on the wall and left the team, unannounced, in late November 1962, with three games left on the schedule. It took four months for Halas and his longtime cohort and companion to make amends. Halas, feeling bad about the situation, put Shaughnessy back on the payroll, paying him $1,000 per game to scout every NFL contest in Los Angeles.[32] Ironically, this responsibility and compensation greatly resembled how Shaughnessy's replacement—George Allen—got his start with the Bears four years before.

Wary of having Allen go it alone, Halas quickly tabbed longtime acquaintance Jumbo Joe Stydahar as the defensive line coach.[33] "Opposing runners averaged 4.7 yards per play against us last fall," he explained. "We are confident he can help us. Nobody ever ran very far against Joe."[34] Indeed, Stydahar's credentials were quite impeccable. He grew up in Kaylor, Pennsylvania, near Altoona, 80 miles west of the Pittsburgh area, and he starred for West Virginia University in football and basketball. Stydahar was the first lineman ever drafted in the NFL, taken in the first round by the Bears in the first ever NFL draft in 1936. He was a second team All-Pro his first year and a first team All-Pro four consecutive years, 1937–1940. He won NFL championships with the Bears in 1940, 1941, and 1946 and won another championship as head coach of the Los Angeles Rams in 1951. Internal issues hastened his departure from the Rams—in spite of the championship—and he left for Green Bay to finish out the 1952 season as a scout and part-time assistant. The Chicago Cardinals hired him in January 1953 as the head coach. Stydahar experienced little success and much frustration; their futility on the field exasperated him so much that before one game in 1953 he threatened to withhold all paychecks if they did not win the following Sunday.[35] In spite of a multi-year contract he was fired by Walter Wolfner in 1954 after a loss to the cross-town Bears, the Cardinals' most hated rival. After leaving the Cardinals Stydahar next got involved with a packing business, Starr Container Corporation, and settled his family in northern suburban Glencoe, Illinois.[36]

The attention given to pro football over these first months of 1963, well after the season's ending, was picked up by the media. The amount of ink given to a Bears coaching change, the huge audience the championship game between Green Bay and New York had, the unfolding of the gambling peril, and the new, lucrative national television contract seemed to point to a new "dominant" pastime in the country. Ollie Kuechle, sports editor of the *Milwaukee Journal*, presented the idea that football had surpassed baseball as the national pastime.[37] The slow pace of action in baseball compared to football, the increase in gate receipts in both the college and the pro game, the dwindling interest in minor league baseball, *Time Magazine*'s tribute to Vince Lombardi, and a declaration that football was the new "sport of the 1960's" all indicated that the gridiron had replaced the diamond.[38] Football advocates ignored some of this and simply cited attendance statistics. Pro football averaged 78 percent capacity per game in 1962 and the Big Ten averaged 82 percent, while major league baseball barely averaged 32 percent. Ed Short, general manager of the White Sox, countered this by saying in 1959 the White Sox and Dodgers drew more than 92,000 on a Sunday, Monday, and Tuesday in the World Series and doubted that if the Packers played the Giants three days in a row the interest would be anywhere near that big.[39] There was also a much higher number of people—children in Little League, teens in baseball programs, adults in softball leagues—playing baseball recreationally than football.[40] Whether baseball was falling by the wayside or not, no one could deny that the growth of the National Football League seemed boundless, both in dollars and human interest.

If the amount of media revenue was to be the yardstick for measuring whether baseball was still dominant with the public, the grand old pastime still seemed to have the upper hand after the major leagues disclosed their expected television revenue for the 1963 season. Under the new agreement the 20 baseball teams would receive $14 million, an average of $700,000 per team, roughly twice the revenue that the NFL's 14 teams would receive. Unlike the NFL, which divided the revenue evenly, each baseball team worked out its own individual contract. These contracts ranged from $300,000 (Washington Senators) to $1,200,000 (New York Yankees).[41]

The revenue disparity between Chicago's two teams was glaring. The White Sox were to receive $800,000 for 56 games, just over $14,000 per contest, and the Cubs' take was $500,000 for 86 games, about $5,800 per contest. Marketing analysts debated what was more advantageous, more broadcast exposure (the Cubs) or more revenue with less exposure (the White Sox). However, neither team could come close to the enviable revenue-per-game amount NFL teams like the Bears would get. Their take of the national television revenue for seven broadcasts was about $330,000, more than $47,000 per contest. The disparity in per-game revenue reinforced the NFL's claim that the viewing public valued pro football over baseball. Not only that, but the television rights for the end-of-season NFL championship game was still being negotiated. The league's expectation was that the contract would be significantly higher than the $615,000 NBC television paid to broadcast each of the last two championship matchups.

In actuality the total television revenue for baseball was actually significantly more than the stated $14 million. Twelve teams would get an additional one million each for their weekend "Game of the Week" appearances, and the league office was to receive $4.25 million for the All-Star game and the World Series. The amount was the same whether the Series lasted the minimum four games or the maximum seven.[42]

While the NFL's corporate office on Park Avenue remained mysteriously silent on the issue of gambling, a serious allegation of corruption by on-field personnel at the college level received national attention. The *Saturday Evening Post*, whose weekly circulation was more than two million, printed "The Story of a College Football Fix" in their March 23, 1963, edition.[43] The article claimed that Georgia's famed athletic director Wally Butts and Alabama football coach Bear Bryant colluded to influence the outcome of the Georgia-Alabama gridiron matchup the previous autumn. The implication was that Butts gave Bryant information about Georgia's offensive plays, updates on its players, and also the defensive schemes in a telephone conversation eight days before Alabama romped to a 35–0 victory. The informant for the article was an Atlanta insurance salesman, George Burnett, who claimed to overhear the entire conversation. He claimed that "an impulsive desire to let the truth be known" convinced him to talk to the *Post*.[44]

Bryant and Butts vehemently denied the charge and asked the magazine for a printed retraction. Georgia governor Carl Sanders ordered an investigation, and the state's attorney general, Eugene Cook, launched a formal investigation. Bryant went on local television in Alabama and explained that he had passed a lie detector test. He pointed out that he was cleared of any suspicion of wrongdoing by University of Alabama president Dr. Frank Rose and also by the commissioner of the Southeastern Conference, Bernie Moore.[45] Butts resigned his position as Georgia's athletic director, ending a 25-year coaching and administrative career.[46]

Both individuals stated their intention to sue the magazine for libel.[47]

Bears fans learned some troubling news when the local Chicago papers updated the situation with perennial All-Pro Bill George. If George Allen's defense was going to duplicate its 1962 effectiveness in the upcoming season the availability and contribution of George would be essential. George was spending the off-season as the Midwestern advertising manager for *Pro Football Illustrated* magazine and still healing up from the serious injuries he suffered in an automobile accident before the 1962 season started.[48] He suffered neck damage between the fifth and sixth vertebrae which impaired the functioning of his arm and shoulder.[49] Although he started 13 of the 14 games in '62, the injury greatly limited his effectiveness the entire season.[50]

Even though George would be 34 during the upcoming season, many saw him as the heart of the Bear defense, since 1963 would be his 12th year with the team.

George was the Bears' second-round draft choice in 1951, after a stellar career as a middle guard at Wake Forest, where he also was a heavyweight wrestling champion. With his agility, huge shoulders, long arms, and quick feet, it soon became apparent that he could do more than just clog the middle of the defensive line.[51] The Waynesburg, Pennsylvania, native started every game in 1952 and had the good fortune of being teamed with and tutored by two future Hall of Famers, Bulldog Turner and George Connor. Nineteen fifty-two was Turner's last season, but George played with Connor through 1955. When George broke into the NFL Clark Shaughnessy offered this glowing evaluation: "He is a rare physical specimen both from the standpoint of power and agility. He is absolutely fearless on the field. He has a brilliant mind, an ability to size up a situation quickly and react to it, and also the ability to retain the complicated details of his job."[52] George's abilities meshed with Shaughnessy's defensive schemes and it quickly became apparent that with his speed and ability he could do just about anything on the field.

Connor, George, and Turner complemented each other very well, and Connor quickly picked up the unique mix of George's abilities. The two of them worked out schemes in which George in essence became the first middle linebacker in football. Sometimes he would line up directly over center and rush; on other occasions he would line up over center and drop back in coverage. Other times George would start off the line, delay a count, and then fill a gap or rush the passer. To make it even harder on the opposing quarterback he might line up well off the line of scrimmage and cover short or medium depth passes. George established himself as the "quarterback" of the Bears' defense, with his athletic versatility and his skill at explaining and understanding Shaughnessy's often maddingly confusing defensive schemes.[53] While the division champion 1956 Bears featured many outstanding players—Doug Atkins, Ed Brown, Rick Casares, J.C. Caroline, Joe Fortunato, Harlan Hill, Stan Jones, and Fred Williams—George was the unquestioned leader of the team, looked up to by fellow players and coaches alike.[54] George's gridiron accomplishments landed him on the cover of *Sport Magazine*'s 1957 pro football preview issue, along with two teammates, Casares and Jones.

Aside from his high football I.Q., another trait that separated George from other players was his ferocity and intensity. He was not above crossing the line on occasion, as the Chicago Cardinals' Carl Brettschneider learned in the huge Bears-Cardinals brawl December 9, 1956, at Wrigley Field. George instantly neutralized the Cardinal linebacker's truculence when he cold-cocked him with a single knockout punch.[55] Bears wide receiver Johnny Morris, who played 10 years in the NFL, declared George to be the most intense player he ever saw.[56] Packer Hall of Famer Paul Hornung, who faced George in 18 games, singled George out as one of the hardest hitters he ever faced.[57] George had his own compliment for Hornung, remembering him as the best roommate he ever had. This impression came from his experiences at the Wilshire Hotel in Los Angeles during a Pro Bowl weekend. George said that what made Hornung so great was his prolonged absence; he was always out running the infamous L.A. nightclub circuit with his buddy Rick Casares.[58]

Toward the end of March the Bears schedule for 1963 came out. Using the Chicago Cubs' Wrigley Field as their home meant every season started with a string of games on the road.

Games in Green Bay, Minnesota, and Detroit started the season, before the Bears played at home October 6 against Baltimore.[59] The last Cub home game that year was September 25; the right field portable bleachers had to be constructed, and the grounds crew always gave the field a minimum of two weeks' rest before football started. As they had in 10 of the last 11 seasons Halas arranged for a two-week road trip for the Los Angeles and San Francisco games. Halas, always looking to save a nickel where he could, would rather save the $15,000 it cost to transport the team from Chicago to the West Coast than worry about the hardship on the players being away for 16 days. The players would reluctantly check in at an inn near Crestline, California, for the week between the 49ers and Rams games.[60] Based on the results of the 1962 season, the last five games in 1963 seemed critical, and they looked difficult: the Packers at Wrigley, the Steelers away during Thanksgiving weekend, then the Vikings, 49ers, and Lions at Wrigley to end the year. These five opponents amassed a 41–28 record in 1962; this end of the schedule would make or break the season. The NFL released its exhibition season schedule shortly thereafter, with the highlight for the Bears scheduled for September 7. On that date, eight days before the critical start of the season in Green Bay, the Bears would go to New Orleans and play the Baltimore Colts in the first game of a rare NFL doubleheader. The nightcap was to feature the Dallas Cowboys playing the Detroit Lions.[61]

With an announcement at the end of the month, it seemed like the Papa Bear's installation of the 41-year-old George Allen to replace the 70-year-old Clark Shaughnessy might be the start of a youth movement for the sideline crew. Halas announced the promotion of ex-Bear Jim Dooley to the full-time position of offensive ends coach.[62] Dooley was Halas' first-round draft choice in 1951 after winning All American honors playing both ways at the University of Miami. He spent the next 10 years being one of Halas' favorites and a good friend and close associate of Papa Bear's prodigal son, Sid Luckman.[63]

Dooley started every game in 1952, his rookie season, as a defensive back. In an era when most defensive backs were under six feet, the 6'4" Dooley led the team with five interceptions.

He moved to offensive end the following year and became a favorite target of quarterback George Blanda, using his speed and height to snare 53 passes, placing him fifth in the NFL in pass receptions for the season. Military commitments took two years out of his fledgling career; he appeared in only three games in 1955 and 1956, all at the end of the 1956 season. It was apparent Dooley had not lost anything with the time off. In the NFL championship game against the New York Giants he gave the Giants' secondary fits, catching six passes for 60 six yards in spite of the frigid conditions. In a game where the Bears endured an historic wipeout, Dooley was one of the few bright spots for the Bears. He went on to finish in the NFL's top 10 for receptions in 1957 and 1959.

By the end of 1961 Dooley's playing career was over. He started only two games and appeared in only four others, catching a career-low six passes, although he did gain a respectable 90 yards on them. Dooley told Halas on several occasions that he wanted to coach when his career was over.

Halas put him on the staff as a "defensive advisor," and Dooley successfully revamped and simplified Shaughnessy's overly complicated schemes.[64] The 33-year-old Dooley would bring playing experience from the current era—and also some young blood—into the offensive coaching room, which at the time included Paddy Driscoll (68), Phil Handler (55), Luke Johnsos (57), and Sid Luckman (47). As the years progressed, few Chicago Bears would experience both triumph and tragedy as keenly as Dooley would.

3

April and May

Hornung and Karras,
Welcome to Shambles

April 1963 became the most significant month of Pete Rozelle's, Paul Hornung's, and Alex Karras' existence. On Wednesday, April 17, Rozelle, making "the most difficult decision" of his life,[1] suspended both Hornung and Karras indefinitely for betting on football games. The definition of "indefinitely" was purposefully not given, although Rozelle clarified things somewhat by adding that "obviously their future conduct and attitude will have a bearing on the matter if I should choose to consider lifting the suspension after the 1963 season."[2]

Rozelle's punishments did not end with these two big stars. The entire Detroit Lions organization was fined $4,000 for failing to forward information to the NFL office about "certain associations by members of the Detroit team, and because certain unauthorized individuals were permitted to sit on the Lions' bench." Also, five members of the Lions were fined $2,000 each for betting $100 on the Giants-Packers championship game at the end of December 1962. Rozelle also updated the situation with three other NFL individuals who had been under investigation. Chicago Bear fullback Rick Casares and San Francisco 49er tackle Bob St. Clair were cleared of any wrongdoing, and the investigation of Baltimore Colts owner Carroll Rosenbloom was not yet completed.[3]

The NFL's investigation over the previous months involved many more than just the abovementioned individuals. Aside from Hornung, Karras, Casares, and St. Clair, the investigation included 48 players on five other NFL teams.[4] Rozelle's explanation about Casares and St. Clair was that they were "cleared of all charges of undesirable association and deportment detrimental to the game."[5] Casares issued a statement to the press, saying that he was "pleased but not surprised." His memory became selective when he added, "all I did was cooperate with their investigation, and that's how I got involved."[6] He seemed to have forgotten that he actually avoided a severe penalty, especially in light of what he revealed three months earlier during his lie detector test.

His head coach issued an even more contradictory statement. Halas said he was "gratified but not surprised," adding that "I also expressed complete confidence in the integrity of our fullback, Rick Casares, who unfortunately was mentioned prominently in some stories because he had volunteered to take several lie detector tests. I know how much these stories hurt Casares, a great player and a tremendous competitor."[7] The reason Casares was "mentioned prominently" was not because of the tests; it was because of Halas himself. It did not take much effort to unravel the spin in Papa Bear's yarn.

A little more than four months before Halas made this statement, he was claiming credit for tipping off Rozelle about his suspicions about a "particular player," namely Casares. The *Chicago Tribune* made a special point of disclosing that Halas' concern was responsible for the story going public.[8] Halas and the *Tribune* seemed to conveniently forget that he also benched Casares in favor of the little used and unproven John Adams a few years before because of Casares' play in two West Coast games. No other local newspaper gave Halas credit for any of this, and it proved that Halas had good friends in high places. One of his closest associates, W. Donald Maxwell, was editor of the *Tribune* from 1955 until 1966.[9]

While gambling was anathema to Halas, going back to the severe warnings he got about it from his father when he was young,[10] the Bears' great success and lopsided scores in the 1930s and '40s would sometimes raise suspicions. Warren Brown, the legendary sportswriter in the *Chicago Herald American,* was convinced that Sid Luckman would intentionally overthrow receivers on occasion to control the score of the game.[11]

Cooper Rollow of the *Chicago Tribune* heard such stories long after Luckman's playing days were over. "There was speculation that Luckman needed one more touchdown for gambling reasons, never proven, but speculated," Rollow explained. "Sid would say in the huddle, 'Okay, guys, one more touchdown, even though it seems we don't need it, I'm gonna take everybody out for a steak dinner tonight.'"[12]

So how did Casares get off while Hornung and Karras received banishments? Shirley Povich of the *Washington Post* had an explanation: Karras' admitted gambling went back to 1958, Hornung's to 1957.[13] Hornung also admitted to associating with, befriending, and gambling with Abe Samuels and also with the notorious Chicago mobster Manny Skar, all while he was still in college.[14] Skar would die in a mob hit two years after Hornung's suspension, shot six times in the courtyard of his high rise at 3800 North Lake Shore Drive, five blocks east of Wrigley Field.[15]

Karras' partners in the Lindell A.C., the Butsicaris brothers, played host to some of the most infamous figures in the Detroit underworld. The figure that particularly caught Rozelle's attention was Anthony "Tony Jack" Gialcone, a Sicilian American who was a major capo in the Detroit Partnership.[16] The Detroit Partnership was the eastern Michigan branch of the Mafia and became the organized crime kingpin in Detroit after the notorious Purple Gang weakened during the Depression. Rozelle felt that having a Manny Skar or a Tony Gialcone in one's history was enough to justify harsh punishment.

Gialcone was also a big part of the reason Rozelle fined the Detroit Lions organization $4,000. On August 18, 1962, Karras and teammate John Gordy were given permission by Lions coach George Wilson to use their own transportation back to Detroit following the completion of the team's exhibition game in Cleveland against the Browns. The transportation was a cross-country luxury bus; its passenger list included, but was not limited to, Gialcone, his henchmen, and the Butsicaris brothers. The bus was trailed by a nondescript sedan during the entire journey, transporting FBI agents.[17] Detroit general manager Edwin Anderson confronted Karras the next day. Rozelle waited until December 31—the day after the Pro Bowl pitting Karras' West Division Pro Bowl squad against their East Division rivals.

Karras recollected that Rozelle asked about the party bus from Cleveland first and about the gambling issues second and that Rozelle seemed more upset about his association with Gialcone than he was about the betting on games.[18] He blamed the Lions organization for this problem as much as blamed Karras. This "laxity in supervision of club personnel"[19] was one of the bases for the $4,000 organizational fine the Lions received. The other was allowing some of the same unsavory individuals on the Lions' bench during a game.

Karras' five teammates received $2,000 fines for placing $50 bets on Green Bay to beat New York in the 1962 championship game. The bets were placed through an acquaintance of Karras. The five players were John Gordy, guard; Gary Lowe, defensive back; Joe Schmidt, middle linebacker; Sam Williams, defensive end; and linebacker Wayne Walker.[20]

NFL owners, the media, and the general public generally applauded Rozelle's move. There was much discussion about "keeping the integrity of the game" intact, in spite of the fact that the investigation of the most serious allegations—the ones involving owner Carroll Rosenbloom throwing games—was not completed. It was actually Rozelle's second major victory in less than two years, his handling of Washington Redskins owner George Preston Marshall being the first.

"The Redskins will start signing Negroes when the Harlem Globetrotters start signing Whites," Marshall once said.[21] The avowed

3. April and May

segregationist billed his franchise as the "team of the South" and as such relied on players from Southern programs, which at the time had no minority players. The Redskins, however, were desperate for a new stadium, and the tract of land for it was owned by the federal government. Marshall's overt racism did not go over well with Attorney General Robert F. Kennedy. Rozelle got involved with this situation and impressed upon Marshall that the NFL vision was national and not provincial. Between governmental pressure and Rozelle's cajoling the Redskins had three Black players in 1962, all running backs: Don Hatcher from Michigan State, Leroy Jackson from Western Illinois, and future Hall of Famer Bobby Mitchell from Illinois.

Hornung's and Karras' eventual reactions to their fate were very different. Hornung was contrite after receiving his punishment. He admitted that he did wrong and felt badly about disappointing his mother, Loretta Hornung.[22] The Associated Press reported that Packer fans all through Wisconsin overwhelmingly supported their fallen hero, as did his teammates, noting that he admitted his mistake and took the punishment "like a man."[23] Vince Lombardi said, "I am shocked and hurt.... However, there was a definite violation of the player contract and constitution and bylaws of this league in regards to gambling.... The commissioner had no other alternative."[24]

Other than apologizing and admitting that he was wrong Hornung had little to say, keeping his feelings about Rozelle to himself as the story broke. Years later, however, he talked more freely about the issue. Hornung felt singled out by Rozelle and forced the commissioner to back down regarding how much he would reveal. If forced to squeal on others, Hornung warned Rozelle, he would then go straight to the McClellan Committee hearings in Congress, talk frankly and freely, and "get this entire league in trouble."[25] This forced Rozelle to back down.

Karras was defiant and denied any serious wrongdoing. He staunchly defended the Lions' organization and his teammates, saying they never should have been punished that it was commonplace for NFL teams to have outsiders on the bench during games.[26] He threatened legal action, insisting that he "hasn't done anything that I am ashamed of and I am not guilty of anything."[27]

Soon after receiving his punishment from Rozelle Karras received a phone call from David Gudelsky, the chairman of the Michigan Athletic Commission. Gudelsky informed him that he had been granted an event license to wrestle Dick the Bruiser at the Olympia in downtown Detroit. Karras had applied for a license two weeks before his meeting with Rozelle, expecting the worst. When word got out that Karras might go back into pro wrestling his phone rang off the hook with offers, including one from the promoter John Doyle for $40,000 per year.[28] In spite of his plans for a lucrative future, trouble found Karras just two days after his suspension.

Dick the Bruiser's real name was Richard Afflis. He had a three-year career as an offensive lineman with the Packers from 1951 to 1954. In the evening of Tuesday, April 23 the Bruiser came into the Lindell A.C. asking to see Karras. Bruiser threatened Karras and punched Jimmy Butsicaris, and a brawl ensued that required eight Detroit patrolmen to break up. The actual match at the Olympia occurred four days later. Bruiser won the dust-up by pinning Karras, after Karras managed to throw him out of the ring. After the match Karras never wrestled again.[29]

The last judgmental word, tainted with a heavy dose of homerism, came from Irv Kupcinet, in his *Chicago Sun-Times* feature, "Kup's Column." With a blatantly provincial display that "our guy is better than those guys," Kupcinet wrote that while the gambling scandal was breaking,

Bears quarterback Billy Wade was in Ft. Lauderdale and Daytona, encouraging vacationing college kids to remember the teachings of the Gospel.

It did not take Bears fans long to start wondering what the absence of two such significant opponents might mean in the upcoming 1963 season. Some borrowed a cliché borne of the Chicago Cubs' futility over the last 17 years: "Our team doesn't have to get better, the other teams just have to get a little bit worse." There would be no question that the Lions would be "a little bit worse" with Karras out of the picture, but the Hornung-less Packers might not suffer at all.

Karras posed significant problems for Bears interior offensive linemen as he did for all offensive lineman that opposed him. At this point in the offseason the Lions planned to replace Karras with Mike Bundra, a rookie, in 1962. Bundra was a sixth-round draft choice from USC who was about Karras' size, 6'3", 255 pounds. In '62 he played in 12 games, had no starts, and recovered one fumble.

Things were not as encouraging regarding future Bear-Packer matchups with Hornung off the team. The Bears lost their two 1962 matchups with Green Bay by a combined score of 87-7. Hornung carried the ball on two occasions in the first game—a 49–0 shutout—and gained only 14 yards. He did not play at all in the second game, a 38–7 Packer victory. His replacement in both contests was Vanderbilt's Tom Moore, a first-round draft pick by Lombardi in 1960. Hornung was injured for much of 1962 and Moore filled in very capably, racking up 377 yards with seven touchdowns to go along with 11 catches good for 100 yards. He outgained Hornung in total yards, 477 to 387. Against the Bears Moore gained 60 yards on 20 carries and caught three passes for 60 yards. Moore complemented pile-driving fullback Jim Taylor perfectly and was selected for the 1962 Pro

Bowl contest, so it was unlikely the Pack would suffer due to Hornung's absence in the backfield. Their kicking game would not miss him either.

In 1962 Jerry Kramer made nine out of 11 field goals and 38 out of 39 extra points.

Those following the discussion whether the NFL had eclipsed baseball as the country's major sports interest took note of a press release from Pete Rozelle's office at the end of April. He mentioned that the NFL had reached an agreement with NBC broadcasting for the television rights to the 1963 championship game scheduled for December 29, 1963. NBC outbid all other networks with an offer of $926,000 for the single Sunday afternoon contest. This amount was a 50 percent increase in the television rights from the last two title games.[30] This amount was the most ever paid for a sporting contest by a wide margin and settled most of the debates about whether pro football was the biggest sports interest of the nation.

The NFL, however, soon got over the good feelings about their financial windfall. On May 10 the sudden death of one of the league's biggest names changed the mood quite suddenly. Eugene "Big Daddy" Liscomb, one of the most famous and beloved linemen ever to play, was found dead in a friend's apartment. One of the few NFL stars to never play in college, the huge (6'6", 285-pound) 10-year veteran went straight to the pros after starring on the Camp Pendleton Marine Corps football squad. Liscomb went on to play for the Los Angeles Rams, Baltimore Colts, and Pittsburgh Steelers. When he was found, comatose, he had three needle marks on his elbows and a homemade syringe was near his body on the floor. Dr. Rudiger Breintecker, the assistant medical examiner, told the Associated Press, "There is a definite suspicion that narcotics are involved in the death."[31] His partying buddy that night, Timothy Black, admitted that he had scored some heroin.[32]

As if the unexpected passing of a big star was not enough, following the gambling scandals the last thing Rozelle and the league needed was a drug-related death, complete with an autopsy and public records for everyone to examine. Those that knew Liscomb well did not believe the facts about his death as they were presented. It was well known that Liscomb was a heavy drinker who loved a party but he was also deathly afraid of needles and had never used hard or even recreational drugs. "I'm a B & B man," Liscomb used to say, "just booze and broads."[33] Liscomb's liver was impaired from his voracious appetite for hard liquor, and one theory about why he succumbed and Black survived was because Liscomb's liver could not expel the amount of heroin quickly enough. The autopsy revealed that he had five times the lethal amount of heroin in his system.[34] George Taliferro, an ex-NFL quarterback who knew Liscomb well, mentioned that Black was a drug dealer who borrowed $1,000 from Liscomb and that the only reason Liscomb was in Black's apartment was to collect the money, which Black did not have at the time. Black, according to Taliferro, took the matter into his own hands, with the result being Liscomb's death.[35]

Sports stories as viscerally jarring as Liscomb's death rarely found their way into print during this era, not just in football, but in all sports. The carousing, drinking, partying, and womanizing were well known but discreetly ignored by the press, while hard drug use by players came as a shock to even the most grizzled sports scribes. It sullied the stereotype of "All-American hero" the NFL strove to foster, compromising the professional athlete's role as ego ideal for the nation's youth. It also had the possibility of bringing before the public the unsavory topic of drug use, legitimate and illegitimate, by the NFL's teams.

In May George Allen went to work establishing the roster for the 1963 season, with training camp about 10 weeks away. His first accomplishment was trading reserve fullback/tight end John Adams to Los Angeles for the Rams' second draft choice. He was expendable because Rick Casares and Joe Marconi were set at fullback, and with Mike Ditka and rookie Bob Jencks—a second-round draft choice four months ago—the Bears were set at tight end. Adams was a fifth-round pick by the Bears in 1959. He learned his craft at San Diego's Herbert Hoover High School, the same institution that graduated Bear great Bill McColl in the late 1940s. He starred as a collegian at Los Angeles State and was chosen for the Little All-America team as a triple-threat, a 6'3" 235-pound fullback skilled at running, throwing, and punting. As a pro he never lived up to his billing, starting two games at fullback and one at tight end over four seasons. With the Bears the 99 yards Adams gained on 41 rushes included a 62-yard run from scrimmage and one touchdown. As a tight end he caught 12 passes for 171 yards, scoring three touchdowns. Adams was interested in playing on the West Coast since he worked at a bank in San Diego in the off-season. The Rams wanted to use him as a tight end and punter.[36]

Allen also revealed that he used his old coaching contacts in Iowa to sign two collegians as free agents, Martin Heerema and Elden Schulte, both from Central College in Pella, Iowa. Heerema was a 6'2", 245-pound tackle and Schulte a 6'2" 234-pound linebacker. Allen was willing to gamble with small college players whose gridiron experience mirrored his previous coaching experiences. In the fourth round of the 1963 draft he chose Stan Sanders, an end from Whittier College, the program he left to join the Rams. Allen felt that small colleges had some players that could be diamonds in the rough. Indeed, four starters in the 1962 championship game bore this idea out: Green Bay's Fuzzy Thurston (Valparaiso); New York's Dick Pesonen (Duluth State); Andy Robustelli (Arnold College); and Bill Winter (St. Olaf).

Allen continued shoring up the offensive line soon after by signing Johnny Johnson, the team's sixth-round pick in the 1963 draft. Johnson chose the Bears over the AFL's New York Jets, which chose him in the 20th round of the AFL draft. The Hobart, Indiana, native, 6'5" and 260 pounds, started at the Indiana University for three years and was so effective his senior year that he was chosen to participate in the Blue-Gray game in Mobile, Alabama. Johnson distinguished himself in that showcase event by blocking a punt which led to the Blue squad's first touchdown. He became the second Bear lineman to hail from the northwest corner of Indiana, one of the football hotbeds of the country in the mid–20th century. Fellow lineman Ted Karras starred at Gary Emerson High School, eight miles from Johnson's Hobart High.[37]

While Halas was finding himself more flush with cash, thanks to the lucrative television contracts, he was not in any mood to spend any of it. For that reason he looked very unfavorably upon a new stadium plan for Chicago that influential Chicago attorney Lewis Jacobson was pushing. Jacobson proposed to the city fathers that a bond issue for $50 million should be created for a universal professional sports stadium to be used by the Bears, Cubs, and White Sox.[38] His plan included the White Sox abandoning Comiskey Park and the Cubs and Bears exiting Wrigley Field, after which the three owners of these franchises would pony up one million dollars each toward the bond issue. The stadium would not be an indoor facility but would have a roof to protect the field and the fans from inclement weather. Halas was concerned; as he was the only team owner who was a tenant, his fate in this matter rested with his landlord, Phil Wrigley, and was not within his control.

Luckily for Halas White Sox owner Arthur C. Allyn was dead set against the idea and clearly spelled out his reasons.[39] Allyn indicated that he was already exploring the architectural and construction feasibility of putting a roof over Comiskey Park. He added that both he and previous owner Bill Veeck had made massive upgrades to the park and that it could now accommodate 14,000 cars in nearby parking lots. The three-year-old Dan Ryan Expressway also made the park much more accessible than it had been. Allyn also praised the general condition and accessibility of Wrigley Field, mentioning that he himself took the CTA elevated trains from his home in Evanston with no difficulty to get to that park. Bob Whitlow, the Cubs athletic director, mentioned that the Cubs were in the process of studying additional land near the ballpark to purchase to ease the parking headaches for Cubs and Bears fans who drove to a game.[40]

The much anticipated NFL owners' meeting occurred in St. Louis at the end of May. There were five issues on the agenda: roster size, the television contracts, contributions to the player benefit plan, the 1925 championship controversy, and the pension plan. Curiously, the elephant in the closet—betting by league personnel—was not listed. The league did not want to draw attention to this persistent negative, and it was common knowledge that the media's questions would raise the sordid subject's profile more than anyone wanted anyway.

The owners quickly decided to increase each team's roster to 37 players in the 1963 season, one more than before. This number excluded any individuals on a reserve list or tax squad.[41]

Since the $9.3 million television contract with CBS would expire in seven months, discussion started regarding how best to negotiate the contract for 1964. The other broadcast agreement—the NBC championship game rights worth almost a million dollars—also came up. The owners, with no input from the players, started to consider what portion of that revenue would go to the players' benefit fund, which covered life insurance ($10,000 for first-year players, $20,000 for veterans)[42] and health benefits.

The most encouraging development for the players coming out of this meeting was the finalization of the players' pension plan. Commissioner Rozelle announced that the Internal Revenue Service had approved the proposed plan, which they reviewed over several years. Under the plan a player with five years of playing time would get $437 a month at age 65; 10 years, $656; 15 years, $821. For comparison's sake, in 1963 the average monthly income for a family of four in the United States was $516.[43] Rozelle told the press that he "preferred not to compare the plan with professional baseball, since the owners feel that our program is more than adequate."[44] It was common knowledge that the major league baseball pension plan was established 16 years earlier, in 1947, and that it was more generous. The NFL issued no press releases about the betting scandal and its consequences, although there was plenty of talk between the owners about the situation. Rozelle also had no updates on the only unfinished betting investigation, the one regarding Colts owner Carroll Rosenbloom. This was clearly a topic he wished to avoid.

An interesting trade rumor, however, did arise as a consequence of Paul Hornung's suspension. Word got out that due to Hornung's absence Vince Lombardi was eager to get the St. Louis Cardinals' star running back John David Crow to shore up the Green Bay running game.

Crow was the eighth most productive rusher in the NFL in 1962, so he could very capably fill Green Bay's backfield void. Also, the Cardinals just completed a dismal 4–9–1 season, so just about anything they could get in return would be an improvement.

Rozelle also announced the creation of a new position in the NFL corporate offices, setting up an intelligence arm to "augment the system of surveillance [the league] has had for more than a decade."[45] He named

53-year-old James E. Hamilton as the new "roving watchdog" to prevent "undesirable associations" by players throughout the league. Hamilton, who started with the Los Angeles Police Department in 1937, was currently the commander of the intelligence division of LAPD, a position he took in 1950. "Many of the players in the league are unaware of undesirable elements in the cities where they play," Rozelle explained, "and we feel Hamilton, because of his extensive background in police work, will be able to steer players away from such bad areas."[46] Rozelle went on to say he would put Hamilton on a schedule where he would visit all 14 NFL cities two or three times a year, meeting with players and coaches. He openly admitted that the Hornung/Karras scandal was a major reason for Hamilton's hiring.[47]

The most interesting story out of the NFL owners' meeting involved an issue that happened 37 years before. By a vote of 12–2 the owners decided to let the Chicago Cardinals keep their 1925 NFL title, which was taken away from the Pottsville Maroons (a team that existed from 1925 to 1929).[48] The Maroons had legitimately beaten the Cardinals on December 6, 1925, 21–7, at Comiskey Park in Chicago, thinking that the title was theirs as they left town. The shenanigans of both teams led to the controversy. To gain a better season record than Pottsville, the Cardinals scheduled two games with weak, disbanded opponents, the Milwaukee Badgers and the Hammond Pros. The Badgers were so disorganized that they put four high school players on their roster. The Pros had folded their tent long before their game with the Cardinals and had not played for six weeks. Pottsville was suspended by NFL president Joseph Carr for playing the Notre Dame All-Stars (beating them, 9–7) in Philadelphia. This game was a complete encroachment on the football territory of the Frankford Yellow Jackets, a team that was active from 1924 to 1931. With this suspension of the Pottsville franchise, the Cardinals—who lost to Pottsville but finished with a better record, thanks to the victories over Milwaukee and Hammond—was given the championship.[49]

In the early 1960s the NFL appointed a special committee to examine the case. After the facts were presented the owners voted on the issue, with the Cardinals keeping the disputed championship by a vote of 12–2. The two dissenting votes were Pittsburgh's Art Rooney, who viewed Pottsville's old claim as an encroachment on his eastern Pennsylvania territory, and George Halas, whose disdain for the Cardinals during the 1950 Walter Wolfner era knew no boundary.

May ended with a press release from George Allen's office that the Bears had 16 rookies signed up for the start of their training camp, which would start in less than two months. While their first-round draft choice, center Dave Behrman of Michigan State, signed with the Buffalo Bills in the AFL, their next three choices—tackle Steve Barnett of Oregon, end Bob Jencks of Miami of Ohio, and defensive back Larry Glueck of Villanova— were all signed. The 13 additional rookies were five halfbacks (Dennis Harmon, Southern Illinois; Gordon Banks, Fisk University; Lowell Caylor, Miami of Ohio; Woody Moore, Indiana; and Bob Yaksick, Rutgers); three offensive lineman (Larry Coleman, Indiana; Martin Heerema, Central of Iowa; and Johnny Johnson, Indiana); three linebackers (Andy VonSonn, UCLA; Elden Schulte, Central of Iowa; and William Tyson, Utah State); one pass receiver (Dennis Andrews, Virginia); and one defensive lineman (Ken Thomas, Grambling College). Out of this group Johnny Johnson would be the only one to play for the Bears. Andy VonSonn played with the Los Angeles Rams in 1964 and Lowell Caylor played one year for the Cleveland Browns, contributing to their 1964 NFL championship. None of the other 11 newcomers ever played in an NFL regular season game.

4

June and July

Mugs Halas, Your Table Is Ready, and Papa Bear's White Whale

As the calendar turned to June George Halas turned to one of his most trusted associates to assist with the herculean task of conquering the Green Bay Packers. Paddy Driscoll, his faithful companion going back 45 years, was named the team's director of research and planning. In taking the position Driscoll was also named vice president of the franchise.[1] "Rapidly developing techniques have heightened the importance of game preparations to the point where a single coordinator should spend all of his time on that job," Halas told the press. "Study of game films and scouting reports has taken on an added dimension, which is the need for translating information into concise, meaningful reports."[2] The 68-year-old Driscoll first joined the Bears' coaching staff in 1940.

John Leo "Paddy" Driscoll had been a gridiron luminary since 1915, when he starred as a triple-threat quarterback and halfback at Northwestern University. Driscoll was the Paul Hornung of his time, with his passing, running, and drop-kicking skills. Like Jim Thorpe, he also played professional baseball. In 1918 Driscoll played second base, shortstop, and third base for the Chicago Cubs, appearing in 13 games. Since he hit only .107 (three for 28, with one double, three runs batted in, six strikeouts, and two stolen bases[3]) he quickly got back into football by joining the Navy, earning a "special services" commission. The "services" he was to render were playing football on the Great Lakes Naval Training Center gridiron squad, which guaranteed him staying stateside during World War I.[4] Driscoll starred on the undefeated 1918 Great Lakes football team, where he met Halas. He duplicated his Big Ten exploits at Great Lakes, once scoring 35 points (five touchdowns and five extra points) against Rutgers. Driscoll was responsible for 10 of the 17 points scored in Great Lakes' 17–0 victory over the Mare Island Marine Base in the 1919 Rose Bowl. He kicked a field goal and passed to teammate Halas for the game's only touchdown.

With the war ending Driscoll realized that football was going to be his life. In 1919 he signed on to play with the Hammond Pros. Driscoll contacted Halas about the team, and Halas joined the northwestern Indiana squad for $100 per game the year before he went to Decatur and established the Staleys. Driscoll's next pro game with Halas occurred under illegal circumstances.

At the time in 1920 Driscoll was under contract as the player/coach of the Racine Avenue/Chicago Cardinals. After the season ended, he got a call from Halas, whose Staleys were going to meet the Akron Pros in a championship game at Wrigley Field. Thinking he needed all the help he could get, Halas violated several APFA[5] league rules by paying his old Navy buddy $300 to play as a single-game, non-rostered ringer. The game ended in a 0–0 tie, but the championship was awarded to Akron, based on their undefeated season. The loosely-run APFA meted out no discipline to either of them.

Driscoll's impressive record from 1920 to 1922 as the Cardinals' coach was 17–8–4. From 1923 to 1925 he gave up his coaching duties and continued to star in their backfield. He joined Halas again in 1926, spending his last three years as a player with the Bears, but in some ways his Bears affiliation went back to 1922. Even while in the employ of the Cardinals the name

"John L. Driscoll, 816 Foster Street, Evanston, Illinois" appears on the original incorporation papers of the Chicago Bears as a minority partner.[6] When Driscoll hung up his spikes in 1930, he had been a first-team All-Pro six times and a second team All-Pro twice and was named to the NFL 1920s All Decade Team; years later, in 1965, he was inducted into the NFL Hall of Fame.

His next venture into coaching occurred in 1937 at Marquette University, which he left in 1941 to become an assistant coach with the Bears. He assisted Hunk Anderson and Luke Johnsos in running the team while Halas was in the service during World War II. Driscoll spent the next 14 years as an assistant, and Halas named him head coach before the 1956 season, after he promised his wife Min that he would quit the sidelines. Many viewed Driscoll's appointment as questionable. He had no contemporary head-coaching experience and was 61 years old. The biggest bullet point on his resume was his 38-year association with Halas. Rick Casares, the Bears most valuable player that year, said, "Paddy Driscoll was one of the sweetest guys who ever lived. But Paddy was just a figurehead. He didn't say ten words."[7] Luke Johnsos and Halas himself pulled most of the strings, as the Bears went 9–2–1 but lost badly to the New York Giants in the title game, 47–7. After Driscoll's Bears went 5–7 in 1957, Halas took over the head coaching duties again and Driscoll was kicked upstairs as a vice president. It was unclear what Driscoll would be doing in his new position as director of planning and research that he had not been doing the previous six years.

While Halas directed his attention to his staff, George Allen kept working at improving the Bears' roster. On June 11 he shifted his attention from the offensive line and traded the Bears' 1964 second-round draft pick to the Pittsburgh Steelers for veteran linebacker Tom Bettis. The eight-year veteran's availability would be insurance if the Bears linebacking corps became thin. For Bettis the trade represented a homecoming.[8]

Thomas William Bettis was born March 17, 1933, in Chicago. He was a West Sider who went to St. Mel High School, a perennial football power in the tough Chicago Catholic League.[9] Bettis' prowess on St. Mel's gridiron earned him a scholarship to Purdue University, where the 6'2", 235-pound linebacker continued to dominate. He became the team captain for the Boilermakers his junior and senior years, winning the team's most valuable player award each season. He was the fifth player taken in the 1955 NFL draft, chosen by the Green Bay Packers, who were 4–8 the previous season and eager to shore up their defense. In his first season Bettis played in all 12 games but started only one contest. From 1957 until 1961, however, he started at linebacker, helping the Packers win a division title in 1960 and become world champions in 1961. After that championship season Vince Lombardi traded Bettis to the Pittsburgh Steelers. During the 1962 season he started 13 of Pittsburgh's 14 games, and more important from the Bears' standpoint, he played all three linebacker positions.[10] His versatility meant he could replace Joe Fortunato, Bill George, or Larry Morris, if need be. He might also be a font of knowledge regarding his old team— Halas' obsession, the Green Bay Packers.

With an eye toward allocating more time planning game strategies with his coaching staff, soon after Allen announced the acquisition of Tom Bettis, Halas announced the promotion of his son Mugs to president of the team.[11] The younger Halas had been serving as team treasurer since 1950. In the years leading up to this promotion, his father, George Sr., incrementally increased Mugs' responsibilities. Arranging pre-season schedules, managing ticket sales, negotiating local radio and television contracts, negotiating some player contracts, talent scouting, and acting as the team's traveling secretary all were the younger Halas' responsibilities at one time or another. The 38-year-old, a 1949 graduate of Loyola University in Chicago and a World War II Navy veteran, became a minority owner in 1954, when father George divided 17 percent of the team's shares of stock equally between him and his older sister Virginia McCaskey.[12] "The change will relieve me of many executive duties and leave me free to concentrate on coaching," Halas Sr. explained. "Mugs has been around the team since he was big enough to walk and I am sure his devotion to the Bears is second only to mine."[13]

Over the years Mugs' devotion to the Bears always seemed more entrenched than his father's devotion to Mugs. When the Bears lost to the expansion Minnesota Vikings for the first time on September 17, 1961, Mugs kicked the wall in the locker room out of frustration and broke his big toe.[14] Also, the relationship between the Papa Bear and Mugs' wife Terry was strained, to the point where she tried to keep her father-in-law from interacting with her two children. Bear executive Jerry Vainisi had his own take on the father-son situation: "He lived all his life being a Junior, son of a famous man with high expectations. His father second-guessed him a lot, and Mugs would take his frustrations out in many ways over the years, either by drinking or by playing the temperamental tough guy whom people feared to cross because of the Old Man."[15] Papa Bear's poor treatment of his son was often out in the open, according to sports journalist Jeannie Morris. "He treated him like shit! It was awful for a parent to do to a child of any age. Who knows what it was like in private, but a lot of people saw the public humiliation."[16] Part of the reason for the apathy between father and son may have stemmed from the near-paternal devotion Halas Sr. felt toward Bears legend Sid Luckman. Luckman treasured a letter he received from Halas just before Halas died which read: "My dear Sid, 'I love you with all my heart.' When I said this to you last night as I kissed you I realized 44 wonderful years of knowing you were summed up by seven words. My boy, my pride in you has no bounds. Remember our word 'now!' Every time I said it to you, you brought me another championship. You added a luster to my life that can never tarnish. My devoted friend, you have a spot in my heart that NO ONE else can claim. God bless you and keep you, my son. I love you with all my heart. Sincerely yours, George."[17] The letter in some ways says as much about Papa Bear's relationship with his son as it does about his relationship with Luckman.

The Bears also got some good news regarding the recuperation of their star halfback, Willie Galimore.[18] Galimore underwent knee surgery twice, in November and December, during the 1962 season. In early June he went back to Florida A&M, his alma mater, to work out with some of their players for the first time since the surgery. "It went great—real great," Galimore reported. "I'd been jogging at half speed but I cut plenty today. And there was no discomfort, no stiffness. I got two touchdowns. After the second one, one of the guys yelled, 'Man, there's nothing wrong with his legs.'"[19]

Galimore was respected throughout the NFL as being—along with the Rams' Jaguar Jon Arnett—the most talented scatback in football. Few could match the 6', 185-pounder's sprints, fewer still his acceleration, and

The immortal Willie Galimore crosses the goal line on November 17, 1963, against the Packers, outrunning everyone on the field, as was his custom. Rick Casares (at left, clapping) cheers him on while Ed O'Bradovich (87) watches approvingly. The lucky lad on the tarp and the Chicago police officer characterize all of Chicago's feelings toward this beloved, tragic running back.

none his ability to cut at top speed. "Willie the Wisp" carried on the Bears' tradition of featuring dominant running backs, a tradition that started in 1925 with Red Grange and continued through the following decades with Bronco Nagurski, Beattie Feathers, George McAfee, Scooter McLean, Bill Osmanski, and Rick Casares.

Willie Galimore was born March 30, 1935, in St. Augustine, Florida, and he starred in football and track at St. Augustine's Excelsior High School. Galimore won a football scholarship to Florida A&M and dominated the Southern Intercollegiate Athletic Conference for four years. He was All-SIAC each year and named a Black College All-American by the *Pittsburgh Courier* in his last three seasons. With Galimore the Florida A&M Rattlers won one Black College National Championship and four conference championships. During his career the Rattlers' record was 33–4–1, in large part due to his 3,596 rushing yards.[20]

The Bears learned about Willie the Wisp on a lucky tip. While vacationing in Florida assistant coach Phil Handler went to Hialeah Park Race Track and got to talking to one of the jockeys. When he learned of Handler's occupation the jockey mentioned that an unstoppable running back with more moves than a fine watch was leaving nearby Florida

A&M and could be a real asset to any team that picked him up. Handler convinced Halas to take Galimore in the fifth round of the 1955 draft as a futures selection. Galimore at the time was only the second Florida A&M player ever drafted by the NFL.[21] Starting all 12 games in 1957, he gained 739 total yards and scored seven touchdowns. Galimore's performance in 1957 cemented him as a fixture in the Bears' backfield, the perfect ying to Rick Casares' yang. He also became one of Halas' favorites, with his sunny disposition, winning smile, and consistently positive attitude. Injuries, however, mostly to his knees, prevented the elusive running back from reaching his full potential.[22]

With training camp less than a month away George Allen was able to sign four more starters by the end of June. Offensive guards Ted Karras and Roger Davis renewed their contracts along with defensive backs J.C. Caroline and Roosevelt Taylor.[23] Caroline, a human Swiss Army Knife of a player, overcame a rough start to become a Bear legend.

A Columbia, South Carolina, native, J.C. Caroline earned a scholarship to the University of Illinois. After leading the nation in rushing in 1953 he was elected captain. Caroline's efforts that season earned him All-American honors. Prejudice, however, interrupted his gridiron success. A bigoted professor who could not fathom the Fightin' Illini having a Black captain gave him a failing grade, rendering him ineligible to play, let alone become captain of the squad.[24] The grade was administratively changed, but by the time the wrong was corrected, Caroline had already signed a very lucrative $15,000 contract to play in the Canadian Football League. After a year with the Toronto Argonauts and the Montreal Alouettes Caroline was drafted by the Bears in 1956. During Caroline's seven subsequent seasons with the Bears he performed admirably on both offense and defense. On offense the former Fighting Illini great gained 263 yards on 68 rushes for a 3.9-yard average, filling in when starting halfbacks Bobby Watkins or Willie Galimore were not available. With most of his playing time in the defensive backfield, Caroline was only one interception shy of tying the team record of 22 career interceptions held by Bear legend Don Kindt. In spite of these impressive contributions his greatest value to the team, many felt, was his special teams' play. Like Doug Atkins, Rick Casares, and Mike Ditka, Caroline was one of the few players not intimidated by Halas; he knew his worth to the team. Halas once tore into him on the sideline during a game against the 49ers when R.C. Owens beat Caroline and caught an alley-oop pass. Standing up to his curmudgeonly coach, Caroline angrily shot back, "Pay me as much to knock down that pass as Owens gets paid to catch it and I'll knock it down."

Roosevelt Taylor, on the other hand, was one of George Allen's success stories, and he owed his career to Allen educating Halas just how talented he was. In 1961 Taylor signed with the Bears as an undrafted free agent out of Grambling College. The diminutive defensive back, acknowledged as one of the fastest defenders in the NFL, was also one of the league's surest tacklers. In 1962 he led the Bears' defense with 95 individual tackles and 17 assists. His pass coverage was so effective in 1962 that only one touchdown pass all season was charged against him. The 5'9" 180-pound speedster worked himself into becoming one of the premier shut-down defensive backs in the league.

Taylor's story serves as inspiration to anyone struggling to overcome personal hardships.[25] He was raised by his mother and sister in New Orleans' 9th Ward, 50 yards from the Mississippi River, in a house that had a kitchen, bedroom, and toilet off the kitchen. A defective roman candle burned his eyes when he was 11, and he narrowly avoided total blindness. Taylor excelled in football, basketball, and track at Joseph S. Clark High School, and at 5' 9" he could dunk a basketball. He was promised a basketball scholarship at Grambling which never came through, but he shined on their gridiron, leading all small college defensive backs in 1960 with 12 interceptions.

George Allen flew down to Grambling to sign their huge defensive tackle, Ernie Ladd, who eventually inked a contract with the San Diego Chargers in the AFL. He asked legendary Grambling coach Eddie Robinson if he had any defensive backs, and Robinson told him about Taylor. When he saw the diminutive speedster hold his own in a track meet against Olympic hopefuls Allen was sold and signed Taylor to a free agent contract. When he made the Bears Taylor took a great deal of pride knowing he was the first Black athlete from New Orleans to play professional football.

Allen got more players in the fold when the calendar turned to July and defensive tackle Fred Williams and the double-duty lineman Stan Jones signed contracts. Williams, a perennial anchor in the Bears' defensive line, would be playing his 12th season with the Bears. Williams excelled in football, basketball, and boxing at Arkansas' Little Rock Central High School, winning championships in boxing and basketball and all-state football honors twice. Little Rock Central had a fantastically successful football program. Williams was the school's 12th alumnus to play in the NFL, a list that included Bears luminary Ken Kavanaugh. "Fat Freddie" continued on a gridiron scholarship at the University of Arkansas and was selected by the Bears in the fifth round of the 1952 draft. He made the NFL Pro Bowl squad in each of his first two seasons and again in 1958 and '59 but started 10 games for the Bears in 1962 due to a knee injury. His fun-loving personality and penchant for high jinks made him as valuable in the locker room as he was on the field. Williams' training camp drinking contests with Doug Atkins became legendary. The cagey veteran's off-season knee surgery was successful, and Allen was counting on big things from Williams in 1963.

Stan Jones came to the Bears through the fifth round of the 1953 NFL draft. His peerless playing at the University of Maryland earned him the Knute Rockne Memorial Trophy as the nation's outstanding lineman. Jones attributed much of his success to a consistent weight training program he followed religiously since he was 14. In the 1950s football training and preparation did not include weight lifting, and he was one of the first proponents of weight training in the NFL.[26] On November 4, 1951, the Bears played the Redskins in Washington, D.C., and the day before Halas decided to see the Georgia vs. Maryland contest. That afternoon he saw Jones sack future Bear quarterback (and Jones' future roommate) Zeke Bratkowski and force an interception.[27] Halas was so impressed that he drafted Jones in 1953 as a futures selection. Jones actually had no intention of playing pro football, hoping to become a pilot in the Air Force after graduation, but he failed the flight physical. When Bears line coach Phil Handler called him and offered him a contract, Jones forgot about flying and started his Hall of Fame NFL career.[28]

Jones found his first training camp at St. Joseph College in Rensselaer unbearable. The non-air-conditioned dormitory reminded him of a penitentiary, complete with a security guard the players called "Dick Tracy" getting a bonus from Halas if he turned in a player for breaking curfew.[29] Yet Jones overcame his training camp miseries to win the starting left tackle slot his first year. He was named to the Pro Bowl for the next seven seasons (1955–1961) and won Associated Press All-Pro honors in 1955, '56, and '59. Jones claimed that his toughest opponents when he played offensive guard were Art Donovan of the Colts, Leo Nomellini of the 49ers, and Bud McFadin of the Rams.[30]

He taught school in the off-season and filed papers to retire from the NFL in December 1962, after a season in which he started only one game due to injuries. Also at that time, he had locked horns with Halas as the team representative of the NFL Players' Association, which was six years old in 1962 and still had no affiliation with the AFL-CIO.[31] George Allen, eager to fill some holes on the defensive line created by injuries to Fred Williams and Maury Youmans, convinced Jones to permanently shift to defensive tackle.[32] This change resulted in Jones agreeing to the $14,000 contract that Halas offered him for the 1963 season.

After hearing about Papa Bear's press conference on July 20, however, Stan Jones may have questioned the wisdom of signing up. Halas said the only veterans guaranteed jobs were tight end Mike Ditka and quarterback Bill Wade. He discussed the pre-workout talk he had with the players to the assembled newsmen, who took note of the fact that the 30-minute contact scrimmage that day was the earliest full-contact exercise they could remember. "A new, impersonal era is at hand. A veteran has to earn his job. No special consideration will be given for his past accomplishments. Pampering is out. There will be no more pussy-foot playing, no more pussy-foot coaching, no more pussy-foot conduct. I've simply decided I've been at this business too long to play the role of nice guy any more. If a newcomer shows more than a veteran, the newcomer gets the job. We are here to develop a winner and the only way to win is to give 100% effort."[33]

The "tough talk" was hard to figure for a team coming off a 9–5 season, a team that got better as the season progressed. It would be hard to envision rookies beating out veterans who just recently achieved that measure of success. Nobody who knew anything about the team could remember when Papa Bear ever played the role of "nice guy." Halas never had a history of "pampering" or "pussy-footing"—whatever that meant—as a coach. Luckily for him, none of the cynical reporters asked him which coaches historically resorted to "pussy-footing," or what the definition of "pussy-foot conduct" was. He also completely ignored the work some of the players had put in during the offseason. Five veterans came in lighter than they had a year ago: Doug Atkins, at 261 pounds, down from 280; Rick Casares, 14 pounds lighter at 221; Bill George, 234, a six-pound reduction; Herman Lee, down to 251 from 265; and Maury Youmans, shedding a significant 15 pounds to get to 255.[34]

Halas' tough-guy demeanor hinted at his obsessive envy of Green Bay's success. Since Vince Lombardi took over as coach and general manager, Halas' record against the Packers was 2–6. One loss was 41–13 and another was 49–0. In the four years Lombardi was in charge up north, the Packers record including all championship games was 41–14, and the Bears were 30–21. In the four years prior to Lombardi's arrival (1955–1958), the Packers' record was 14–33 and the Bears were 30–17. While on a personal level Halas liked Lombardi, Lombardi's superiority conjured up too many sobering truths Halas did not want to face.

Lombardi's success made Green Bay the capital of the NFL world when for decades Chicago enjoyed that status. Lombardi's total domination in head-to-head contests raised the issue that coaching strategy and game planning in the modern era was now beyond Halas; nice to have a George Allen around, but Lombardi could do it himself. Lombardi was also part of the NFL's now more influential younger generation; Halas was a relic of the old guard, and it seemed like the torch had been passed. Allie Sherman was 39 and Lombardi was 49; they were the coaches in the last two championship games. Commissioner Rozelle was 36. In the old guard, Bert Bell was gone, Halas was 67, Washington's George Preston Marshall was 66, and Pittsburgh's Art Rooney, Sr., was 61. The face of pro football, in Halas' eyes, was changing, and he no longer seemed a part of it. Lombardi loomed over all of it, and Halas became obsessed with beating him. Vince Lombardi had become George Halas' White Whale.

Evidence of this first surfaced in January 1962.[35] Halas told assistant coach Chuck Mather to comb through the playbook and find plays that he thought would work against Green Bay. These plays would be practiced continuously in training camp but not used in any games except the Green Bay contests.[36] Offensive lineman Bob Wetoska reminisced, "Halas said we were going to dedicate this training camp to beating the Packers in the opening game. Every practice included at least fifteen minutes of practicing against the Packers' offense. Every day we did that, building through all the exhibition season to beat Green Bay. Psychologically he was preparing us to do that."[37]

When news of Papa Bear's press conference reached the Packers' training camp at St. Norbert's College, the world champions were quick with praise and eager to not provide any bulletin board material. Defensive tackle Dave Hanner said, "I'd rather tackle anybody in the league than Rick Casares. He hits like a thunderbolt." Offensive tackle Norm Masters added, "Doug Atkins is big and tough and mean. If he wanted to, he could kill you. That's why I always give him a little sweet talk." Linebacker Ray Nitschke, never one to praise an opponent, opined, "Tom Bettis should help them a lot. He'll be valuable insurance because he can play either side or the middle." Lastly, center Jim Ringo added, "Bill George is one of the truly great craftsmen in the history of football."[38] The B.S. was getting piled pretty high with the Bears/Packers season opener less than two months away on September 15. While the Packers seemed to go out of their way with polite praise and correctness about their worthy opponent, no Bears response was forthcoming. None was needed; the Packers' recent successes said it all.

On Thursday, July 25, the Bears got their first real test when the College All-Stars travelled to Rensselaer for a full contact, controlled scrimmage.[39] In 90-degree heat the Bears prevailed, 13–12, when J.C. Caroline blocked an extra point attempt by the collegians. This was the also the big test for the All-Stars before they played the world champion Packers eight days later on Friday, August 2, at Chicago's Soldier Field.

The College All-Star game was the creation of the *Chicago Tribune*'s Arch Ward, who previously had established the Major League Baseball All-Star game between the American League and the National League as part of the Chicago World's Fair in 1933. The game typically attracted huge crowds—Soldier Field's bleachers held more than 100,000—and the game became a significant moneymaker for Chicago charities. The *Tribune* featured articles about the All-Stars and their exploits weeks before the contest was scheduled to enhance ticket sales, sometimes exaggerating the skills of the All-Stars to convince readers that it would be a close contest. By 1963, however, the superiority of the NFL champions was clearly established on an almost annual basis. In the 29 previous games before the August 2 matchup with the Packers, the NFL's record was 19–8–2. The last time the All-Stars won was in 1958, when they beat the error-prone Detroit Lions, 35–19. This was the game in which Lions quarterback Bobby Layne allegedly gambled on and significantly affected the final score.[40]

The controlled scrimmage was limited to each team running 72 plays in 10-play increments, starting from the offensive team's 30-yard line. The All-Stars' passing game was very effective, as four passers—Glynn Griffing of Mississippi (seven completions), Ron Vander Kelen of Wisconsin (six), Sonny Gibbs of Texas (six) and Terry Baker of Oregon (five)—completed 24 passes on 36 attempts. For the Bears, quarterback Rudy Bukich was 10 for 22 and Wade was eight for 15. The collegians held their own on defense and also on pass protection. Bob Jencks staked the All-Stars to a 6–0 lead with 27- and 40-yard field goals in the second quarter. The Bears answered when wideout Charlie Bivins took a lateral from Mike Ditka and scored the first touchdown of the day. Roger Leclerc's extra point attempt was low and the half ended at 6–6. In the third quarter Bill Wade connected with Ditka for a 16-yard touchdown and Leclerc was able to convert the extra point; after three quarters, Bears 13, All-Stars 6. In the fourth, Washington's speedy Charley Mitchell—who had been drafted in the fourth round by the Bears but decided to sign with the Denver Broncos—cut sharply off-tackle and finished off a 14-yard run to the end zone, making the score 13–12. On the extra point attempt, the crafty Caroline juked around the right end and blocked Bob Jencks' extra point, and giving the Bears 13–12 bragging rights. The *Tribune*'s enthusiasm for the All-Stars continued throughout their entire coverage. Sportswriter Roy Damer's final line was "All in all, it was a day on which the All-Stars won their spurs. With a little more improvement, they'll qualify as worthy opponents for the mighty Packers."[41]

The Bears were impressed with two All-Stars that they would be welcoming to their training camp after August 2, Larry Glueck, the defensive back from Villanova, and Jencks, the tall offensive end/place kicker from Miami of Ohio.[42] A grueling five weeks awaited, with preseason tiffs against the Giants, Redskins, Packers, Cardinals, and Colts affording the only time away from the heat and humidity of Rensselaer.

5

August

Back Home Again, in Indiana

Unfortunately for the Monsters of the Midway, turning the calendar to August meant a return to the humid plains of northwest Indiana for a series of very slow-moving weeks at St. Joseph's College in Rensselaer, Indiana. Rensselaer, 70 miles southeast of Chicago's city limits, had a population of 4,740 in 1960, with the total being closer to 6,000 when college was in session. Halas loved the place; the Bears started using it as their preseason base in 1944. To Papa Bear, the big advantage was the college's distance from urban distractions. Lafayette, Indiana, the home of Purdue University, was 42 miles south, and Gary, Indiana, was 54 miles north. With Halas' strict curfew and security crew there was not much for the players to do but think about football.

First order of business was running the infamous "Halas Mile." In the heat and humidity which that area of the Midwest is famous for, Halas had everyone run a timed mile to get an early gauge on their conditioning. He told the press that seven players did not reach the elapsed times he expected and that they would continue with the run until they did. He referred to them as the "slothful seven," adding that he would love to embarrass them by posting their names but he did not want Bears opponents to know their identity.[1] This was old-school Halas at its best, with the negative aspects of shaming to elicit change a wholly unfamiliar theory to the owner/coach.

The sole objective for this training camp was to mold a team that could conquer the Green Bay Packers, and on the night of Friday, August 2, that goal seemed a little more plausible. The Green Bay Packers settled into the Drake Hotel, their usual digs when playing in Chicago, for what they thought would be another ho-hum preseason tune-up against a bunch of amateurs. College All-Stars, yes, but still not pro football players. They apparently paid little attention to the collegians' showing in Rensselaer.

The All-Stars' surprisingly strong showing against the Bears bolstered their confidence against the Packers. Their coach, Otto Graham, said, "The main thing left for us is to acquire finesse in our play. The boys did a good job against the Bears, but we can't afford to rest on that performance. We still haven't reached our peak."[2] Daryl Sanders, the Detroit Lions first-round draft pick who played offensive tackle against the Bears' Maury Youmans, added, "We went down there expecting to get hit and we did. I learned a lot in that scrimmage, playing opposite Youmans. After the game he showed me a few things on how I could improve myself. In rushing passes, they don't power you as much as finesse you, but our line coach Dick Stanfel has taught us a few tricks and I thought we did pretty well." Quarterback Terry Baker, headed for the Los Angeles Rams after the Packer game, talked about the confidence the Bears' scrimmage provided. "A great indoctrination to pro ball for us. It showed most of us we could play this game." He admitted to some apprehension facing the Bears' defense but the performance all the collegians gave turned out to be a huge morale booster. Ed Budde, the Kansas City Chiefs' and Philadelphia Eagles' first-round draft choice, played all day against the Bears' Earl Leggett. "The Bears did not hit as hard as expected," Budde explained, "but they did show me some real good moves without concentrating on power."[3]

In the Packer contest Sanders would be going against Bill Quinlan, Baker and the other quarterbacks would be staring across the line at Henry Jordan and Ray Nitschke, and Budde's assignment was to neutralize Dave "Hog" Hanner. To Lombardi's great irritation and Graham's jubilation, the All-Stars beat the Packers, 20–17, in front 65,000, most of whom made the pilgrimage down from Green Bay.[4] In spite of the close score it was a valid conquest by the collegians, who outgained the Packers on the ground, 141 yards to 96, and also in the air, 183–169. Two All-Stars shined the brightest, placekicker Bob Jencks and a Green Bay native who was hoping to be drafted by the Packers, Wisconsin quarterback Ron Vander Kelen. Vander Kelen, who left the next day for the Minnesota Vikings' training camp, keyed the victory with his accurate passes and a critical touchdown pass to Pat Richter for the decisive touchdown in the fourth quarter. Disappointed Packer fans had seen the Vander Kelen to Richter act many times before and welcomed it. Those two gridiron stars were largely responsible for the University of Wisconsin winning the Big Ten title and going on to a narrow defeat against USC in the Rose Bowl just eight months earlier.

There were reports that Jim Taylor was not at his best with an injured knee, Ray Nitschke was suffering from a back ailment,[5] and the Packers had less preparation time than the All-Stars, but Lombardi manned up to the situation. "We have no excuses," he said. "It was a fine All-Star squad and Vander Kelen is a great pro prospect."[6] Vander Kelen was carried off the field on his teammates' shoulders but took no credit. "I got real good protection," he beamed. "The guys up front—Ed Budde, Dave Behrman, Don Chuy, and Daryl Sanders—did a great job. I can't say anything bad about the Packers—we Vikings have to play them two more times in the season."[7] The game was the first Packer loss in their last 18 preseason contests, and coach Lombardi was furious.[8]

Lombardi invited the three All-Stars he had drafted—Tony Liscio of Tulsa, Chuck Morris of Ole Miss, and future Hall of Famer Dave Robinson—to the team's post-game buffet at the Drake after the game. Robinson remembered that "Lombard was so mad he wouldn't even speak to me. He was so mad because of the game he wouldn't speak with any of us ... he looked at us, turned and walked away. We were like lepers, sitting by ourselves. A couple of players came over and said welcome to the team, but they weren't real happy. They knew we created havoc and there would be hell to pay next week at training camp."[9]

Lombardi's treatment of Robinson indicated how obsessed he was about a third straight NFL title. Robinson was one of the most highly-touted defenders leaving college in 1963, and to lure him away from the San Diego Chargers in the AFL, Lombardi, by 1963 standards, gave him the store. Robinson got a $45,000 two-year contract that included a $15,000 signing bonus and the use of a new Pontiac Bonneville convertible from one of Lombardi's favorite connections, Jake Stathas of Brown County Motors.[10] Syndicated sports columnist Dick Hackenberg pointed out that in spite of the embarrassment to the NFL, Pete Rozelle must have secretly been glad about the game's outcome, since it showed that the Packers could not have possibly bet on themselves.[11]

Meanwhile, at Rensselaer, George Allen was getting worried about his linebacking corps. Larry Morris had not yet reported to camp due to his business partner in Georgia suffering a heart attack. To make matters much worse, Tom Bettis, obtained from the Packers to shore up the depth at all three linebacking positions, suffered a dislocated elbow and might miss the next seven weeks.[12] This development put Coach Halas in an even fouler mood than he had been. The first exhibition game against the Giants was three days away and the injuries were piling up at an alarming rate. Bettis would miss the trip, along with Ed O'Bradovich, Willie Galimore, Charlie Bivins, and rookie John Gregory. Halas did not seem to understand the correlation between the excessive number of full-contact scrimmages he was scheduling and the health of the team. "We've tightened up considerably and are out to improve our execution and general technique. We've decided this is the way to do it; scrimmage, scrimmage, scrimmage."[13] Halas felt a little better as the team departed to Ithaca, New York, for an exhibition game against the New York Giants on August 10.

Dr. Ted Fox had informed him that Bettis' elbow injury was a sprain, not a tear or dislocation, and that the veteran linebacker would be ready very soon, possibly for the second pre-season game against the Washington Redskins.[14] While he still fumed about all the players who would not make the trip to New York, columnist William N. Wallace in the *New York Times* offered the coach some good reasons why he should be pleased that O'Bradovich would not grace the field.

Many thought the feisty young defensive end cost the Bears a victory in their grudge match at Wrigley Field against the Giants the previous season on December 2, 1962.[15] In front of 49,000 screaming Bears fans and referee Bill Downes, O'Bradovich landed a barrage of punches on Giant halfback Phil King. His behavior got him kicked out of the game and a $50 fine by the NFL, and it cost his team 15 yards, allowing the Giants to move from the 45- to the 30-yard line. At the time the Bears had a one-point lead, 24–23. Don Chandler changed that with a field goal and the Giants limped home with a 26–24 victory, the Bears' only loss in the last six weeks of the season.

O'Bradovich was roundly criticized by his teammates but had what seemed like a reasonable explanation. The Bears' defensive tackle Fred Williams had been hooking, poking, and provoking King all through the game, and after King complained in the huddle, Frank Gifford, who undoubtedly had his own score that he wanted to settle with O'Bradovich, told King that O'Bradovich was King's harasser and aggressor. So "the play ends and I'm walking back to the huddle, and all of a sudden this King comes up and pops me right in the back of the head. I admit I got a short temper; I blew, I went for him," landing some punches, O'Bradovich explained. Referee Downes immediately kicked O'Bradovich out of the game and Giants head coach Allie Sherman replaced King with Joe Morrison. The 15-yard penalty was assessed, and Chandler kicked the winning field goal.

O'Bradovich, however, never calmed down. He walked over to the Giants' locker room after the game looking for King. Giants veteran Jack Stroud, shorter than O'Bradovich but heavier and 12 years older, intervened, and O'Bradovich did no further damage. Over the summer King, a Vanderbilt alum like the Bears' Bill Wade, told Wade to tell O'Bradovich he apologized and that the embroglio was the result of a misunderstanding on his part. O'Bradovich took the news with a question: "What about Gifford? I think he's a guy who owes me $50." Wallace asked Gifford about it the next day at Giants training camp. "Not a chance, I'll send him a case of bubble gum."[16] It might only be the first exhibition game of the 1963 season, but the Bears-Giants affair did not seem like it would be for the faint of heart.

The Chicagoans flew to Syracuse on Friday, August 9, and then took a 50-mile bus trip to the dormitories of Ithaca College, their headquarters for the weekend. At the other side of town was Cornell's Schoellkopf Field, where portable bleachers were added to the stadium's permanent seats, in anticipation of perhaps 25,000 for the game. It was the first Bears game in an Ivy League facility but the third for the Giants, who previously had games at Princeton and Yale.[17]

The hype for this contest was extremely high, considering it was a preseason contest. While they had no championships to show for it, the New Yorkers had a phenomenal .770 winning percentage (47–14–1) over the last five years with four Eastern Division championships, 1958, '59, '61, and '62. Their winning percentage was more than 100 points better than the next most successful team over that period, the Cleveland Browns (39–22–1, .639) The game also featured two record-breaking quarterbacks facing off: in 1962 Y.A. Tittle set an NFL record by throwing 33 touchdown passes, and Bill Wade shattered Sid Luckman's 15-year-old team records for completion percentage and passing yards. In 1961 Wade led the NFL in passer rating, comeback victories, and long pass completions. In 1962 he was the league's best in comeback victories, game-winning drives, and passes completed. The studious, young Allie Sherman was a coaching contrast to Papa Bear Halas. The game featured two of the best four defenses in the NFL, if one included Green Bay and Detroit in the mix. Arguments abounded; was Huff better than George, Robustelli more effective than Atkins, Johnny Morris equal to Frank Gifford? These issues were all front and center, with the backdrop being the bad blood between the teams going back to at least 1956, greatly intensified in 1962.

A crowd of 21,00 mostly Giants aficionados settled into their seats on a beautiful summer afternoon and saw their heroes from Gotham beaten up and outplayed by the Chicagoans, 17–7. The Bears outrushed the Giants, 192 to 69 yards, as Ronnie Bull, Rudy Bukich, and Bo Farrington stole the offensive show in Ithaca. Bull rushed for 86 yards on 15 carries, while Bukich, the Bears' veteran second string quarterback, completed seven of nine passes for 116 yards. Bo Farrington caught six of seven passes, two of them for touchdowns from Bukich.

Even with O'Bradovich back in Chicago the Bears had plenty of combatants who were more than willing to intimidate their foes.[18] Offensive guard Roger Davis cold-cocked Giants defensive back Erich Barnes when he thought Barnes had unnecessarily roughed up Wade after he was already out of bounds. Ditka had enough of the Giants' Tom Scott holding him and rudely put him down. Guard Ted Karras took offense at New York's legendary roughneck Andy Robustelli, and their fisticuffs ended in a brawl. Even Bears rookie kicker Bob Jencks, playing in his first professional game, got physical with Giants veteran Tom Lynch.[19] Since Karras threw the last punch in his dust-up with Robustelli and it was the only one seen by the referees, he was thrown out of the game and fined $50.[20]

Halas was pleased with the afternoon's proceedings and was loquacious with the press after the game. "I have not had a chance to discuss [the ejection] with Karras," he told the press, going on to effuse, "Bull, he's going to be a great one," referring to the performance by the 1962 NFL Rookie of the Year.[21] The Karras ejection brought back unpleasant memories of O'Bradovich's rage nine months earlier which many thought cost the Bears a victory.

It was not all negative for the New Yorkers. Coach Allie Sherman did not make a big deal out of Don Chandler's four missed field goals and was pleased with the three spectacular catches for 77 yards made by rookie Roger Reynolds, a Bowling Green alum slated to be Frank Gifford's understudy. But the superiority of the Midwesterners was obvious on this day and Robustelli summed it up the best: "This one's over and thank goodness we don't have to play them again."[22] While they lost the personal battles as well as the contest, the Giants could feel good about their post-game health. "This is the first time in 35 years," stated Giants team physician Dr. Francis J. Sweeney, "that we played the Bears and didn't need X-rays afterward."[23]

On the way back to Chicago Halas wasted little time paring down his preseason roster. Rensselaer would be short six rookies the following week, as end Dennis Andrews (Virginia), linebacker Bobby Marshall (Virginia Union), defensive back Dennis Harmon (Southern Illinois), guard Larry Coleman (Indiana), defensive back Woody Moore (Indiana), and tackle Ken Thomas (Grambling) were all cut. None of these individuals caught on with other NFL teams.

Doug Atkins broke Rensselaer's humid drudgery after the team returned from Ithaca. As his teammates readied for a 9:00 a.m., full-padded practice, Atkins waltzed out toward the field with spikes, shorts, a t-shirt, and a shiny helmet. He went right past Halas, ignoring him completely, not saying a word, and then went into a slow-motion trot around the field. His curious teammates could not stop themselves from occasional glimpses of Atkins' unusual performance, followed by a stolen glance at Papa Bear to gauge his disgust with this act of disobedience. The speed, noise, and violence of the contact drills were in direct contrast to the serene slow-jogger who endlessly circled the field. After practice Halas chose to avoid a confrontation with his giant nemesis, but a teammate went up to Atkins and asked him what was going on. "Oh, I just decided to break in a new helmet this morning," Atkins explained.[24]

On Monday afternoon Halas met with the press and changed his tune somewhat about the preseason win over the Giants. "We are not too elated over our victory though it was a nice win," he explained. "We took 48 men to Ithaca and managed to use 45 of them and now we know a bit more about all of our squad members."[25] The Bears' infirmary list got smaller as the week went on, with only Willie Galimore, Ed O'Bradovich, and John Johnson scheduled to miss the second exhibition game Thursday, August 15, against the Redskins.

The game would feature the return of halfback Charlie Bivins, who missed the trip to Ithaca. His presence was a welcome sight for Ronnie Bull and Johnny Morris. With Galimore and Bivins out, Bull did the lion's share of the rushing against the tough Giants. Bivins' absence also left a big hole, filled by Morris, on kickoff returns. He was the Bears' seventh-round pick in the 1960 draft after finishing his college career at Morris Brown in Atlanta. While Bivins was picked in the second round by the Buffalo Bills, he eschewed more money to play with the Bears in the more established NFL. Bivins attracted attention because of his size and speed. At 6'1", 212 pounds, he was big for a running back, and while lacking the acceleration of a Willie Galimore or the sprint swiftness of a Johnny Morris, Bivins could run a 9.6-second 100-yard dash. For an athlete of Bivins' size this timing was exceptional. The Bears put Bivins' abilities to good use; he returned 52 kickoffs his first two years in the NFL for an admirable 1,273 yards, averaging almost 25 yards per return, with only one fumble, and a long run of 78 yards in 1962. On offense Bivins could fill in at either half-back or fullback. Since joining the Bears he had 48 rushes for 221 yards and two touchdowns along with seven pass receptions for 33 yards.

The Bears lost a squeaker to Washington in the 1962 preseason, 29–28, in Norfolk, Virginia, so Halas was eager to settle the score with his long-time rival, Redskins owner George Preston Marshall. The two teams had not met in the regular season since December 10, 1957, when Halas' game of musical chairs with the quarterback position led to the "Three B's"—Zeke Bartkowski, George Blanda, and Ed Brown—all playing ineffectively. Fans were mystified why Halas would not stick with Brown, who led the entire NFL in passing the year before, and the result was a rare 14–3 Redskin victory. With Pete Rozelle in charge Marshall's influence in the NFL was waning, and the Redskins of late had the sorriest record of all the established teams in the league. Since 1958 their five-year winning percentage was .241, 14–44–6; the 'Skins won fewer than one out of every four contests. The only team in the NFL with a worse record over that period was the Minnesota Vikings—and they had only been in the league one year, going 2–11–1 in 1962. The Redskins had not been to the postseason since 1946; Marshall had only himself to blame, refusing to integrate the roster and insisting on loading up on non-minority players from Southern colleges and universities.

Pressure by Rozelle did lead to the Redskins having some Black players on the roster, most notably halfback Bobby Mitchell, whom Washington got in a trade with the Browns for their first-round pick, Syracuse's Ernie Davis. While Marshall refused minority players, he had no issue with individuals exemplifying America's melting pot. Perennial All-Pro defensive tackle Bob Toneff, one of a few widely heralded Redskins, fit the bill more than any other NFL player. The Detroit native's father was from Bulgaria and his mother from Serbia. He starred for the Irish at Notre Dame, was drafted into the military and played in Germany, and went on to play in the nation's capital.[26] The Redskins slated second-year Wake Forest alum Norm Snead as the quarterback to face the Bears. Snead was a first-round choice by the Redskins. At 6'4" he had excellent field vision and durability, but he threw three interceptions in the three games he played in 1962. Snead's offense featured the newly acquired Mitchell at flanker and the rookie sensation from the University of Wisconsin at end, Pat Richter. The game was the nation's capital's annual Shrine Benefit Game, and 40,000 were expected in the D.C. Stadium, which became the Redskins' new home three years earlier. This game would be the Bears' first appearance in what was considered one of the finest NFL facilities, their previous encounters in the nation's capital being at antiquated Griffith Stadium, baseball home of the Washington Senators.

The Bears played two good quarters and two rather forgettable ones against the Redskins and prevailed for the victory, 28–26. The scoring started after Roosevelt Taylor intercepted a Snead pass, which gave Wade and the Bear offense the ball at the Redskins' six-yard line and an easy touchdown. Wade engineered a well-executed 79-yard drive toward the end of the first period that ended with Casares plunging over from the one, to put the Bears up 14–0.

Snead and the Redskins came to life, however, in the second quarter, when the 'Skins got three touchdowns and a Bob Khayat field goal to go up 23–14 at halftime. Two pass interference penalties on Bennie McRae set up the first two Washington tallies and a third pass interference call—against rookie Larry Glueck with only 13 seconds left—set up the third score. Khayat's field goal came between the second and third touchdowns.

Early in the third quarter the Bears' special teams' unit provided a big boost when Billy Martin ran back a punt 77 yards for a touchdown. After Jencks converted for his third extra point the Bears were within two, 23–21. Rudy Bukich, starting at quarterback for Halas in the second half, pulled out the victory with a perfect 68-yard bomb to Bo Farrington—shades of the Giants game the week before. Khayat kicked another field goal in the fourth quarter to bring Washington within two points, and the Redskins were threatening to score late in the fourth when Davey Whitsell intercepted Snead's pass intended for Fred Dugan, sealing a sloppy, 28–26 preseason victory. The biggest casualty from the game was the loss of reserve defensive back and special teams return man Tommy Neck, who successfully ran back three punts for 72 yards against the Giants and Redskins. Neck would be out indefinitely with torn knee ligaments.[27]

Halas had little to say about the Washington game, his mind preoccupied with the upcoming Milwaukee matchup with the Green Bay Packers. He was quite pleased, however, with the performance of Farrington and Martin, whose contributions indicated that the Bears' offense could be stronger than predicted. John "Bo" Farrington was born January 18, 1936, in DeWalt, Texas. Farrington prepped at Houston's football factory, Yates High School, and was the first of the school's 23 alumni who have played in the NFL. Farrington's labors on Yates' gridiron earned him a scholarship to Prairie View A&M, where he rose to become their premiere pass catcher. Farrington's Prairie View team went undefeated in 1958, and he played a prominent role in their Orange Blossom Bowl victory in 1959. The Bears drafted him in the 16th round in 1960, and he became a reliable receiver right from the start of his career. In his 45 games with the Bears he had seven touchdowns and only one fumble. His 98-yard reception in 1961 was the longest in the NFL that season.

Billy Martin was one of four Bears—along with Tom Bettis, Ed O'Bradovich, and Mike Pyle—to have grown up in the Chicago area. Martin was the only one who was a South Side Chicagoan, from the Bronzeville neighborhood. He graduated from the storied Wendell Phillips High School, whose alumni include Gwendolyn Brooks, Nat "King" Cole, Dinah Washington, and NFL Hall of Famer Buddy Young. Phillips was a football power in the Chicago Public League, which over the years had been almost a minor league for the NFL. Since the NFL's inception 38 of the 78 high schools in the Chicago Public League have contributed 194 players to NFL rosters, including Bears fixtures like George Halas (Crane Tech) and Dick Butkus (Chicago Vocational). Martin was the seventh prep gridder from Phillips to play professionally. The shifty 5'11", 197-pound running back won a football scholarship to Minnesota, and under the tutelage of legendary coach Murray Warmath, he became a favorite target of quarterback Sandy Stephens. After Minnesota's 1961 Rose Bowl loss to Washington Martin began his professional career, having been drafted in the fourth round by the Bears in 1960 as a future selection. In his rookie season Martin was fourth in the NFL in total kick returns, behind Abe Woodson of the 49ers, Dick James of the Redskins, and Pat Studstill of the Lions. His 17 punt returns and 25 kickoff runbacks netted 515 yards, the longest scamper a 47-yard kickoff return. Martin even saw some spot duty behind the line of scrimmage, rushing nine times for 25 yards and one touchdown. After his showing against Washington Martin proved he was a threat every time he touched the ball in the open field.

Unfortunately, back in Chicago, the name of one of the Bears' key players came up in the Chicago press.[28] Mike Ditka served as president of Mike Ditka's Willowbrook Lanes, an $800,000 bowling alley in west suburban Willowbrook, Illinois. Ditka owned 20 percent of the stock in this venture. Anton Borse, the village president, and his wife, Florence, the village clerk, were charged with demanding a $7,000 payment to grant Willowbrook Lanes a $750 annual liquor license. R. Lee Huszagh, an attorney from nearby Wheaton, Illinois, acted as the intermediary. Huszagh apparently had a change of heart after delivering half the funds to the Borse home and spoke with William V. Hopf, the assistant state's attorney of DuPage County. Hopf also revealed that a grand jury was being summoned to investigate the matter; he also pointed out that neither Ditka nor any other members of the board of Willowbrook Lanes were under any suspicion of guilt.[29] This was the kind of negative publicity and bad press Halas dreaded. The Willowbrook Lanes would be back in the news at the end of the season, with far-reaching implications.

During the game in Washington defensive end Maury Youmans suffered a left knee injury which at the time was considered minor. However, when he came on the practice field at Rensselaer on Monday, August 20, his knee locked up and he underwent emergency orthopedic surgery that evening.[30] This injury left the Bears very thin at the left defensive end position with a preseason game against Green Bay just five days away. Ed O'Bradovich was still unavailable due to health issues, so Bob Kilcullen, the veteran with experience at all four defensive line spots, would have to step in. It also meant that the untested Luther Jeralds might see significant playing time against the world champions.[31] Jeralds was a training camp invitee who had not played since 1961, when he appeared in nine games for the AFL's Dallas Texans. At this point Allen, Halas, Stydahar, and the rest of the coaching staff were glad the Green Bay matchup was only a preseason game.

The Bears' defensive brain trust, however, had a lot to be pleased about with the play of second-year defensive back Bennie McRae.[32] The 23-year-old, six-foot, 180-pound Michigan alum was taken in the second round in the 1962 draft. McRae excelled as a two-sport athlete in the Big Ten. In the fall he was the feature back in Bump Elliott's offense, earning AP and UPI first-team All-Big Ten honors. McRae also gained 230 yards catching passes. His athleticism was not limited to the gridiron; he was also one of the most significant collegiate track men of his time. McRae was listed as one of the top 10 low hurdlers in the world in the spring of 1961.[33]

While McRae saw action in every game during his rookie season in 1962, he only started one game, making an interception with a 47-yard run back and recovering one fumble. His play during the 1963 preseason thus far had been extremely impressive. He started against the Giants in the Ithaca preseason opener, replacing Davey Whitsell, and was given the thankless task of covering the Giants' All-Pro Del Shofner. Y.A. Tittle tried to connect five times with Shofner during the contest but McRae shut him out completely. The following week against the Redskins he replaced J.C. Caroline in the defensive backfield and had to match the steps of Washington's peerless future Hall of Famer Bobby Mitchell. Norm Snead threw 21 times to Mitchell but was successful only eight times, each for short yardage. McRae was making his presence known, and at this point it was a toss-up whether Allen would decide on Caroline, McRae, or Whitsell as his two starting defensive backs—a nice decision to make, indeed.

Next on the training camp schedule was the biggest test of the Bears' preseason, Saturday night, August 24, the 14th Annual Midwest Shrine Classic against the Packers in Milwaukee County Stadium, the home of baseball's Milwaukee Braves. The Packers always drew well in Milwaukee and a sellout of more than 46,000 was expected.[34] Bears fans could hear the game live on WGN Radio and watch a delayed television broadcast at 10:30 p.m. on Chicago's CBS outlet, WBBM-TV.[35]

WGN announcer Jack Brickhouse would have one of the busiest weekends of his career, broadcasting four baseball games and one football contest over span of 52 hours. On Friday afternoon, August 23, he was assigned to the televised Cubs-Mets game in Wrigley Field, after which he would fly to New York to broadcast the White Sox night game against the Yankees in the Bronx. Brickhouse was then to fly back to Chicago early Saturday morning and cover the Saturday afternoon Cubs-Mets contest on TV, then drive to Milwaukee to broadcast the Bears-Packers game on the WGN radio. His weekend would end late in the afternoon Sunday, a Sunday which included a drive back from Milwaukee to Chicago and a televised broadcast of the series finale between the Cubs and Mets Sunday afternoon.[36]

After their All-Star game disappointment the Packers preseason consisted of two easy conquests, victories over the Pittsburgh Steelers, 27–7, and the Dallas Cowboys, 31–10. In spite of their victories after the All-Star surprise, Vince Lombardi was not a happy camper coming into the Bears game. On several occasions he told the press that he was "far from pleased" with his team's performance, which he called "spotty" at best.[37] He also singled out one of Green Bay's best players, fullback Jimmy Taylor, for criticism, complaining that Taylor has been loafing in practice and not "stinging tacklers with his old authority."[38] The Packers entered the contest at full strength, with the exception of halfback Elijah Pitts, who was out with a shoulder separation.

The Bears' injury report had more names. Maury Youmans and Ed O'Bradovich were out with injuries, and Bob Kilcullen would fill in at left defensive end. Halas decided to keep Willie Galimore out of the contest as well, wary about risking him against the Packers in a preseason game after his knee surgeries. He also made it clear that Stan Jones had beaten out veteran Fred Williams for the starting left defensive tackle position, Bennie McRae would start at left cornerback, and Joe Marconi would get his first preseason start at fullback. For some unexplained reason Halas also revealed a new wrinkle in the game plan, explaining that he may at times have Marconi and first-string fullback Rick Casares on offense at the same time, displaying a "power backfield" for the Packers to contend with.[39] It was unclear whether this plan was a smoke screen intended to distract the Packers or if he was serious. Why he would present this in a preseason game instead of saving it as a surprise in the season opener in Green Bay was a mystery.

The game was not unlike other Bear-Packer games of the previous years, with the champions prevailing 26–7. It was evident throughout the game that Halas did not reach deeply into the Bears' bag of tricks, content to have matched the Packers through the first half. In the first quarter the Bears thwarted a Packer scoring opportunity when Dave Whitsell blocked Jerry Kramer's attempted 33-yard field goal, moving the ball back to the Bears' 43, where the offense took over. Bill Wade engineered a 57-yard drive at that point, highlighted by a spectacular catch by Ditka over Jesse Whittenton at the Packer 16, and then some patented Wade fakery at the four-yard line, ending in a bullet pass to Ditka at the back of the end zone to put the Bears ahead, 7–0.

In the second quarter the Packers drove the length of the field on the legs of Tom Moore and Jim Taylor; Kramer tried a field goal from the 18 but his kick was wide of the mark. The Bears went nowhere offensively after the miss, and when Bobby Joe Green's poor punt landed on the Bear 41, the Packers had great field position. The Packers' drive was helped by a roughness call, after which Bart Starr hit a streaking Ron Kramer between the uprights to put the Packers on the board. Jerry Kramer's extra point attempt was blocked by J.C. Caroline, so the Bears held the lead, 7–6. The Packers took note that in less than one half of football the Bears special teams' unit had kept four points off the board; the half ended with the Chicagoans ahead by one point.

After that it was all downhill for the Monsters of the Midway. Bukich replaced Wade and Casares replaced Marconi; the "power backfield" of Marconi and Casares never materialized in the contest. Catches by Boyd Dowler and Max McGee, coupled with the strong running of Moore and Taylor, resulted in a 10-play, 76-yard touchdown drive ending in McGee's end zone catch that put the Packers ahead for good, 13–7. Bukich led a nice drive soon after that got the ball to the Packers one-yard line. On second down, Ronnie Bull could not nudge across for the score; on third, Casares did not make it either. On fourth down, Bukich once more called Bull's number, but he was stopped short of the goal line. The Packers immediately picked up the pace when they took over on their own one-yard line. Bart Starr's pass to Tom Moore was good for 22 yards. Passes to Dowler and Kramer, coupled with a 12-yard burst from Jim Taylor, had the ball on the Bears' 20 as the third period ended. Dowler then got into it with Bears linebacker Larry Morris and drew a penalty, moving the ball back to the 30 and costing Dowler any opportunity to continue in the contest. Jerry Kramer then kicked a field goal to put the Packers in complete command, 16–7. Another Kramer field goal and a pick-six interception by Dave Robinson, the Packers' prized rookie defensive end, made the final score 26–7.

While Mike Ditka caught four passes and Ronnie Bull gained 101 yards on 18 carries and two pass receptions, with the exception of their special teams' kick defense the Bears did not distinguish themselves in this outing whatsoever. The Packers got 24 first downs to the Bears' 16, they outgained the Bears in total yards, 375 to 219, and and Bart Starr outclassed Wade in the first half and Bukich in the second, completing 19 of 27 passes while the Bear quarterbacks managed only nine of 22. Rick Casares took some of the blame, claiming that the game would have been different if he had scored late in the third period.

"I've learned my lesson," he said. "I saw Willie Wood [Packers defensive back] behind the goal post and as soon as I drove my head into him I stopped charging, thinking I was over. Next time I won't stop running until I hit the grandstand."[40] While a touchdown at that point would have put the Bears ahead 14–13, both teams were freely substituting after that point, and the Packer offense had their way with the Bears' second teamers. Bukich's errant pass, picked off by Robinson, sealed their fate. Legendary broadcaster Jack Brickhouse's frenetic weekend was kind of a bust. Chicago teams were 2–7 in the games he covered, with the Sox being swept in the Bronx by the Yankees, the Bears losing badly in Milwaukee, and the Cubs taking two out of three from the Mets. The only bright spot for Windy City fans was the pitching of the classy lefty Dick Ellsworth in the Cubs' 3–1 victory over the Mets on Sunday, the 25th. Ellsworth won his

18th game two weeks before Labor Day for a fading seventh-place team, lowering his ERA to 2.03, bested only by Sandy Koufax.

Afterward George Halas kept a lower profile than expected, considering that the Bears lost so convincingly to the team he never stopped obsessing over. "In three exhibition games opponents have completed 51 of 103 passes for 744 yards and four touchdowns," he told the press.[41] "We will concentrate on closing some of the leaks in pass defense."[42] There were four issues causing this poor performance.

George Allen was still experimenting with the personnel in the defensive backfield. While rookie Larry Glueck was unlikely to start, he got playing time on defense, taking time away from Caroline, McRae, Petitbon, Taylor, and Whitsell. The coaching staff had to see what Glueck could do, especially since he was taken so early in the draft. Secondly, the starting core four was not completely established. Taylor and Petitbon were solid at the two safety positions, but the choice between Caroline, McRae, and Whitsell for the two defensive halfback slots—not to mention who fit best on which side—was still not established. The third point was that Allen was having the Bears work on more intricate and varied defenses in Rensselaer than he was bringing into the exhibition games. Lastly, the defensive line in some ways was as unsettled as the defensive backfield.

Injuries had created a hole in the left defensive end position with O'Bradovich still not available and Youmans needing emergency knee surgery. Even with the other positions settled with Doug Atkins, Earl Leggett, and Stan Jones, the unit was not as cohesive as it could be without consistency in the other end position. Once the position was more settled the teamwork of that end with the outside linebacker—whether it was Joe Fortunato, Larry Morris, or the recently returned Tom Bettis—would be much more effective. Also, the emphasis in the exhibition games so far was not on pass rushing and stunts but on being more effective against the run. In 1962, in spite of their excellent record, the Bears defense ranked 13th out of 14 teams against the run. "We're through being patsies," Halas declared. "We're starting to make the other guys stop and think before they run into the middle of our line." Defensive line coach Jumbo Joe Stydahar added, "we're paying more attention to the little details—the proper use of forearms, the use of the head." In the three preseason games the emphasis on improving the run defense seemed to be paying off. In 14 games in 1962 the Bears gave up an average of 4.7 yards per opponents' carry; for the three exhibition games the average was only 3.2, an improvement of almost a third.[43] They also had good depth on the line, with Fred Williams, four-year veteran Stan Fanning, and Luther Jeralds, a camp invitee from North Carolina who had played with the Dallas Texans in 1961, being capable backups.

Some of this explained the Bears' poor defense against the world champions, but the offense only scored seven points and was not immune to criticism with the season opener less than three weeks away. Quarterback Bill Wade answered questions from the press about this while he prepared for the preseason matchup with the Cardinals.[44] "There's a very good reason [for the offense being unproductive]. I have often called running plays in situations where, if it were a league game, a pass might have been better. We need the practice in our ground game; it's a belief in the system." Wade went on to explain, "We are developing and polishing a new system; certain changes have been blocking assignments, and our linemen and backs must have experience in the new system. The blocking techniques are more complicated than those on pass protection, and I feel it is vitally necessary that we perfect our ground before the regular season."[45] Both he and Rudy Bukich were forbidden from reaching deep in the playbook against Green Bay, especially with a matchup against them two weeks later in the season opener. Wade was considered one of the most analytical and introspective quarterbacks in the NFL at the time, and he ended with a universal question the league would wait 23 years to address. "I fully believe Casares scored in the third period, but I can't prove it. Why can't a photographic device be installed on both goal lines to take a picture of a close play, just as the cameras record a dead heat at Arlington Park?"[46]

Focusing on the upcoming 18th Annual Armed Forces Football Game in Soldier Field against the Cardinals, Halas announced that Willie Galimore would play for the first time this preseason. Offensive line coach Phil Handler praised the progress of their prized rookie Steve Barnett, and George Allen remarked on the successful efforts of linebacker Tom Bettis against his old team in the Bears' loss to the Packers.[47] While the newcomers on the team may not have sensed it, to Papa Bear the Cardinal rivalry meant almost as much as his animus toward the Packers.

From 1921 through 1960 George Halas' chief gridiron rivalry was not Green Bay but the other professional team calling Chicago home, the Chicago Cardinals. The Bears and the Cards competed in the same division of the NFL from 1921 through 1949. There were at least five contests between the teams at a season's culmination which had direct bearing on who would be the division champion. Halas owed his economic survival in many ways to his friendship with and the generosity of the Cardinals' owner, Charles W. Bidwill, Sr., who, during his ownership from 1933 until his untimely death in 1947, was one of the wealthiest individuals in professional sports.

Bidwill was also a minority owner of the Chicago Bears.[48] In 1931 Halas had to raise $38,000, half the value of the franchise at the time, to buy out his original partner, Carl "Dutch" Sternaman. He borrowed money from everyone he could—including his mother—and Bidwill's contribution was $5,000. Right before Bidwill's death in 1947 he and Halas agreed that Bidwill's share of the team had appreciated 10-fold, to $50,000. When Bidwill died that April his substantial estate was frozen and put in probate, and hiw wife Violet Bidwill asked Halas for the $50,000 he owed for the stock.

This put Papa Bear in perhaps the most difficult financial bind of his life. In the immediate post-war years Halas was still taking out loans every off-season from the American National Bank to keep the team solvent until season ticket revenues arrived.[49] He did not have the cash, but, like Connie Mack in Philadelphia, could raise funds by selling players. Violet knew that Halas had the most promising young quarterback in the NFL at the time, Bobby Layne, and mentioned to him that she would settle the debt if Layne simply came to the South Side, to lead the Cardinals. There was no way Halas would agree to this. The Cardinals were on the upswing, on the verge of two championship seasons, and he could not envision strengthening his in-city rival any further; enter Ted Collins and his failing Boston Yanks/New York Bulldogs.

Ted Collins was an impresario involved with the singer Kate Smith who was losing close to $300,00 a year with his Boston Yanks, an NFL team that moved to New York, changing their name to the Bulldogs in 1949.[50] He needed a star to take some attention away from the long-established New York Giants. Halas made him an offer he could not refuse. Take Layne, give me two number-one draft choices and $50,000 cash, and you can have the most promising quarterback in the NFL. There was only one additional stipulation: Layne could never be traded to the Cardinals. Collins took the deal, Layne was never to haunt Halas from Chicago's South Side, and Halas could now pay off Violet Bidwill.

This settled an immediate crisis between the Cardinals and the Bears, but the relationship between the franchises only got worse. The rivalry on the field continued well after Bidwill's passing; the good relations between the Bears and the Cardinals ended at the same time.[51]

When Bidwill died in April 1947 he missed seeing the Cardinals win their first championship since 1925 by eight months. Violet Bidwill became the team owner, inheriting 85 percent of the stock, and enjoyed the championship victory in December 1947 and the return trip to the NFL championship game the following year, when they lost to the Philadelphia Eagles, 7–0, in a game that came to be known as the "Blizzard Bowl."

Violet married Walter Wolfner, her financial consultant, who had made money investing in World War I surplus materiel and coffee imports, in 1949. She also named him managing director of the Cardinals, a position for which he was ill-prepared. Wolfner fought with the press,

Cardinal staff, Halas, and the NFL establishment, claiming that commissioner Bert Bell had it out for the Cards and favored Halas at every turn. The Cardinals had the poorest attendance in the NFL during Wolfner's time, and the league lost money because of it. The revenue sharing policy at that time dictated that the visiting team receive 40 percent of the gate, or a $20,000 guarantee. Since almost all Cardinal games resulted in the $20,000 being more than 40 percent of the Cards' measly attendance, visiting teams barely broke even when they came to play at Comiskey Park—expenses for an NFL team's road trip in that era was around $15,000.[52]

Wolfner worked out a plan to move the team to nearby Northwestern University and play in Dyche Stadium, in Chicago's leafy lakefront suburban area. Halas wanted no part of the Cardinals playing in a stadium larger than Wrigley Field, with easy transportation access, in an area where many of his season ticket holders resided, Chicago's north shore. He dusted off an old agreement he had with Charles Bidwill saying that the Cardinals must stay south of Madison Street (the north-south demarcation for Chicago's city limits) and the Bears must stay north. Wolfner told Halas that the old agreement was null and void, since he would not be in Chicago but Evanston, Illinois. The matter was taken up by the NFL office, and Bell sided with his old comrade, Halas, and the Cards had to stay put in Comiskey Park.

Bell put more pressure to get Wolfner to move the franchise in 1958. He scheduled the Cardinals' first home game for September 28, the same day that the White Sox had their last home game, beating the Kansas City Athletics in front of only 4,100 fans.[53] The enraged Wolfner had to find a venue for that date, and the Big Red had their home season opener 540 miles east in Buffalo, New York.[54] Even in Buffalo's War Memorial Stadium, with a 46,000 capacity, the Cards drew fewer than 22,000 for a game against the home-state Giants.

Complicating matters even further was the NFL's rule that no road game could be televised if the team's host city had an NFL game that weekend; protecting the gate took priority over television revenue. So when the Cardinals were home no Bears games were televised, and when the Bears were home no Cardinals games were on the air. This arrangement hurt the Bears, the Cardinals even more, and the entire NFL as well. Wolfner offered Halas half a million to move out of Chicago, and, upon his refusal, raised it to a million.[55]

By the end of the 1958 season Wolfner knew his time was up in Comiskey Park and possibly Chicago. Their last home game at Comiskey was November 30, 1958, a 20–14 loss to the Los Angeles Rams, with only 13,014 in attendance. They averaged fewer than 20,000 for their five home games, and barely 17,000 if the crowd of 32,000 that came for a loss to the

Browns on October 26 was not counted. In 1959 Wolfner worked out an agreement with the Chicago Park District to play four home games in Soldier Field and the other two in the new Metropolitan Stadium in Minneapolis. The gate improved with the four games at Soldier Field, but not by a lot, the total attendance inflated by the 48,000 Bear fans that came to see a north side–south side rivalry match in the last game of the season. Halas himself kicked in half a million dollars to hasten the team's move to Missouri and commented to the press about the Cardinals' departure: "This is the best thing that's happened to St. Louis since Lindbergh."[56]

The Cardinals found more fans and more gridiron success their first two years in St. Louis, going 6–5–1 in their debut season in 1960 and 7–7 in 1961. However, six weeks after they closed out the '61 season with a 20–0 shutout of the Steelers, the team faced a new crisis when Violet Bidwill died on January 29, 1962. Her vast estate, which included race tracks, real estate, and oil wells as well as the Cardinals franchise, was largely left to her two sons, Charles II and William. Her personal possessions included a huge wardrobe; in the third-floor ballroom of her lakefront estate on Michigan Avenue in Wilmette, Illinois, was $40,000 worth of clothes, including 1,500 pairs of shoes and 1,000 coats.[57] Violet's 85 percent control of the Cardinals was equally divided between her two sons, engendering Wolfner's ire, and he immediately went to court to vacate the will and get control of the team.

Wolfner's legal tactics to get the team were cruel and harsh. He claimed in court that both Bidwill sons were adopted, that the adoption was not executed with all legal documentation, and that the will was therefore null and void. These allegations hit like a bombshell. Neither Charles nor William were ever told by their parents that they had been adopted; to learn such a fact in a probate hearing in front of a judge determining ownership of the family's possessions was unconscionable. The tactic spoke volumes about Wolfner's character. Eventually the Illinois Appellate Court, First District, Second Division heard the case and ruled in the Bidwill sons' favor. Wolfner was out, and Charles Bidwill II took over as president and younger brother Bill as general manager. Charles and Bill worked on burying the hatchet with Mugs Halas to see about restoring a Bears-Cardinals rivalry in the Armed Forces Football Game, which made the charity contest for the evening of Saturday, August 31, in the Cardinals' last Chicago home, come to fruition.[58]

On the field the Cardinals entered the 1963 season in better shape than they had been in the last seven years, when they finished second in the East Division at 7–5. Head coach Wally Lemm was starting his second year in charge, after leading the Houston Oilers to the 1961 AFL title. Lemm made grizzled veteran Ed Henke a player-coach, doubling as left defensive end and also the Big Red's defensive line coach. Henke was one of four players from the defunct All-America conference (Los Angeles Dons, 1950) still active in the NFL. At 35, Henke may have lost a step or two but could make up for it in other ways. His resume included teaching hand-to-hand combat to new recruits during the Korean War.[59] The Cards' offensive line featured local boy Ken Panfil, the pride of the Chicago Public League and Gage Park High School. The Purdue alum was one of the best blocking offensive tackles in the NFL. On offense Bobby Joe Conrad kicked field goals and extra points, could return kicks and punts, and would occasionally catch a pass or rush from scrimmage. The Cardinals' roster was full of quality running backs, led by one of the most dominant rushers in the league, John David Crow.[60] Many put Crow, who overcame Bell's Palsy to become an All-Pro, in the same category as the Packers' Jim Taylor. In Sonny Randle the Cardinals had one of the best receivers in the NFL; he was also the favorite target of their brainy quarterback, Charley Johnson. During the offseason Johnson earned his master's degree in chemical engineering from Washington University in St. Louis.[61]

As was his custom before many home games, Halas put the entire team up at the Edgewater Beach Hotel the day before the game to help keep their mind "on football." He himself lived on the grounds of the resort, on the top two floors of the southeast tower in the nearby Edgewater Beach Cooperative.[62] The contest was a homecoming for the Cardinals, whose last game in Chicago was November 29, 1959, when more than 48,000—their biggest crowd in years—saw them get drubbed by the Bears in their Soldier Field home, 31–7. The Big Red had something to prove, and the intensity was significant for a preseason game. A huge crowd of 60,884 saw the Cardinals rally back after the Bears scored first on a Ronnie Bull four-yard plunge followed by a spectacular 61-yard Bill Wade to Johnny Morris pass, the Big Red overcame a 14–0 deficit to beat the Bears, 17–14. During the scoring drive the Bears benefited from some extracurricular activity between Mike Ditka and Cardinals defensive back Jimmy Hill. Ditka roughed up the eight-year veteran on a pass play and Hill most aggressively retaliated. The Cards were penalized 15 yards and Hill was ejected from the game. Later in the contest Ditka sent his apologies to the Cardinal bench.[63] Right before the start of the game Halas took Doug Atkins and Roosevelt Taylor out of the action. Their absence at defensive end and defensive back made it easier for Johnson to connect with Billy Gambrel and Sonny Randle to tie the contest. A field goal by Jim Bakken was the margin of victory. Cooper Rollow, writing in the *Chicago Tribune*, wrote that the absence of Taylor and Atkins impacted the outcome of the game. Johnson often targeted their replacements, Luther Jeralds at right defensive end and Larry Glueck in the defensive backfield. It was a sweet win for the Cardinals, even though some wondered if they would have beaten the "real" Bears, with Atkins, Morris, and Taylor able to play. But nobody begrudged the Cardinals this victory. Head coach Wally Lemm said it meant maybe more than winning a regular season game, and quarterback Charley Johnson won the Eisenhower Trophy, voted by the media as the best player in the Armed Forces matchup.[64]

Halas was infuriated with the loss. He barred the press from the Bears' locker room after the final gun sounded and was in no mood to talk to anyone when he finally opened the door.[65]

He pulled himself together enough the next day to make some cuts and reduce the roster to 42. Waived were center Bill Worrell, halfback John Szumczyk, linebacker Eldon Schulte, offensive tackle Johnny Johnson, defensive tackle John Kenerson, quarterback Val Keckin, and defensive back Lowell Caylor. Along with these cuts Maury Youmans and Tommy Neck were placed on injured reserve.[66] Worrell, Szumczyk, and Schulte were never picked up by another team. Kenerson, previously on the Rams, the AFL's New York Titans, and the Steelers, was now out of pro football. Keckin, a reserve quarterback with the San Diego Chargers in 1962, was also through. Johnny Johnson would come back to the Bears in a few months, the start of a successful six-year NFL career, and Lowell Caylor helped the Cleveland Browns win the NFL championship in 1964.

As August ended the Bears had one preseason game left to play in Baltimore followed by many players' happiest day of the year, the exodus from St. Joseph College. The August to-do list was to succeed injury-free in four preseason games, revamp the running game, and tighten the run defense. They would not know if this was a good August for two weeks, when they would open the season in one of their two biggest games of the year, on the shores of Green Bay.

6

September

Best Start in 15 Years!

George Halas took a brief break from his coaching duties at the end of August to be enshrined in the newly finished Pro Football Hall of Fame in Canton, Ohio.[1] Halas was one of 17 individuals, five deceased and 12 living, to be so honored. Eleven of the 12 living Hall of Famers would attend the ceremony; Washington Redskins owner George Preston Marshall was too ill to travel.

The deceased members of this first Hall of Fame class were Bert Bell, Joe Carr, Wilbur "Fats" Henry, Timothy Mara, and Jim Thorpe. The living members who attended were Sammy Baugh, Earl "Dutch" Clark, Red Grange, George Halas, Mel Hein, Cal Hubbard, Don Hutson, Earl "Curly" Lambeau, Johnny "Blood" McNally, Bronko Nagurski, and Ernie Nevers. Eleven of these initial 17 enshrinees were from just three teams. The New York Giants had four representatives (Hein, Henry, Mara, and Thorpe); the Packers had four (Hubbard, Hutson, Lambeau, and McNally); and the Bears had three (Grange, Halas, and Nagurski).[2] Halas hurried back to Chicago after the conclusion of the ceremonies.

A rather meaningless contest against the Baltimore Colts in hot, humid Tulane Stadium was all that stood between the Bears and the start of the 1963 NFL season. Prior to the team's departure to Louisiana George Allen cut two capable defenders, linebacker Andy Von Sonn and defensive tackle Stan Fanning. Von Sonn was a rookie, drafted in the 14th round, who had a distinguished college career at UCLA. With Tom Bettis backing up the starting trio of Fortunato, George, and Morris he was considered expendable. The release of Fanning was more of a surprise. The giant (6'7", 270 pounds) Peoria, Illinois, native had filled in capably on the defensive line every season after he was drafted in the 11th round in 1960. When he lined up next to Doug Atkins opposing quarterbacks found it almost impossible to pass on the left side, given their tremendous height. Both Von Sonn and Fanning were immediately snatched off the waiver wire by the Los Angeles Rams, and both contributed to the Rams during the 1963 season. The Rams' quick move to claim them opened Allen up to second-guessing about why he did not try to trade them.

During the first week of September shock waves were felt in team offices throughout the NFL when the Philadelphia Eagles' two quarterbacks, starter Sonny Jurgensen and backup King Hill, staged a double walkout from the Eagles' training camp in Hershey, Pennsylvania.[3] Jurgensen, who in 1961 set an NFL record with 235 completions for 3,707 yards and 32 touchdowns, wanted an increase in his $26,000 salary. Hill, the first player picked in the 1958 draft, was upset about the Eagles wanting to reduce the $18,000 he made in 1962. In 1963 a player could participate in training camp and preseason games without a contract but had to be signed before the start of the regular season.[4] Players were also bound to their club under the option clause of the standard NFL contract for one year after their contract ran out, with a reduction in pay being an option each club had. This clause bound the player to the team for one year's service in addition to the actual term of the contract and greatly limited the players' options if they were unhappy. A player could either play out his option under the previous year's contract or sit out the ensuing season.[5] Hill and Jurgensen decided their only leverage was to abandon camp together and leave the team without a quarterback.

Owner Jerry Wolman and general manager Vince McNally had a real problem on their hands; aside from Hill and Jurgensen, four other veteran Eagles were also unsigned, and McNally upped the hostilities by announcing to the press he had "contacted number of NFL clubs in an effort to deal for a quarterback."[6] This ham-handed maneuver by the Eagles' front office served no purpose whatsoever. If it were a means to intimidate Hill and Jurgensen into a quick settlement, they should have known better. With an exhibition game in two days against the Giants and the season starting in nine days, no quarterback in the league could join the Eagles with that short amount of preparation and hope to succeed. The Eagles' brass came to their senses the next day and gave both Jurgensen and Hill what they wanted but not without bitterness and rancor. The negotiations got so heated that McNally at one point tore the arm off his swivel chair and threw it across the room.[7] Caught in the middle, head coach Nick Skorich breathed a sigh of relief that they would both be ready for the Eagles' final preseason game against the Giants in Princeton, New Jersey, a game in which they were thoroughly outclassed by the Giants, 34–10.

The Bears-Colts matchup at Tulane University was the second game of a football doubleheader, promoted by the New Orleans business establishment, which was eager to land an NFL team.[8] Preseason doubleheaders were held the last two years in Cleveland's huge Municipal Stadium and both events drew more than 75,000 fans. In the first game the Dallas Cowboys took care of the Detroit Lions, 27–17. Heavy rain and wind dominated the second half of this contest, delaying the start of the Bears game by almost an hour.[9] Rick Casares bulled into the end zone from eight yards out for the first score and Ronnie Bull threw a left-handed option pass to Bo Farrington for the second. The game did little to prepare the Bears for their two regular-season matchups against the Colts because Johnny Unitas was held out of the action, replaced by the veteran Lamar McHan and the undrafted free agent rookie Gary Cuozzo.

The preseason win came with a cost. Halfback Billy Martin broke his fibula and would be out for an indefinite period. Linebacker Tom Bettis, filling in for the injured Larry Morris, re-injured his elbow.[10] The injury to Bettis could not have come at a worse time, since just a few days before the Bears released Von Sonn. Halas breathed a sigh of relief Monday, September 9, however, when he learned that both halfback Charley Bivins and Morris would be ready for the season opener against the Packers, so the ramifications of Martin's broken leg and Bettis' injured arm were lessened. This second Monday in September was celebrated for a different reason also; the team vacated Rensselaer and set up temporary headquarters at Northern Illinois University in DeKalb. To get down to the 37-player roster limit, veteran offensive tackle Art Anderson, who lost his starting job to rookie Steve Barnett, was traded to the Pittsburgh Steelers for a draft choice.[11]

With the season opener just a few days away both the Packers and Bears started preparing in earnest for what was one of the most important games of the year for either team. Coach Lombardi had a habit of giving his players a day off on Mondays, but this was not the case September 9, six days before the game. He scheduled a 50-minute scrimmage Monday morning followed by a skull session for the entire team in which they would go over scouting reports and tendencies of the Bears.[12] The Packers were fresh off an easy victory over the Redskins in their last preseason tune-up and were remarkably healthy. Defensive tackle Dave Hanner needed six stitches for a forehead laceration and also suffered a broken thumb but was expected to be available by Sunday.[13] To get some insurance for his roster Lombardi obtained 10-year veteran defensive back Jerry Norton from the Cowboys.

The only Bears that would not be available were halfback Billy Martin and end Ed O'Bradovich, still suffering from a stomach ailment; both were put on the injured reserve list, joining the previously incapacitated Maury Youmans and Tommy Neck. The injured reserve list dictated that a player was ineligible to perform for four weeks, which meant that the earliest any one of this injured quartet could play was Sunday, October 13, for the game in Los Angeles.

After two days of arduous workouts on the Northern Illinois gridiron Halas, perhaps intrigued by some of the names on the NFL waiver wire, cut defensive end Luther Jeralds. With Youmans and O'Bradovich out for at least four weeks, some sportswriters were confounded by this roster move.[14] Halas explained that he would be starting Atkins and Bob Kilcullen as the two defensive ends in Green Bay, with defensive linemen Roger Leclerc and Fred Williams—who lost his starting tackle position to Stan Jones—as their backups. Halas also gave no hint whether or not some recent NFL castoff had intrigued him, playing it close to the vest, knowing that other teams needed defensive linemen as well. Jeralds was not unemployed for very long. He immediately signed a contract with the Ottawa Roughriders in the Canadian Football League.[15]

Halas had a policy of limiting any distractions after the Wednesday evening of a week with a Sunday afternoon game. Maury Youmans remembered a command from the Papa Bear at the start of each season: "You know, we are in Chicago now.... I want you guys to get rid of that dreaded disease before Thursday, *Penis Erecta*, because I want you guys ready to play."[16] Halas took this mistaken belief about abstaining to extremes. Min Halas, being a good spouse, had a luncheon before the season for all the players' wives which the players named the "Nothing After Wednesday Club." At the luncheon Mrs. Halas told the wives not to have sex after Wednesday evenings since it will sap the players' strength for Sunday.[17]

As the season opener drew nearer the Bears practices intensified, with a Saturday morning session planned prior to the team flying to Green Bay that afternoon. Halas had an extra-long skull session with the team at the DeKalb Holiday Inn before any breakfast was served. He ended the meeting asking if there were any questions, and J.C. Caroline asked, "When are we going to eat?" Halas looked at him scornfully and said, "J.C., Mahatma Gandhi went 40 days and nights without any bread and water. The least you can do is wait five more minutes for breakfast." Caroline followed his query with another question: "What team did Mahatma Gandhi play for?"[18]

The Packers were just as focused and continued to offer verbal respect for their upcoming foes. "They are dedicated to two things this year, winning the West Division and beating us," tackle Forrest Gregg told the press. "Their running game is much better with the improved play of Ronnie Bull," he continued, "and their defense has settled down and stopped running around,"[19] he added, the last comment a reference to George Allen's modernization of the antiquated and complicated Clark Shaughnessy schemes he inherited when he became defensive coordinator.

While the Bears game was Sunday the 1963 NFL season actually started the night before, with St. Louis playing in Dallas and Detroit visiting Los Angeles. The oddsmakers favored the Cowboys and the Lions by a slight margin in those contests. In the Sunday matchups, the Packers were picked over the Bears; the Giants and Colts were pick 'em's; the Vikings were favored over the 49ers; the Steelers were expected to edge the Eagles; and the Browns were an easy favorite over the Redskins.[20]

The Bears settled in to the Hotel Northland late Saturday afternoon. The Northland was within walking distance of the Packers' old home, City Stadium, but several miles northeast and across the Fox River from New City Stadium. It would be two years—1965—before the stadium was re-christened Lambeau Field. For the '63 season seating capacity of the facility was raised to 42,327. The south end zone was the only area without seating. The Packers were taking this contest very seriously. Two weeks earlier when the Bears played the Cardinals at Soldier Field, Packer head scout Wally Cruice had four assistants in the press box taking notes on the Bears.[21]

The starting lineups for the season opener:

Bears	Pos.	Packers
John Farrington	LE	Max McGee
Herman Lee	LT	Bob Skoronski
Ted Karras	LG	Fuzzy Thurston
Mike Pyle	C	Jim Ringo
Bob Wetoska	RG	Jerry Kramer
Steve Barnett	RT	Forrest Gregg
Mike Ditka	TE	Ron Kramer
Bill Wade	QB	Bart Starr
Ronnie Bull	LH	Tom Moore
Johnny Morris	RH	Boyd Dowler
Rick Casares	FB	Jim Taylor

Cruice may have recruited the minds of many to study the Bears, but the Packers were not aware of how much the Bears had prepared for this opening contest. Schemes specifically for the Packers were practiced every day in preseason. Tom Bettis had a score to settle with Lombardi and was only too eager to divulge some details and tendencies of Green Bay's offense. George Allen felt he had cracked the code to the Packers' schemes and had some novel new defenses to thwart them. One of these innovations was removing Joe Fortunato in passing situations and replacing him with a fifth defensive back, J.C. Caroline. Another was to confuse opposing quarterbacks by varying pass-rush and pass-defense schemes. He might have all linebackers rush the passer while defensive ends dropped into coverage. Keeping the linebackers in place for a and blitzing a defensive back or two was another one.[22] Allen was very eager to see what Bart Starr might do with these innovative looks.

The Bears and Packers meet at midfield prior to the November 17, 1963, matchup at Wrigley Field. Mike Ditka (89), Mike Pyle (50), Joe Fortunato (31) and Larry Morris (33) of the Bears meet with Bill Forester (71) and Jim Ringo (51) of the Packers, while Bill George (61), Doug Atkins (81), Rudy Bukich (14), and Larry Glueck (43) watch from the Bears' sideline.

The largest football crowd in Green Bay history, 42,327, filled the new stadium with great anticipation. From the beginning most of them did not like what they saw, as the Packers were thoroughly outclassed, 10–3, in a game not as close as the score indicated. Caroline outfoxed the Packers' wedge on the opening kickoff and viciously tripped up return man Herb Adderley well short of the 20-yard line. The Packers tried to exploit a supposed weakness on the left side of the Bears' defensive line—where Stan Jones and Bob Kilcullen had replaced Earl Leggett and Ed O'Bradovich—and avoid the right side, where Atkins and Leggett were perched. It didn't work. Jones and Kilcullen worked in perfect harmony with the Bears' great linebacking crew and held the Packers to only 77 yards on 21 rushes. Also, throughout the game the Packers were clearly not ready for the Bears' pre-snap shifts and gap clogging assignments.

Bart Starr had even less success against this George-Allen revamped defense. While he was sacked only once, Starr was confounded by the Bears' pass defense schemes, completing only 11 of 22 attempts for 83 yards. Four defenders—Rosey Taylor, Richie Petitbon, Dave Whitsell, and Bill George—made interceptions, four picks off a quarterback who threw only nine interceptions in 15 games the season before. Starr connected with McGee, his favorite receiver, on only one pass; Ron Kramer only caught three. It was only the third time in their last 51 games in which the Packers were held to 160 yards or less. Remarkably, the Bears did not make one substitution on defense throughout all four quarters.

While the scoreboard did not indicate any similar offensive domination by the Chicagoans, quite simply the Bears' offense beat up the Packers' defense. Bull, Casares, Marconi, and Wade combined for 107 yards on the ground and Wade was brilliant, completing 18 of 24 passes. In spite of only 10 points being scored, Halas said it was Wade's best game to date as a Bear.[23] Wade engineered the ball-control, clock-eating offense perfectly. Knowing that Green Bay often would be dropping back linebackers to thwart the longer passes to Ditka, Morris, and Farrington, Wade concentrated on throwing underneath, piling up the yards with shorter completions, making drives last longer and the ball move consistently down the field. Green Bay made no adjustments to this short-pass scheme throughout the whole game. The Bears' deep threats—Ditka, Farrington, Galimore, and Morris—had only one reception each, while Bull had six, Marconi four, and Casares four. Ditka and Morris both blocked like men possessed, with Ditka on one play springing Bull for a long gain with a block that almost annihilated Ray Nitschke.

The battles between Ditka and Nitschke in every Bear-Packer game were intense. Ditka loved to prove himself against the best, and along with his reputation for being a fearsome, ornery bully,[24] Nitschke was one of the most talented linebackers of his time. Sam Huff got all the media attention, many said based solely on where he played, but the likes of Nitschke, Bill George, and Detroit's Joe Schmidt were the most respected. Lombardi thought so much of Nitschke's play that he made him one of the highest paid defenders in the league, $45,000 for two years, matching the outrageous compensation rookie Dave Robinson got to ignore offers from the AFL.[25]

In the first half rookie Steve Barnett was having a difficult time with Packer veteran Dave Hanner, who recovered a fumble just as the Bears were about to score. Barnett came out with an injury, and line coach Joe Stydahar moved starting guard Bob Wetoska to tackle and put second-year man Jim Cadile at guard. This move greatly neutralized the Packer front four, and Wetoska successfully handled Hanner.

Lombardi acted like a man with his hair on fire after the game. Pat Peppler, the Packers' director of player personnel, said the coach was "beside himself, like a man possessed," in the locker room after the loss.[26] He told the press that no defensive changes were made at halftime because the Bears' short-passing offense was gaining so few yards per play and

Ray Nitschke (66) meets his match as Ted Karras (67) clears a path for Joe Marconi (34). Herman Lee (70) leads Marconi while Bill Forrester (71) and Dan Currie (58) watch.

not changing the course of the game. The Packers knew they were physically beaten and outclassed throughout the game. "When you give up four interceptions," Bart Starr said, "you don't deserve to win."[27]

The Bears, on the other hand, were ecstatic, loud, and relieved. Defensive captain Joe Fortunato gave the game ball to Halas. Halas had the ball inscribed "Greatest team effort, 10–3," and for years it sat in the Halas Hall trophy case.[28] He apologized to the team for only having beer and no champagne available to them. Johnny Morris gave all the credit to the defense, but defensive back Dave Whitsell said "the offense got the ball and stuffed it down their throats."[29] Everyone praised the signals that Fortunato called on defense. Stan Jones, playing in his 112th game as a Bear, called it the greatest thrill of his life. He was so taken with the teamwork he and Kilcullen achieved that he asked Kilcullen to be his presenter when he was inducted into the Pro Football Hall of Fame 28 years later.[30]

The Bears took the Chicago Northwestern Railway home to Chicago and began to prepare for next week's trip to Minnesota. They learned enroute that the Cardinals easily dispatched the Cowboys, 34–7; the Lions toyed with the Rams 23–2; the Vikings squeaked by the 49ers, as Fran Tarkenton passed for 262 yards on the road in San Francisco; the Steelers and Eagles tied, 21 apiece; the Browns thrashed the Redskins, 37–14;

and the Giants, on the strength of Y.A. Tittle's three touchdown passes, defeated the Colts 37–28. Other than the Bears' upset of the world champions, the biggest surprises were the Cardinals decisive victory on the road in Dallas and the Vikings' conquest of the 49ers in Kezar Stadium, a hard place for any visiting team to emerge victorious.

Some of the first week's contests got dangerously brutal.[31] Eagles defensive captain Don Burroughs completely lost it and attacked head linesman Dan Tehan and struck referee Bill Downes as they were heading to the locker room after the Steelers-Eagles tie. Rozelle suspended Burroughs one game, without pay, for the behavior.[32] Y.A. Tittle was hospitalized with a bruised sternum and bruised ribs. Johnny Unitas dislocated a finger and had it snapped back in place while on the sidelines. The Cardinals' running back Prentice Gautt suffered a kidney injury so serious the team physician said he was through for the year. And, worst of all, Pittsburgh's team physician had to perform an emergency tracheotomy on the Steelers' lineman John Reger *while he was on the field* to prevent him from choking to death after he swallowed his tongue.[33]

Packer fans and Wisconsinites had more bad news to swallow after the loss when they learned Governor John Reynolds wanted to involve the U.S. Congress and Attorney General Robert F. Kennedy in the fight to keep the Milwaukee Braves from moving to Atlanta.[34] Chairman of the board William Bartholomay and team president John McHale were involved in shameless double talk about the future of Wisconsin's beloved baseball team. The greedy dream of having the entire Southland as a television market meant more to them than being honest with the most loyal fans in baseball.

The Bears moved their practices from DeKalb to Chicago, where the players could finally settle in for the season, with practices moving to Soldier Field. Many players and their wives made their in-season living quarters at the New Lawrence Hotel or the Lawrence House Apartments. The New Lawrence, 1020 West Lawrence Avenue, was an art-deco 12-story high rise built in 1928 at the intersection of Lawrence and Kenmore avenues, 10 blocks north of Wrigley Field. Kenmore's southernmost intersection is at Waveland Avenue, bordering the ballpark; Kenmore Avenue would bisect Wrigley Field's end zone if it went further south. The huge hotel was designed by the firm of Husazgh & Hill, the same firm that designed the world-famous Aragon Ballroom, which was nearby. Many members of the Chicago Cubs and Bears had made the New Lawrence their Chicago home since the 1930s. In its day it was one of the more fashionable facilities on Chicago's north side, featuring an indoor swimming pool, golf practice center, handball courts, an exercise gym, and a rooftop garden with views of Lake Michigan. Its first-floor tavern and lobby were the scene of many a professional ballplayer's social activities, noble and otherwise, over the years.[35] The Lawrence House was an apartment hotel that catered to the players who had wives or family. The leases were short-term, length-of-season arrangements. It was a smaller venue without the amenities of the New Lawrence but was also less institutional. Both facilities still exist and have been converted to longer-lease apartments.

While the players all preferred having the weekday practices in Chicago instead of Rensselaer, practices in Chicago meant the presence of an individual that Papa Bear Halas worshipped but the players found insufferable: Sid Luckman.[36] Halas had given Luckman the "title" of quarterback coach, with compensation at one dollar a year. Center Mike Pyle pointed out that Luckman did not get involved with the coaches' meetings and offered nothing in the way of offensive strategy. The offensive game plan was emphasized only on Wednesday practices. Luckman would show up an hour before practice and insist that there be full speed passing drills while he often paid no attention, talking to Halas or his buddies on the sidelines. Halas held Luckman in such high regard that no other coaches were allowed to speak while Luckman was around. Assistant coach Luke Johnsos in particular resented Luckman's presence, flanker Angelo Coia found Luckman's consultations useless, and Bill Wade himself got nothing out of it either. Jim Dooley derisively referred to it as "The Luckman Day Quarterback-Testing Thing." Years later Wade summed up everyone's frustration as follows: "It's like me trying to help Brett Favre today. I mean, what kind of help can I give him? You got to be out there, committed, you got to react to what is happening on the field."[37] It did not matter to Halas that Luckman had not been the Bears' regular starting quarterback since 1947. Halas ignored how much the game and the quarterback position had changed in 16 seasons; he needed his favorite son in the fold. The old man was extremely fortunate to have Jim Dooley and George Allen on his staff.

A trip to Minnesota was up next for the Bears, an away game in Bloomington, Minnesota, against the two-year old Minnesota Vikings. Pro football started in the Twin Cities in 1921, when the Minneapolis Marines played 23 games between 1921 and 1924, finishing with a record of 4–17–2. The organization folded for five years, playing again in 1929 in Minneapolis' old Nicolet Park as the Red Jackets. The franchise folded for good in 1930; their record for those last two years was a sorry 2–16–1. In some ways the Vikings owed their existence to the creation of the AFL.[38]

The Minnesota football franchise was actually a charter member of the fledgling AFL while the league was still in its embryonic stage. Pete Rozelle and the progressive faction of NFL owners were intent on expansion, concerned about cornering markets like Dallas, St. Louis, and the Twin Cities, while oil baron Lamar Hunt already had AFL franchise rights in Dallas and a group headed by William Boyer, H.P. Skoglund and Max Winter had the rights in Minneapolis. Rozelle undercut the AFL's market in Dallas by awarding a new NFL franchise, the Dallas Cowboys, to another Texas oilman, Clint Murchison. To make matters worse for Hunt's Dallas Texans the Cowboys' first season, 1960, coincided with the AFL's first season. By 1962 Hunt moved the Texans to Kansas City, changing the name to the Chiefs.

The NFL also cornered the St. Louis market when Walter Wolfner and his Chicago Cardinals succumbed to the tremendous pressure the league put on them and finally moved to St. Louis. The NFL's capture of the Twin Cities market, however, was more complicated. The NFL promised the Viking group that they could join the Western Division in 1961, one year after the Cowboys, and play home and away games against Chicago and Green Bay every year. In spite of the NFL franchise fee being 24 times that of the AFL amount—$600,000 versus $25,000—the Viking group longed for the prestige and security of the old league and courageously announced the defection at the AFL owners' meeting in Minneapolis.[39]

The Vikings started their existence with one of the most significant upsets in NFL history, beating the visiting Bears on September 17, 1961, in Metropolitan Stadium 37–13. The Vikings went 3–11 that first year and 2–11–1 in 1962, with their debut contest being the only win in four tries against the Chicagoans. The 1963 edition of the Vikings were the youngest NFL team in history.[40] Head coach Norm Van Brocklin, with 12 years of Hall of Fame–caliber quarterbacking under his belt, was mentoring the most dazzling young quarterback in football, Fran Tarkenton. Tarkenton could give opposing defenses fits with his scrambling ability, cutting and veering to avoid danger and somehow often finishing the choreography with an accurate pass. Their receiving corps featured the recent College All-Star game hero Paul Flatley and Jerry Reichow, while first-round pick Tommy Mason and former Illini star (and Bears castoff) Bill Brown were competent ball carriers. In 1962 only four backs in the NFL—Tim Brown, Amos Marsh, Dick Bass, and Bobby Mitchell—amassed more total yards than Mason's 1,696. Their defense was still somewhat of a work in progress, although they were strong at four positions. Third-year man Jim Marshall was effective at right defensive end. Two young linebackers, Rip Hawkins and Steve Stonebreaker, were highly regarded, and defensive back Ed Sharockman had five interceptions in 1962, two off Wade in the Wrigley Field matchup. The Vikings continued their pattern of opening day upsets on September 15 when they surprised the 49ers at San Francisco, 24–20, on the strength of Brown's 77 rushing yards and Flatley's five catches. "Keep telling those Bears how great they are," Van Brocklin told the press. "We were very impressed with their victory over Green Bay, I think everybody in the league welcomed it."⁴¹ Halas had little to share with the press as the game got closer. "We have some things in mind," he told the media, not revealing if the Bears would concentrate on ball control and a conservative offense like they did against Green Bay or if they would open things up against an admittedly more porous Vikings defensive group.⁴² He also had fun with the Twin Cities reporters, telling them, "We have reformed. The Bears now play with finesse ... we can't get anywhere with that rough-house stuff."⁴³ The oddsmakers made the Bears a seven-point favorite.

The offensive lineups for the contest:

Bears	*Pos.*	*Vikings*
John Farrington	LE	Paul Flatley
Herman Lee	LT	Grady Alderman
Ted Karras	LG	Gerry Huth
Mike Pyle	C	Mick Tingelhoff
Bob Wetoska	RG	Larry Bowie
Steve Barnett	RT	Errol Linden
Mike Ditka	RE	Jerry Reichow
Bill Wade	QB	Fran Tarkenton
Ronnie Bull	LH	Tommy Mason
Johnny Morris	RH	Ray Poage
Rick Casares	FB	Bill Brown

On a cool 51-degree autumn afternoon 33,933 Vikings fans went home disappointed, as their heroes could not match the magic they had the week before in San Francisco and lost a one-sided contest to the Bears, 28–7. The Bears pulled ahead in the first quarter when Roosevelt Taylor recovered a Tommy Mason fumble and returned it 29 yards to the Vikings' 26. Wade hit Ronnie Bull with a swing pass at the 24, beating the Vikings' left linebacker Roy Winston badly on the play, and Bull cruised into the end zone, outrunning two other Vikings for an easy score.

Soon after, the Vikings' Jerry Reichow beat Richie Petitbon in the end zone on a 24-yard pass from Tarkenton to tie the score. The Bears had two drives ending in missed field goal attempts by Bob Jencks, and after the second one Dave Whitsell intercepted a Tarkenton aerial but fumbled when he was tackled. Vikings fullback Bill Brown recovered, ran it back 20 yards, and was taken down by Bill George. The Bears' Larry Morris thought there was interference on the play, lost his cool, and pushed umpire Frank Sinkovitz during their animated discussion of the play. Morris paid for his anger by getting ejected for the rest of the game. In the third quarter Wade hit Ditka with a beautiful 35-yard pass that Ditka took behind a sprawling Ed Sharockman at the 10. Ditka then outmuscled defensive back Terry Kosens into the end zone: 14–7 Bears. Mason's second fumble came in the fourth quarter and was recovered by Bears defensive captain Joe Fortunato. Seven plays later the Bears were at the Vikings one, and Wade crept in behind the dominant blocking of guard Bob Wetoska and center Mike Pyle. Rosey Taylor, all over the field on this day, intercepted a Tarkenton pass and ran it back to the Vikings' 20. When the Bears got to the 10, Wade hit Ditka once again in the end zone, making the final score 28–7.

Nobody was surprised about the final score but some found the Bears' domination surprising. Bull and Casares rushed for a combined 106 yards—Casares gaining 53 on just seven carries—and each of them also caught six passes. Wade completed 23 of 32 passes for 253 yards, threw three touchdowns, was not sacked all afternoon, and finished the game with a passer rating of 126.2. Ditka had eight receptions and Johnny Morris had seven. Tarkenton was only 13 for 22, throwing three interceptions, and was sacked once. The Bears' front seven controlled his scrambling to the extent that he gained only nine yards on the ground. While Tommy Mason gained 60 yards, he also had two costly fumbles, and Bill Brown gained only 24 yards on 12 rushes.

Halas was uncharacteristically pleased with his squad for the second week in a row. "[We were] almost as good as against Green Bay," he gushed. "Wade called a splendid game. He was extremely accurate and picked the Vikings secondary to pieces."[44] Norm Van Brocklin had little to say but did point out that it was a mistake to think that linebacker Steve Stonebreaker could adequately cover Mike Ditka. Fran Tarkenton said the Vikings beat themselves: "You can't give up the ball as we did and win."[45]

In other games the Redskins beat the Rams, 37–14; the Browns pushed over the Cowboys, 41–24; the Cardinals edged the Eagles, 28–24; the Colts bested the winless 49ers, 20–14; the Steelers crushed the Tittle-less Giants, 31–0, in the upset surprise of the week; and the Packers humiliated the visiting Lions, 31–10. The Packers defensive domination held the Lions to just 147 offensive yards, 71 on the ground and 76 in the air. Milt Plum had one of the worst games of his career, completing just six of 26 passes and having four intercepted. The 46,000 rabid Green Bay fans loved every minute of it, a revenge match given to the team that had humiliated their heroes on Thanksgiving Day 10 months before.

The Bears' win in Minnesota was not without a price. Veteran defensive tackle Fred Williams separated his shoulder during the Bears' last defensive stand in what Dr. Theodore Fox called a "complete clavicular separation" and had surgery at Illinois Masonic Hospital on Tuesday, September 24.[46] Following the surgery hospital staff revealed that Williams also suffered two torn shoulder ligaments, which were repaired during the surgery, and that he would be out of action at least seven weeks.[47] The earliest Williams, the backup to starting defensive tackle Stan Jones, could be available would be November 17, when Green Bay was scheduled to come to Wrigley Field.

Halas and Allen acted quickly to fill the void on the defensive line.[48] They put Williams on waivers and called up Johnny Johnson from the taxi squad to take his place on the roster. The Indiana alum, a sixth-round draft choice eight months earlier, impressed Allen during training camp with his mobility and tremendous size; Johnson stood 6'5" and weighed 260 pounds. Halas had also grown tired of Williams, in spite of his 11 years of valuable service which included four Pro Bowl seasons. The high jinks and shenanigans that Doug Atkins engaged in often included Williams, so the waiver wire may have offered Halas an opportunity to help rein in Atkins, the player Halas always had the most difficult time controlling.

The dark cloud of gambling once again hovered over the NFL during the second week of the season. Published reports claimed that recently retired Giants quarterback Charlie Conerly, one of the most significant NFL players during his 14-year career, was involved with one Maurice Lewis, an alleged high-roller and known gambler from Memphis. Lewis was indicted in January 1963 on gambling charges. He promptly filed for bankruptcy, and the legal proceedings that followed the filing yielded five personal checks written to Conerly totaling $9,575. The largest amount was for the sale of a 1959 Cadillac convertible Lewis bought, a gift Conerly received from the Giants on "Charlie Conerly Day" in 1960. Rozelle had his chief investigator, James Hamilton, interrogate Conerly and look into all the transactions, instructing Conerly not to talk; the investigation was uncovered after a tip to a Memphis newspaper. On September 24 the NFL cleared Conerly of any wrongdoing, and Rozelle issued a statement saying Conerly "is and always has been a credit to the National Football League."[49]

The Detroit Lions were up next for the Bears, closing out the month on September 29 in the Lions' den, Tiger Stadium in downtown Detroit. Their head coach, George Wilson, probably knew the Bears better than any other coach in the NFL. A native of Chicago's West Side, Wilson played in the Chicago Public League at Austin High School, spent some time at St. John's Military Academy in Delafield, Wisconsin, and then starred at Northwestern before putting in 10 seasons as one of Sid Luckman's favorite receivers on the Bears. The Bears with Wilson won four NFL championships, and during his first year as Lions head coach in 1957, he won the NFL championship and was named Coach of the Year. Wilson was as stunned as anyone with how badly the Packers beat his charges during week two. He tried to put some lipstick on the pig by saying that every team is better this season, and he predicted a "five team race" for the Western Division crown. "I think you've got to throw the Bears, Green Bay, Detroit, Baltimore, and now Minnesota into it. It's going to be a close one."[50] In spite of the drubbing his team got in the Green Bay game, Wilson said the Packers did not beat them as much as the Lions beat themselves.[51] He made no prediction about the upcoming match with the Bears.

Halas prepped his men early in the week by having the entire team watch the films of the Lions-Packers game together. "We wanted every man on the squad to see the fierceness of every play, whether on offense or defense," he explained, singling out linebackers Joe Schmidt and Carl Brettschneider along with the Lions' behemoth right defensive tackle Roger Brown.[52] For this game and the entire '63 season Brown did not have the luxury of playing next to Alex Karras. To fill the gaping hole on the defensive line that Karras' indefinite suspension created, the Lions got the promising Floyd Peters from the Cleveland Browns. The 300-pound Brown gave every opponent fits, but in the two Lions-Bears games in 1962, Ted Karras gave Brown all that he could handle. Halas announced that the scheme against Brown would be different this year with Ted's brother Alex out of the picture. Karras and center Mike Pyle would double-team Brown on some plays, while Karras and offensive tackle Herman Lee would double-team him on others, the thinking being that Peters could be easily handled by guard Bob Wetoska or tackle Steve Barnett. Something new had to be tried; the Bears had not scored a touchdown against the tough Lions defense in their last three games.

On the other side of the ball, however, the Bears themselves had only given up three touchdowns in their last four games. In 1962 the Rams had two touchdowns in their loss to the Bears in week 13; the Lions were shut out by Halas' men in week 14; the Packers put up only one field goal the first week of 1963;and the Vikings scored a meaningless touchdown in week two. Dick Hackenberg of the *Chicago Sun-Times* gave all the credit to George Allen and the tough-minded defensive line coach, Jumbo Joe Stydahar. "There has to be something more than sheer coincidence in the fact that, in retrospect, the improvement in the Bears' defense dates back to the entrusting of these departmental duties to George Allen, and the addition of Joe Stydahar to the coaching staff has helped tighten the screws."[53]

The Bears flew into Detroit Saturday, September 28, and settled into the Sheraton Cadillac Hotel, at Michigan and Washington avenues, a little more than a mile east of Tiger Stadium, which was at Trumbull and Michigan. Tiger Stadium was a tough place to play. The second deck in the outfield overhung the field level seats, giving the sensation that some of the 55,000 fans were literally on top of you if you were on the sideline or the field. In spite of the Bears' impressive win over the Packers, their easy rout of the Vikings, and the Lions' poor showing against the Packers, the odd-smakers rated the game a toss-up.[54] The only explanation seemed to be the Bears' recent inability to score against the Lions and the reputation of the Lions' defense.

When the Lions were introduced before the kickoff, 50,000-plus frustrated Lions fans booed quarterback Milt Plum and fullback Nick Pietrosante, remembering that in the Packer wipeout one week before Plum was intercepted four times and completed five of 21 passes for 63 yards, while Pietrosante, a first-round draft pick out of Notre Dame just three years before, gained 35 yards on 10 carries. It did not take the Bears long to get the crowd booing a second time.

On the 13th play of the game Wade hit Angelo Coia, who got the split end starting nod over Bo Farrington, with a beautifully thrown 18-yard touchdown pass that Lions defensive back Gary Lowe had no chance to defend. The Bears followed that up with one of the best second quarters in their history. Wade hit Morris with a 16-yard touchdown strike made possible by Morris' speed, leaving the Lions' 33-year old safety Yale Lary far behind, and his leg and head fake getting the 35-year old Night Train Lane completely turned around. Morris, one of the most difficult men in the NFL to cover in the open field, took complete advantage of the Lions' aging secondary: Bears 14, Lions 0. After the kickoff the Bears' defense stifled Plum and the Lions, and Wade drove the Bears down to the Lions' 13-yard line. Finding Ditka one on one with the already victimized Gary Lowe, Wade struck fast, hitting Ditka with a dart at the goal line two yards in front of the hapless cornerback. The Lions finally got it together after the kickoff and were putting a decent drive together when Plum decided to throw to end Jim Gibbons at the Bears' 34-yard line. Richie Petitbon spoiled their chances with a well-timed interception and took off down the sideline. He side-stepped the humiliated Plum at the 20, leaving the Lions' quarterback with a face mask full of turf. Cutting inside after that, he picked up two crushing blocks from Bears defensive end Bob Kilcullen and defensive tackle Earl Leggett at the 10 and easily waltzed into the end zone.

The Lions went nowhere after the kickoff, and Yale Lary's muffed punt gave the Bears the ball at midfield. Halas' men drove down the field with very little resistance, and Wade snuck over from the one-yard line to make the halftime score Bears 35, Lions 0.

Lions fans found their heroes' performance intolerable, and the boos for Plum were so vociferous—he had three completions in nine attempts with two interceptions and one sack—that Wilson took him out and put Earl Morrall in at quarterback. Halas substituted for the second half as well, replacing Casares with fullback Joe Marconi and halfback Ronnie

Bull with Charlie Bivins. The changes resulted in the Lions actually winning the second half but still losing the game badly. Terry Barr was all alone on a deep route after Bears cornerback Bennie McRae got his feet tangled, and Barr scored on a 60-yard touchdown. Morrall picked on the Bears' cornerback Dave Whitsell repeatedly, knowing that Whitsell had a badly sprained ankle suffered in a practice four days before.[55] After Barr's touchdown, Morrall found Gail Cogdill, who faked out Whitsell and scored from 67 yards out: Bears 35, Lions 14.

The Bears, however, were not finished. In the fourth quarter Doug Atkins, who was having his way with the Lions' rookie left tackle Daryl Sanders, roughed up Morrall for a safety. The Lions got a garbage-time score when Cogdill once again got the better of Whitsell. Whitsell actually intercepted Morrall's offering to the tall split end, but as he turned to take off, Cogdill wrestled the ball out of his hands and ran 38 yards for the score.

Not that it mattered. For the second week in a row the vaunted Detroit defense had given up more than 30 points. They had consecutive losses to the Packers and Bears, their main rivals for the Western Division title, and, worst of all, their starting quarterback had eight completions in 30 attempts and six interceptions in his last six quarters of football. Plum's passer rating for his last two outings was a pathetic 13.2, while Morrall's, in two quarters of work, was 99.

Wilson had no explanation for his team's rather complete failure in front of a very displeased and vocally demonstrative home crowd. He unrealistically said that McRae's interception was the turning point in the game, giving the Bears an easy seven points.[56] Halas was both pleased and relieved, explaining that he was perfectly content to win the first half and let the Lions win the second half. He also admitted to having a minor panic until Atkins notched the safety.[57] His Bears were 3–0 for the first time since 1948, they were in first place, and they could now finally move into Wrigley Field. Wrigley would be waiting for them because the Chicago Cubs last game was also on this date, a 2–0, four-hit shutout by Milwaukee's Warren Spahn, who, at the age of 42, won his 23rd game against only seven losses.

Another battle played out on this day, however, a battle between two very proud western Michigan athletes who would face each other repeatedly. Dave Whitsell was a smallish halfback from Indiana, drafted in the 24th round as an afterthought by the Lions in 1958. Whitsell was the greatest athlete to ever hail from little Shelby, Michigan, a tiny hamlet near the shores of Lake Michigan, "where the north begins and the fine fruit grows," and the only professional athlete to call ever call Shelby home. Earl Morrall was a first-round draft choice of the San Francisco 49ers in

1956 after a successful, nationally-recognized collegiate career at Michigan State. Morrall in his youth was the best athlete in gritty Muskegon, Michigan, an industrial hub 12 times the size of Shelby, 26 miles away, down the Lake Michigan shore. The pride of their heritage came out when they faced each other, with Morrall throwing and Whitsell defending. Morrall got the better of things on this day, while Whitsell and his mates walked off with the win. Their battles would play out in a much larger fashion, and on a more historically significant day, before the year was out.

The third week of the 1963 season ended the month of September with only one surprise and the dominant teams having their way. Y.A. Tittle came back to lead the Giants over the Eagles, 27–14. The Redskins took care of the Cowboys, 21–14, and the Steelers dominated the Cardinals, 23–10. Cleveland punished Los Angeles, 20–6, and the Vikings surprised the entire NFL with an easy 45–14 pantsing of the 49ers on the strength of Fran Tarkenton's performance. The Packers looked like their old selves for the second week in a row, rallying to beat the Colts, 31–20. George Halas and his minions took special interest in that last score; one could never pay too much attention to the Packers, and the Colts would open their home season at Wrigley Field the following week.

7

October

The NFL Takes Notice

In October 1963, with the first three games of the 14-game 1963 NFL season completed, there was an undefeated team in each division, the Cleveland Browns in the East and the Chicago Bears in the West. "While we were all ganging up on Green Bay," one scout said in the Detroit press box while the Bears were thrashing the Lions, "Halas slipped in on us with just about as good a team as ever came out of Chicago."[1] The experts had rated the Packers and Lions as the teams to beat in the Western Division, and the Bears had already dominated both of them, with both wins coming on the road, the first time since 1958 that they were victorious in both cities in the same season. Three factors loomed large in the Bears' surprising success.

The first was the good fortune of having a relatively injury-free August and September and having enough depth to overcome what injuries they had. With defensive ends Maury Youmans out for the year with knee surgery and Ed O'Bradovich out with an unspecified medical ailment, veteran tackle Bob Kilcullen stepped in and had great outings in all three September games. The second success was the new sophistication and simplification of the offensive and defensive schemes. Jim Dooley, Phil Handler, and Luke Johnsos got the credit for the successful offensive game planning while George Allen's and Joe Stydahar's fresh ideas allowed the talented veterans like Doug Atkins, Joe Fortunato, Larry Morris, Richie Petitbon, and Dave Whitsell to all reach their tremendous potential. Noticeably unmentioned was Halas, who may have been the biggest contributor simply by staying out of the way. The third was the significant contributions by the younger players. Steve Barnett, Ronnie Bull, Angelo Coia, Mike Ditka, Bennie McRae, and Roosevelt Taylor were becoming significant fixtures at their positions, and with Billy Wade leading the NFL in quarterbacking, the Bears experienced no major challenges in the first month of the season.[2] The fact that their success came in spite of the continued absence of Willie Galimore, one of the most feared break-away runners in the league, was even more remarkable.

While the Bears were basking in their continued success, George Wilson, the Lions' head coach, was fuming about his team's poor showing and what he considered a lack of respect.[3] After the Packers had their way with Wilson's Lions, *The Football News* ran an article on Vince Lombardi titled "Lombardi Knows How to Win." Wilson was so upset he called the writer and said, "Lombardi doesn't know how to win any better than any other coach. Remember just two weeks ago? Remember Thanksgiving Day?" Roger Stanton, the paper's editor, wrote back to Wilson: "We know that you know how to win, too. But please show us again soon so we won't forget."[4]

The pressure was getting to both Wilson and the Lions. They finished second in the Western Division last three seasons. They entered 1963 with high expectations but lost their best player to a gambling suspension and had a starting lineup that was getting older. A key member of their defensive secondary, 29-year-old Gary Lowe, was out for the year after tearing his Achilles' tendon in their loss to the Bears.[5] It was bad enough that in the first three weeks of the season they lost to their two biggest division rivals, but the way they lost made the situation much worse. Without Karras the Lions also lacked the discipline that was a hallmark of their defensive squad the last few years. In the Bears game Wade was able to draw them offside twice with long counts.[6] The Lions had their next two games against winless teams, San Francisco and Dallas, so they had the chance of being 3–2 by mid–October, with nine games left. The only problem was that they were already two games behind the Bears and were behind both the Bears and the Packers in head-to-head competition. They needed the Bears' and Packers' high level of play to come back down to earth, which was completely out of their control.

With the Chicago Cubs' season ending, and the team once again for the 18th consecutive season not being in the World Series, the Bears could finally move into their real home, Wrigley Field. By 1963 the terms of the lease that Halas had with P.K. Wrigley changed somewhat. The rent was paid directly to Wrigley himself, not to the Cubs team, as he had inherited the field directly from his father, William Wrigley, and not as an asset in the family trust. Changing the park from a baseball venue to a gridiron was a major undertaking.[7]

The first step in creating the north-south gridiron in the stadium was to level off the dirt part of the infield so there is no trace of the diamond, its base paths, the pitching mound, or the batter's box. Readying the pitcher's mound and batter's box involved removing a great deal of hardened clay. Next, 1,500 yards of sod were put down to completely cover the dirt.[8] The dugouts were covered with wooden structures; a small opening was left in the visitor's (first base side) dugout leading to the staircase to the visitor's locker room. The gridiron was jammed so tightly into the field that a part of the east corner of the south end zone was the wood covering the dugout. While the field was striped with lime, another crew put the huge portable bleachers up in right and right center field. Halas then added two seats in each of the railed-off boxes in the box seat area, storing the 21-inch seats the Cubs had in the boxes and replacing them with 15-inch ones, increasing the number of seats in each box from six to eight.[9] This practice of selling more tickets at the expense of the fans' comfort reflected the different attitudes toward the paying customer that Wrigley and Halas had.

In 1932, when P.K. Wrigley took over the Cubs, one of the first changes he made was to reduce the number of seats in each box from eight to six. His thinking was that it was not a good business practice to annoy the highest-paying customers by cramming them closer together for short-term financial benefit.[10] Until the lucrative television contracts Halas did not have the luxury to consider that, but he also never reduced the number of seats for the benefit of his patrons. Over the years the lease agreement between Wrigley and Halas proved beneficial to both parties.

Halas had a lease agreement for the stadium that dated back to 1921. The original lease specified the rent would be 15 percent of the gross receipts, raising to 20 percent if the take was more than $10,000. The Cubs got the concessions revenue but the Bears kept anything generated from the sale of programs.[11] In later years Halas would pay P.K. Wrigley directly a base rental fee and small percentage of the gate. In 1948 Halas got permission to build portable bleachers in right and right-center field. He also removed the 21-inch folding chairs in the box seat sections with 15-inch chairs.[12] This meant that eight instead of six individuals could sit in the railed-off box, albeit more uncomfortably than before. This raised the football capacity to more than 47,000. Cramped quarters in the box seats notwithstanding, Wrigley Field could not have been more perfect for the fans.

In 1963 Wrigley Field was one of the most convenient sports venues in the country. It was located a half-block west of the Addison Street CTA Red Line station, 15 minutes from Chicago's Loop and 25 minutes from Howard Street, Chicago's northern boundary. The line continued through Evanston, the northern terminus being in Wilmette, Illinois. Until its abandonment in January 1963 these same tracks carried the North Shore Line electric interurbans that ran regularly throughout the day from Milwaukee to Chicago. If they wished, fans could board the North Shore in downtown Milwaukee and stay seated until their train stopped about 100 feet from Wrigley Field's main gate. Feeding into the Red Line at the nearby Belmont station was CTA's Brown Line, serving neighborhoods as far northwest as Albany Park. Bus service on Addison and streetcars on Clark Street were also very frequent, and the Suburban Motor Coach bus company stopped four blocks away, at Irving Park Road and Clark streets.

Once inside the stadium fans were so close to the action that many claimed they could hear the players talk to each other. The first row down the left field line—which was the sideline the Bears were on—was about six feet from the Bears bench. The gridiron was such a snug fit that fans in the first rows on the first base side near the dugout were practically in the end zone. The north end zone's backline was about five feet from the ivy-covered left field wall; fans in that part of bleachers would bring fishing nets to catch extra points.

Most patrons were season ticket holders, and Halas tried to control every aspect of the precious ticket revenue stream. Bears programs had the following warning: "Tickets for home games at Wrigley are sold only through our business office and the Wrigley Field Box Office. No outside ticket agencies are authorized to sell Bears' tickets. If you purchase tickets from a ticket outlet, and if you pay more than the face value of the tickets, you may purchase the same ticket locations on a season ticket basis next year. Evidence of purchase, such as a receipt issued showing number of tickets, date of purchase, amount paid, and office from which tickets were purchased, must be presented. The original owner will lose his right to the tickets, and the tickets will be assigned to you."[13] The few box seat tickets available were $5, the same price for a place in the portable bleachers, officially referred to as the East Stands. Grandstand seats were $4, and standing room was $2.50.

Enterprising youngsters, however, often found a way to beat the system. Chicago sports radio personality Mike North explained: "We used to go through the double doors by the player entrance on Waveland Avenue near the firehouse. We'd stand on the right side and wait for the Burny Brothers bakery truck when it made a delivery. We'd walk alongside the truck as it pulled in. Another way [to get in] was a guy would have one ticket. He'd put the re-admittance stub in a cup and throw it over the wall. We'd get in with the stub, one at a time, keep passing the stub back outside the ballpark. We'd keep telling the [usher] that we had forgotten stuff from outside the park and had to use the stub to get back in."[14]

It was a different story, however, for the players. The visitor's locker room was up a long flight of stairs behind the first base (visitor's) dugout. The staircase for many years was exposed, allowing the Bears fans to hurl expletives and—if they wished—projectiles from the concourse below. The locker room itself was too small for a baseball team with 25 players and was exponentially more inadequate for 40-plus bigger-bodied football players. The Bears locker room was down the left field line, accessible through a small door near the northwest corner of the field, down the left field line. While larger than the visitor's locker room, the Bears had to shower in shifts, form a long line to access the trainers' small quarters, and hope that the two toilets available for more than 40 players and coaches always worked. Red Mottlow was the first sports reporter in Chicago to use a tape recorder. The Bears' locker room was so cramped with players, media, and hangers-on after a game that Mottlow was not allowed inside with his equipment. He conducted his taped interviews at the top of the staircase leading into the clubhouse, catching the players as he departed.[15] The south end zone, affording the fans a thrillingly close view of the action, was a health hazard to any pass receiver who forgot where they were. Bears defensive back Dave Whitsell was to use this to a huge advantage in the title game at the end of the season. In colder weather the shadows from the upper deck would often cause the south end of the field to freeze, making things difficult and miserable for both teams. In spite of these hardships the players loved the locale.

Wrigley Field was practically walking distance to the Lawrence House and Sheridan Plaza and less than four miles from Halas' penthouse at the Edgewater Beach cooperative apartments. The players made Johnny's Cottage Restaurant, three blocks south of Wrigley at 3174 North Clark Street, their haunt and hideout. For the most part the players found Wrigley Field and the Lakeview neighborhood environs a very comfortable venue.

The Bears experienced a good measure of success against the Baltimore Colts, their first home opponent in 1963, during the previous four years. The Colts won back-to-back NFL championships in 1958 and '59, but were a .500 team in 1960, 8–6 in '61 and .500 in '62. Over that span the Bears and Colts were 5–3 against each other. The Colts spent the winter pointing to this October 6 contest, since the Bears obliterated them in their last matchup. On November 25, 1962, the Bears racked up four sacks, had one interception and held the Colts offense to 152 yards and Johnny Unitas to a 38.7 passer rating. On the other side of the ball the Bear offense gained 505 yards, Wade had one of the best days of his career—passing for three touchdowns with a passer rating of 135.9—while his "mercy" replacement, Rudy Bukich, passed for another touchdown and achieved a rating of 124.4. The humiliated Colts went down to defeat, 57–0.

During the off season the Colts replaced head coach Weeb Eubank with Don Shula. Shula had a very successful career as a defensive back for the Browns, Colts, and Redskins before he went into coaching. When hired by Baltimore he was a successful defensive coordinator for the Detroit Lions. The Colts' All-Pro receiver Raymond Berry would not be playing due to injury. His absence limited Unitas' options, but the great quarterback still had Alex Hawkins, Tom Matte, Lenny Moore, Jimmy Orr, and R.C. Owens to help him out, along with one of the best tackles in the league, 275-pound Jim Parker, to protect him. The Colts also featured an exciting newcomer on offense, rookie John Mackey from Syracuse, starting his eventual Hall of Fame career. On defense the Colts still had the legendary Gino Marchetti at end, and Bill Pellington, whom Mike Ditka referred to as one of the toughest linebackers in the NFL. Pellington was a 12-year veteran, feared throughout the NFL for his clothesline tackles.[16] The Colts' front office choice of Don Shula to run the team was made with an eye toward shoring up the defense. However, the Colts had already given up 82 points in their first three games in 1963; the defense was still very much a work in progress. Before the game little was said about Colts owner Carroll Rosenbloom's troubles with the gambling investigation.

The oddsmakers made the Bears nine-point favorites. One reason for the spread was Shula's announcement that defensive starters Gino Marchetti, Bill Pellington, and Don Shinnick were banged up and may not be able to play.[17] All standing room and restricted grandstand seats were sold out and the Bears made an announcement encouraging people to stay away from the area unless they had a ticket to the game. The team also announced that the only other game that was sold out was the contest with the Packers on November 17.[18] Since the game was blacked out in the Chicago area, one would have to travel to Rockford, Illinois, or South Bend, Indiana, to see it on television.

The lineups:

Colts	Pos.	Bears
Lenny Moore	LE	Angelo Coia
Bob Vogel	LT	Herman Lee
Jim Parker	LG	Ted Karras
Dick Szymanski	C	Mike Pyle
Alex Sandusky	RG	Bob Wetoska
George Preas	RT	Steve Barnett
John Mackey	RE	Mike Ditka
Johnny Unitas	QB	Bill Wade
Tom Matte	LH	Ronnie Bull
W. Richardson	RH	Johnny Morris
J.W. Lockett	FB	Rick Casares

In stifling 90-degree heat the Colts gave the Bears all they could handle before the Chicagoans prevailed at the end, 10–3. Baltimore's defense coordinator Charley Winner mapped out a strategy to completely baffle Wade, who entered the game with a phenomenal 65.6 completion percentage. In spite of being limited both Marchetti and Pellington played, and Winner's defense men allowed Wade to complete only five of 21 pass attempts, including a timely interception by cornerback Jim Welch. Wade was harassed by the Colts' defensive line more than he had been so far in the 1963 season.

Each team managed only five first downs in the first half, and during those two periods the Bears held the Colts to a net rushing total of one yard and were allowing Unitas to have success only on short passes. He was also sacked early on by Bill George and intercepted by Roosevelt Taylor. The great quarterback drove the Colts to the Bears' 34 right before halftime and the Colts hurriedly lined up to kick a field goal. Bill Martin's kick was good from 41 yards out, but the referee Norm Schachter ruled time had expired: 0–0 at halftime.

When the second half began Unitas drove the offense to the Bears nine-yard line; when they could get no further Martin successfully kicked a 16-yard field goal to make it 3–0. Suddenly the Bears were behind for the first time in 1963 and the first time in 20 quarters, going back to December 9, 1962. Halas made a surprising move, taking Wade—and his 19.7 passer rating—out and putting in Rudy Bukich. Bukich hit Ditka with a 14-yard pass which put the Bears on the Colts' 42. Another Casares run followed by a Bukich completion to Bo Farrington got the Bears down to the 27, but a holding penalty and a sack by Colts defensive end Ordell Braase had them back at the 48. Bukich responded with a great pass to Farrington, who didn't go down until he reached the Baltimore 21, but Bob Jencks' 28-yard field goal was wide and the Colts, with their slim lead, took over.

Early in the fourth period Bukich engineered a brilliant 80-yard drive in 10 plays which changed the momentum of the contest. Another pass to Farrington and successful rushes by fullback Joe Marconi and Ronnie Bull moved the ball to the Colts' 36, where Bukich found Johnny Morris with a pass over the middle, putting the Bears at the 23. At this point 48,998 fans thought the bottom had dropped out. A holding penalty cost Halas' men 15 yards, and then the Colts sniffed out a power sweep, dumping Bull for a seven-yard loss, putting the ball back at the 45. The Bears now had 32 yards to go for a first down and were well out of field goal range. Sensing that the Colts were expecting a long pass attempt, Rudy the Rifle hit Bull over the middle with a nine-yard pass. Baltimore safety Andy Nelson was waiting for him at the 30, but Bull gave a brilliant fake, slowing his stride and offering his left leg, which Nelson dove for just as Bull pulled it away and spun around.[19] Defensive back Bobby Boyd was the only one left to preserve the Colts' lead. Boyd was pancaked by a perfectly-executed open field block by Ditka, as Bull cruised into the end zone, and Jencks' extra point to put the Bears ahead 7–3.

The Colts got the ball back and kept it until defensive end Bob Kilcullen sacked a fumbling Unitas and recovered the ball at the Baltimore

25. Unitas went into a frenzy arguing with the officials, claiming that it was an incomplete pass, not a fumble, but the call went the Bears' way. Bukich took over at the Baltimore 25, and after two plays the Bears were at the 10, thanks to the rushing of Bull and Marconi. Halas, proud of his decision to substitute Bukich for Wade, now substituted Roger Leclerc for Jencks. Leclerc, who had lost his field goal assignment to Jencks, kicked a 17-yarder to put the Bears up 10–3 with four minutes and 24 seconds remaining. Unitas brilliantly drove the Colts down the field, but a short pass to Willie Richardson was two yards short of a first down and the Bears took over at their own 31. Pulling out all the stops, Colts head coach Don Shula instructed defensive tackle Fred Miller to "get injured" to stop the clock. Writhing on the turf in feigned pain, Miller did not fool the referees. When the gun sounded at the end of the game Miller got up and trotted off the field with no trace of even a limp.[20]

Rudolph Andrew Bukich was picked in the second round of the 1953 NFL draft—the fifth quarterback taken—by the Los Angeles Rams. His successful college career included being named the Most Valuable Player in the 1952 Rose Bowl when he led USC to victory over Wisconsin. Nicknamed "Rudy the Rifle," Bukich had one of the strongest throwing arms in the league. The Bears were his fourth NFL stop; he was a Ram from 1953 to 1956, played for Washington in 1957, and had two homes during the 1958 season, 11games with the Redskins, the last game of the season with the Bears. In 1959 and '60 Bukich was in Pittsburgh, and the Bears reacquired him in 1962 to serve as Bill Wade's understudy. This Baltimore game was only his 60th appearance since 1953, and over that span he only started eight games in his career. The Baltimore game was also the one in which Bukich, with his 158.3 passer rating, showed the Bears did not need to dominate an entire game to win. Enjoying his time in Chicago, Bukich and his family settled in nearby Morton Grove, Illinois, not far from Bill George. The Colts heard about their poor offensive showing from the Baltimore press. The team was criticized for only having eight touchdowns in four games, and former NFL great Buddy Young wrote that the team had "lethargic ways … and an I don't care attitude."[21]

Halas told the press after the game, "We were a little flat. I had a hard time getting the boys 'up' in the first half. Our offense was just off. Both defenses—ours and the Colts'—did a great job. Bill [Wade] just wasn't throwing the ball well and the receivers were dropping passes."[22] Bukich's performance did not go unnoticed. The *Chicago Daily Defender, New York Times*, and *Christian Science Monitor* all took note of his heroics.

Bukich was not the only "relief pitcher" to meet with success in week four. King Hill came off the bench for Philadelphia after Sonny Jurgensen was injured and led the Eagles to their first victory, coming at the expense of the winless Dallas Cowboys, 24–21. Green Bay, New York, and St. Louis all improved to 3–1. Green Bay crushed the Rams, 42–10, while the Giants bested the Redskins, 24–14, and Charley Johnson accounted for 301 yards as the Cardinals walloped the Minnesota Vikings, 56–14. The Lions atoned for their poor play against Green Bay and Chicago with a 26–3 mauling of the 49ers, and Cleveland kept pace with the Bears as the only undefeated team in the NFL by beating the visiting Pittsburgh Steelers, 35–23.

The Bears had a lot to feel good about as they prepared for their annual two-week West Coast road trip for games against the Los Angeles Rams and San Francisco 49ers. Since 1959 only four teams in the NFL managed to win three consecutive road games, and the Bears had a shot at it. The Packers did it three times (1959, '60, and '62) and the Giants twice (1960 and '62). The Eagles did it in 1961 and the Lions in 1962. The Bears were a game up on Green Bay, their chief rival, and were looking forward to their next two games against winless teams. Two of their four wins featured a virtually impenetrable defense against two of the best quarterbacks in the NFL, Bart Starr and Johnny Unitas. With four games under their belts the Bears lead the league in eight of the 19 defensive categories listed by the NFL, including pass interceptions, defense against the rush, opponents' points scored, and first downs allowed. Equally important was the discipline the defense displayed; they allowed only two first downs on penalties.[23] The other victories showcased an offense with peerless performances by quarterback Bill Wade, a deep receiving corps, and a consistently effective ground game. Rick Casares' yards per carry average trailed only Jim Brown's after four games. With the exception of the Baltimore contest, Wade showed the versatility he brought to his craft. Against Green Bay he effectively ran a ball-control offense with short-pass artistry, while against Minnesota and Detroit he aired it out more often with equally successful results. He was handcuffed by the Baltimore defense; his absence in the second half showed how deep the Bears' offense was, with Rudy Bukich coming in, controlling the game, and rallying to a hard-fought victory. The Bears' offense accomplished all this while still awaiting the 1963 debut of the NFL's most dangerous open-field runner, Willie Galimore. Galimore's introduction into this offense would make the Bears even more effective.

As they had been for several years, the Los Angeles Rams figured to be one of the easiest opponents the Bears would face in 1963. In the previous four seasons the Rams sported a dismal .294 winning percentage, going 15–36–3. During the offseason they fired their head coach, Bob Waterfield, who when released still held the club records for total points, field goals, and extra points. Waterfield quarterbacked the Rams to a championship in 1945 and led them to another championship matchup in 1951, when they lost to Philadelphia. He was replaced by Harland Svare, a star linebacker for the Rams in the 1950s, who at 32 was the youngest coach in the NFL.

Svare had a hard time settling on a quarterback at the beginning of the 1963 season. In their first loss against the Lions, Roman Gabriel and rookie Terry Baker split the assignment. The Rams offense was shut out by Detroit in that game, so Svare turned to former Bear Zeke Bratkowski for their second game, against Washington. The Rams offense scored twice in that loss, so Bratkowski got the start in the game three loss against Cleveland—when they managed only two field goals—and game four, their loss to Green Bay. Svare replaced Bratkowski with Gabriel during the Green Bay contest, who actually fared worse as the game went on.

The Rams' beleaguered head coach announced that he would start Bratkowski against the Bears. On paper the Rams did not look nearly as bad as their record. Their fullback Dick Bass was proof that small college stars could make it in the NFL. The College of the Pacific alum gained 1033 rushing yards in 1962 and 262 more on pass catches. Only Philadelphia's Timmy Brown and the Dallas' Amos Marsh amassed more all-purpose yards in 1962 than Bass did, a nice accomplishment for a team that won only one game. At halfback the Rams still had Jaguar Jon Arnett, one of the most elusive open-field runners in league history. Offensive end Carroll Dale was so highly regarded by the Rams that they traded the great Del Shofner to the Giants. Only three receivers in 1962 caught more passes than the Rams' tight end, Red Phillips. The Rams definitely had the personnel to sneak up on an unsuspecting opponent when they had the ball. Their weak defense, though, was another story, and a big reason why Svare was selected to be the head coach. Svare could consistently count on only two defensive performers, both linebackers: Les Richter, who had lost a step or two from his glory years, and five-year veteran Jack Pardee, one of the original Junction Boys in his collegiate years.

The fact that two former Ram quarterbacks were fairing so well in this '63 season did not sit well with their fans.[24] Bill Wade's performance with the Bears thus far was phenomenal and so was Cleveland's Frank Ryan. Both were flourishing on undefeated teams, and Ryan served up the indignity of beating his old team 20–6 just the week before. If Wade were to be successful in week five against Los Angeles, the Rams would have the rare indignity of losing two consecutive games to quarterbacks they used to employ.

The press had fun with the fact that Halas was more than twice as old as Svare. Asked why Halas was allowed to roam and chase down referees past the 40-yard lines, Svare said, "Well, he's an old man. I suppose the officials have to cater to his whims."[25] Halas ignored the comments and avoided giving the Rams any bulletin board material. "The Rams are just the type of team that can explode on you. They played a terrific first half against the Packers at Green Bay last week," he tried to explain.[26] Halas was unconvincingly referring to the Packers' 42–10 pasting in Green Bay on October 6, trying to pass the first half, in which the Packers outscored the Rams 16–10, as two periods of excellent play by the visitors.

The lineups:

Bears	Pos.	Rams
Angelo Coia	LE	Carroll Dale
Herman Lee	LT	Joe Carollo
Ted Karras	LG	Charlie Cowan
Mike Pyle	C	Art Hunter
Bob Wetoska	RG	Joe Scibelli
Steve Barnett	RT	Frank Varrichione
Mike Ditka	RE	Red Phillips
Bill Wade	QB	Roman Gabriel
Ronnie Bull	LH	Jon Arnett
Johnny Morris	RH	Pervis Atkins
Rick Casares	FB	Dick Bass

Los Angeles' huge Memorial Coliseum was less than half full for the Bears-Rams game, but that still meant 40,476 endured a sweltering sun to watch their hometown favorites suffer one of the worst defeats in team history, 52–14. The Bears scored virtually at will all afternoon while the Rams' offense could do nothing against their swarming defense. It was the worst Rams home loss in their history and the most points the Bears had ever scored while playing them.[27]

Billy Wade, Rudy Bukich, Mike Ditka, and Johnny Morris carried the day for the Bears' offense. Ditka tied a team record with four touchdown catches, three from Wade and one from Bukich. Two of his scores came when three-time Pro Bowler Linden Crow, the Rams' left safety, found him impossible to cover.[28] The only other Bear in history with four TD passes in one game was Harlon Hill, who accomplished the feat nine years before, in October 1954, against San Francisco. Bukich connected with Bo Farrington for the other Bears score through the air; their sixth touchdown was on a four-yard run by Willie Galimore, making his 1963 season debut, long after the outcome of the game had been decided.

On defense the Bears gave up their first touchdown of the season on the ground, when Dick Bass cruised in from the four-yard line in the fourth quarter.[29] Rams left tackle Joe Carollo and left guard Charlie Cowan double-teamed Bears defensive guard Earl Leggett, while Rams center Larry Hayes screened tackle Stan Jones to allow Bass to slip into the end zone. The Bears defensive unit had not given up a rushing touchdown in an amazing 26 quarters, dating back to December 9, 1962, when Bass scored against them in the first quarter from 17 yards out in the Rams' loss at Wrigley Field.

Bass' score was the Rams' only offensive highlight. The Bears got six interceptions—two by Bennie McRae (one of which he ran back for a 35-yard touchdown), and one each by Doug Atkins, Richie Petitbon, Rosey Taylor (who proceeded to run his back 46 yards), and rookie Larry Glueck. After only five games the Bears had 17 interceptions. They also caused five Ram fumbles, recovering three of them. Joe Fortunato's first quarter fumble recovery set up the Bears' first touchdown, and another led to Bob Jencks' 31-yard field goal in the third period.

Halas was elated after the game but reserved judgement as to how great his current squad was. "You can't judge a team until it has played 14 games … [they are] just a helluva good team on five days this year."[30] He went on to single out Wade, Ditka, and Bukich for their consistently excellent play, saying that Ditka had something to prove after taking his eye off the first pass he was thrown and consequently missing it. The Rams' young coach saw things a little differently. Svare called the Bears' defense the best he ever saw, better than any of those great New York Giants' units. "They are much better. The Bears have so much more speed in the secondary. And they're powerful. That secondary will drive you crazy."[31] Svare went on to single out Atkins and the Bears' three linebackers—Fortunato, George, and Morris—for special praise.

A large measure of the undefeated Chicago Bears' success was due to William James Wade. Wade was born October 4, 1930, in Nashville, Tennessee. His father, W.J. Wade, was the captain of the undefeated 1921 Vanderbilt University football team and later became a judge. Wade went to the highly regarded Montgomery Bell Academy for high school and was named the Most Valuable Player of his football conference.[32] Following in his father's footsteps, Wade went to Vanderbilt and was elected president of his freshman class.[33] On the gridiron he won MVP honors in the football-crazed SEC Conference, earned second-team All-American honors, was named MVP of the 1951 North-South Shrine Game, and played in the Senior Bowl and also the College All-Star game in Chicago against the NFL champion Rams. At Vanderbilt he amassed 3,396 passing yards, a record that stood for 30 years.[34] The Rams drafted him in the first round in 1952, after winning a lottery for the first overall bonus pick. Wade was so sought after that he was first player selected that year, a year in which seven future Hall of Famers (Les Richter, Ollie Matson, Hugh McElhenny, Frank Gifford, Gino Marchetti, Bobby Dillon, and Yale Lary) were picked after him. A two-year stint in the Navy at the Coronado Naval Base followed, as he kept sharp playing military camp football.

Wade alternated with Norm Van Brocklin at the quarterback position until 1958, when he led the NFL in passing, thriving under head coach Sid Gillman and becoming disappointed when Gillman left. "I didn't like the way things were going in Los Angeles. We had a new coach, Bob Waterfield, and a new general manager, Elroy Hirsch, and nothing was settled. I wanted to be with a team that had one coach, one person you answered to."[35] He also thought the ownership trio—Dan Reeves, Edwin Pauley, and Bob Hope—was problematic. George Allen, whose first experience in the NFL was with the Rams when Wade was there, convinced George Halas to go after him and move beyond alternating the "Three B's"—Zeke Bartkowski, George Blanda, and Ed Brown—at quarterback. Right after the 1960 season Allen got his way, and in a three-way trade the top-flight cornerback Erich Barnes went to New York, Bartkowski went to the Rams, and Wade came to the Bears. Wade worked out all summer before training camp opened with the Bears first-round draft pick, Mike Ditka, throwing passes to the converted linebacker from Pitt repeatedly. He beat out Ed Brown for the starting role and led the NFL in passer rating (93.7) in 1961.

Wade had the respect and admiration of both his coaching staff

Underappreciated and largely forgotten today, Bill Wade (9), shown here with Packers' Henry Jordan (74) and Lionel Aldridge (62) in hot pursuit, was a great passer, intelligent signal caller, and talented ball carrier. Stan Jones (78), Joe Marconi (34), Bob Kilcullen (74), and Larry Glueck (43) watch from the sidelines.

and his teammates. Halas took a liking to this practicing Presbyterian, impressed with both his athletic ability and his character. Halas saw him as a contrast to Brown, who enjoyed the night life with his buddy Rick Casares and at times got too Bacchanalian for Halas' tastes.[36] "Bill Wade could throw the ball on a hook-and-out better than anyone. I watch guys today, and there's nobody that can throw the ball any better than Wade. He was a very accurate passer, and a tough guy," Angelo Coia said. [37] The extent of Wade's influence on his teammates and on George Halas would become apparent four years later.

After the victory in Los Angeles the Bears travelled to Sonoma, California, in the Valley of the Moon, 50 miles from San Francisco, as they had for several years. Halas had an agreement with Sonoma High School to use their field and facilities.[38] The schedule makers linked the two West Coast games on successive Sundays, and this arrangement served two purposes for Halas. First, it kept his players away from the bright lights, fun, and distractions of L.A. and San Francisco, keeping the likes of a Doug Atkins, Rick Casares, Freddy Williams, and whomever else from non-football related activities and amusements. Second, Halas saved a huge amount of money not having to fly a contingent of some 45 team personnel on a second round-trip between Chicago and the West Coast. Travel was a huge expenditure out of the team budget—roughly $11,000 per road trip in those days—[39] and the penurious head coach would save every way he could.

There were two surprises in the outcomes of the other NFL games in week five. Nobody was surprised that visiting Baltimore would put down San Francisco, 20–3, or Philadelphia's rudeness toward their hosts, the Redskins, 37–24, or that the Packers went to the Twin Cities and beat the Vikings, 37–28—after which Vince Lombardi declared his team to be the best one he had had in his five years in Green Bay.[40] The surprises came in Detroit and Pittsburgh. In Detroit, the Cowboys pulled a major upset, 17–14, and in Pittsburgh, St. Louis prevailed in the closest game of the week, 24–23. While the Bears finished the week as the only undefeated team in the West, the Cleveland Browns matched their success in the East, beating the New York Giants in perhaps the most significant game of the week rather easily, 35–24. The Giants were not used to losing by double-digits in Yankee Stadium; the Browns pulled it off after being behind 17–7, midway through the second quarter. Jim Brown and Ernie Green led a Cleveland rushing offense that gained 210 yards, eating up the clock and wearing out New York's possibly overrated defense. The Giants rushed for only 72 yards through the entire game, as the Browns matched the Bears record and were in control of the Eastern Division.

With their loss to the Colts the San Francisco 49ers were winless after their first five games for the second time in their 17-year history. Their poor start in 1963 matched the futility they had in 1950, when they dropped their first five in a row. In between those seasons the 49ers suffered two other five-game losing streaks, one occurring in 1956 between week three and week seven, and the other in 1955, from week seven through week 11. While parity was not a hallmark of the NFL in the 1950s, it was rare for any team to drop five consecutive games. They had performed slightly above the norm in their four most recent seasons, making a 27–24–1 record. Against the Bears, San Francisco was winless in Chicago the last four years but were 3–1 while hosting the Bears at home in Kezar Stadium.

San Francisco's front office aggravation boiled over in late September, three weeks earlier, and they fired head coach Red Hickey and put Jack Christiansen at the helm. Hickey owned the 27–24–1 record of the team's last four years, his only head coaching experience. The 46-year-old distinguished himself on the gridiron in Los Angeles in the 1940s playing end for one year before World War II and from 1945 through 1948. Christiansen joined the 49ers' coaching staff in 1959, handling the defensive backfield. He was one of the greatest defensive backs in the NFL throughout the 1950s. Christiansen was a fixture in the Lions defense; in future years he was named to the NFL's All-Decade 1950 team and also elected to the Pro Football Hall of Fame.

The team's woes continued after Christiansen took the helm when his quarterback, John Brodie, suffered a broken arm in the team's disastrous 45–14 loss to the visiting Minnesota Vikings. San Francisco hurriedly made a trade with Baltimore to get Johnny Unitas' backup, the veteran Lamar McHan, to run the show. The Bears would be no stranger to the eight-year veteran. Since joining the NFL in 1954 McHan started seven games against the Bears, five while playing with the Chicago Cardinals and two in 1959 before his lost his starting job in Green Bay to Bart Starr. Historically he fared poorly against them, sporting a 2–5 record in his seven starts with only three touchdown passes and 12 interceptions. In fairness six of the interceptions came in his rookie year, 1954, when the Bears smothered their cross-town rivals 29–7. McHan would be ready to face his adversaries; the proud veteran had something to prove.

The 49ers actually had a handful of players more significant than McHan that the Bears had to worry about. The veteran defensive tackle Leo Nomellini was finishing out his Hall of Fame career and closing in on his 40th birthday. The native of Lucca, Italy, grew up in Chicago and was one of the most illustrious products of the Chicago Public League, prepping at George Halas' alma mater, Crane Tech. San Francisco also boasted the only man in the NFL taller than Doug Atkins, 6'9" Bob St. Clair. St. Clair, who claimed a steady diet of raw meat gave him the strength to play pro football, had already carved out a post-playing career, having been elected mayor of suburban Daly City.[41] In the defensive backfield Abe Woodson was a perennial Pro-Bowler and rookie Kermit Alexander showed a lot of promise. The 49ers' kicker, Tommy Davis, was considered one of the most consistent in the NFL, and McHan could rely on end Monte Stickles, a former Notre Dame star who could also kick field goals in a pinch.

Halas was concerned about his charges being overconfident. To pass the time in Sonoma he had extra film study of the 49ers' loss to Baltimore and several practices in rainy weather.[42] He gave the San Francisco sporting press a good giggle by saying, "We're worried about the 49ers."[43] The West Coast media were merciless in their criticism of the Bay Area squad, calling them the "worst team in NFL history"; one San Francisco column was titled "Does Halas Know This Is Be Kind to 49ers Week?"[44]

With the Bears relegated to one of the last games to be played in week six, a great deal of NFL attention was being given to a matchup of two 4–1 teams in St. Louis, where the world champion Packers would play the surprisingly successful Cardinals. Injury-wise the Bears were in good shape for the Kezar Stadium matchup, with Bill George's five-stitch cut on his hand their most serious injury—although it would not prevent him from playing.

The lineups:

Bears	Pos.	49ers
Angelo Coia	LE	Clyde Conner
Herman Lee	LT	Leo Rohde
Ted Karras	LG	Bruce Beasley
Mike Pyle	C	Karl Rubke
Bob Wetoska	RG	Leon Donohue
Steve Barnett	RT	Bob St. Clair
Mike Ditka	RE	Gary Knaflec
Bill Wade	QB	Lamar McHan
Ronnie Bull	LH	Jim Vollenweider
Johnny Morris	RH	Bernie Casey
Rick Casares	FB	J.D. Smith

Fullback J.D. Smith would be looking once again for a little revenge. The Bears drafted him in the 15th round in 1956 but traded him to San Francisco after he started three games for them. The 49ers were throwing a new wrinkle at the Bears' defense by lining up two fullbacks at the same time in the backfield, putting second-year man Jim Vollenweider in the right halfback spot. Halas considered this "power backfield" alignment in the preseason but never utilized it. Christiansen, at the helm of a winless team, figured he had nothing to lose with the experiment; the oddsmakers had the Bears as 17-point favorites.[45]

Reinforcing the adage that on any given Sunday any team could win, San Francisco stunned the professional football world with a convincing 20–14 victory over the Bears. Lamar McHan had one of the best days of his career, engineering drives of 59, 78, and 84 yards, to lead his team to victory for the first time in 12 games, if one included the preseason. McHan's opening drive to start the game went 59 yards in only nine plays. It was fueled by a 23-yard run by fullback J.D. Smith to the Bears' four-yard line. From there the 49ers' other fullback, Jim Vollenweider, went in between guard and tackle for the first score. Six minutes later Tommy Davis booted a 25-yard field goal: San Francisco 10, Bears 0. In the second quarter McHan hit the usually starting halfback, Don Lisbon, with a screen pass around the 49ers' 42-yard line. Lisbon juked and used his blockers effectively and was not hauled down until he reached the Bears' seven-yard line. On the next play McHan rolled out to his left, with guard John Thomas ahead of him for protection. Offensive tackle Leo Rohde effectively sealed off Doug Atkins, giving McHan time to pick out Gary Knafelc, who had beaten safety Richie Petitbon to the middle of the end zone. He caught the pass a split second before linebacker Larry Morris caught up to him. Suddenly, after Davis' extra point, the score was 17–0, and the upset of the year was unfolding. The Bears' offense finally came around at this point, when Wade started a drive from the Bears' 20. Wade hit Morris with a 38-yard strike and a 49er penalty moved the ball to the one. Wade surprised the San Francisco defense at this point. Expecting a run, they were unprepared for the quick strike Wade threw to Bo Farrington for the touchdown. At halftime: San Francisco 17, Bears 7.

In the second half the Bears continued having difficult stopping the run, with the 49ers' two barreling fullbacks moving the ball consistently. With only three minutes gone in the second half Davis hit on his second field goal from 46 yards out, putting the Bears 13 points behind.

Halas replaced Wade with Bukich, but it was not until the waning moments of the third quarter when their offense started to click. With some consistent rushes from Bull and Casares, and Bukich hitting on three successive passes, Bukich scored on a quarterback sneak from the one-yard line. After Jencks' successful extra point, the Bears were down by only six, 20–14, with a whole quarter to play.

The Bukich magic, however, was not about to occur on this day. The Bears drove to midfield but Ditka dropped a well-thrown ball from Bukich and on the next play he overshot a wide-open Johnny Morris, who had faked out and gotten behind cornerback Kermit Alexander.

The 49ers went nowhere on their next possession and the Bears again mounted a drive. When they reached the 47-yard line Bukich thought he had Morris in his sights, but Alexander, not about to be burned again, laid back until the last instant and with a burst of speed cut in front of Morris and intercepted the pass. The Bears did not get the ball back again until there was only one minute left in the game. After connecting for 17 yards to Morris, Bukich called for a screen pass in the left flat. It was played perfectly by 49er linebacker Ed Pine, who picked it off, sealing San Francisco's first victory of the season.

The Bears were stunned until they looked at the stat sheet; the 49ers effectively stopped the rush, something the Bears could not do all afternoon. J.D. Smith got a good measure of revenge against Halas, leading all rushers with 93 yards on 17 attempts. Vollenweider gained another 59 yards on the ground and Lisbon, on top of the 51-yard pass completion, gained 40 yards on 12 rushes. San Francisco amassed 192 yards on the ground while the Bears managed but 71 in 17 attempts.

Halas' reaction to this first loss was very reserved. He had nothing but praise for the 49ers, and, incredibly, did not think it was the Bears' worst game of the year. It was "simply a question of a team I worried about all week."[46] Johnny Morris led all receivers with six catches for 107 yards; the 49ers secondary played intentionally deep, limiting the Bears' long passing game, and their defensive plan worked.

"We will play them one at a time. We were flat and they were aroused. Such a combination of circumstances invariably produces an unexpected result," a rationalizing Halas told the press after the game. "The 49ers were being ridiculed by their press and that just aroused them."[47]

The Bears' loss not only dropped them from the ranks of the undefeated, it also allowed Green Bay to move into a statistical tie for first place. In a showdown of 4–1 teams the Packers were rude guests at St. Louis, holding the Cardinals to only 40 yards on the ground in an easy 30–7 victory. Their victory, however, came at a huge cost. Cardinal's defensive back Jimmy Hill bounced Bart Starr out of bounds after he made a 15-yard run.[48] Starr did not take kindly to what he considered Hill's rough treatment and kicked him while they were both on the ground. As they were getting up both were swinging their fists, and Starr ended up with a broken hand. The NFL's leading passer in 1962 would be out of action for an indefinite period with the injury. The Packers also lost another key cog in their offense when halfback Tom Moore, filling in brilliantly all season for Paul Hornung, injured his back in the first period and never returned to the game. Lombardi was closed-mouthed about both developments after the game, saying only that 30-year-old John Roach would replace Starr at quarterback.

There was one other upset during week six, albeit not as surprising as the Bears' loss, as the Los Angeles Rams finally got in the win column with a 27–24 victory over visiting Minnesota. In other games New York got past Dallas, 37–21; Pittsburgh remained in the title hunt with a decisive win at home over Washington, 38–27; Baltimore rudely moved their hosts,

Detroit, further from any title consideration, winning 25–21; and Cleveland remained the only undefeated team in the NFL with a too-easy 37–7 slaughter of the Eagles. In a battle of the "Browns" it was no contest; Philadelphia's Timmy Brown was held to just 38 yards by the tough Browns defense, while Cleveland's Jim Brown was unstoppable, gaining 144 yards in the game. Like the Packers, the Eagles suffered a devastating loss in this game, when the Browns roughed up quarterback Sonny Jurgensen, causing him to leave the game. Jurgensen suffered a bruised right deltoid and a bone chip fracture of his humerus. The injury occurred when he was crushed between 500 pounds of Cleveland defensive lineman, Bob Gain and Bob Wiggin. The Bears paid particular attention to this, for it meant that for the second straight week they would be looking at a substitute quarterback they knew from their cross-town rivalry with the Cardinals: King Hill.

A negative development coming out of week six's games arose when the bad feelings between the Packers and Cardinals became apparent. Cardinals coach Wally Lemm told the St. Louis press that he thought Packer fullback Jim Taylor was a "dirty player," a charge that Vince Lombardi seized upon. Lombardi said that if Lemm meant what he said, "then he's an unstable man running off at the mouth."[49] This verbal dust-up was seen as a release of mutual frustrations, Lombardi's being his irritation with Starr's serious injury, and Lemm's stemming from his team's disappointing showing after such an impressive start.

The players took matters into their own hands after this first loss of the season. On the bus trip back to the airport, the Bears' four captains—Mike Ditka, Joe Fortunato, Larry Morris, and Mike Pyle—called for a players-only meeting Wednesday morning, October 23.[50] The purpose was to "discuss what went wrong last Sunday. If anybody has any suggestions or ideas they can speak up," explained a reluctant Larry Morris to the press. After a half hour the meeting was over, and the players revealed very little about what was discussed. Pyle said, "It's a chance to get braced again and start fresh." Roger Davis added, "it was a real good meeting." Fortunato explained that "A lot of things came up. It was a kind of pep rally," and Ditka briefly mentioned, "No recriminations, no hard feelings, just a good get-together."[51]

Probably the best thing about the meeting was the players realizing that it was needed. In the first game of the season, the Bears' ground game was ineffective and their defense could not stop the run—two areas of significant concern.

Down to just one quarterback for a tough road matchup in Wrigley Field, the Eagles signed the recently retired Ralph Guglielmi to a contract to back up King Hill.[52] Guglielmi was traded from the Giants to San Francisco in September but chose not to relocate all the way across the country, opting to retire instead. The Eagles were desperate, so Guglielmi, having the upper hand in negotiations, insisted on a contract that extended to the end of the season. The grizzled veteran needed only one more game to be eligible for a full share of his NFL pension, and playing in Philadelphia also meant that he could continue his lucrative insurance business in Washington, D.C.[53]

In an effort to ensure that the Eagles were not handed any bulletin board material and to ward off any trace of overconfidence, the Bears emphasized that there was virtually no difference between facing King Hill instead of first stringer Sonny Jurgensen on October 27. Jurgensen excelled at throwing the long ball, but Hill was just as adept at every other quarterback task.[54] Also, with targets like Timmy Brown, Tommy McDonald, and Pete Retzlaff, many thought the strength of the Eagles' passing was due more to their receiving corps than to who was doing the throwing. If they were superstitious, Halas and his charges could also consider an "ex-Cardinal" hex. The week before, Lamar McHan's performance against them had earned him NFL Player of the Week honors.

In actuality King Hill presented less of a threat than McHan. The first pick in the first round in the 1958 draft, Hill played the entire season behind McHan but assumed the starting role in 1959 when McHan went to Green Bay. That year the Cards were 2–10 and Hill threw 13 interceptions and only seven touchdown passes and he had a quarterback rating of 46.2 for the season. He lost his starting role to John Roach in 1960 and was off to Philadelphia in 1961, content with being Jurgensen's understudy, never starting a game in 1961 and starting only one in 1962.

While the Eagles in the last four years were a very respectable 30–21–1, the team was trending downward, with a significant slide in 1962. They were the NFL champions in 1960, holding off the upstart Packers in Franklin Field to win their first title since 1949 under the leadership of their legendary head coach, Buck Shaw. Shaw retired on top and their line coach, Nick Skorich, took over in 1962. They slipped to 10–4 that year, losing the two contests they had with the Giants, which cost them another chance at a title and relegated them to second place. The bottom fell out in 1962, when their defense ranked last against the rush and second to last in first downs allowed. Their entire '62 season was summarized in their mid-season loss to the Packers, a 49–0 humiliation in which the Eagles gained 30 yards on the ground and 24 in the air and managed but three first downs. While that was going on the Packers rushed for 294 and threw for another 334, for an unheard-of 628 yards of total offense. Philadelphia had played the Bears only once since 1959, beating them in Philadelphia, 16–14. That game was only the second victory the Eagles ever had against the Bears, a 15-game history going back to 1935.[55]

Gone from the Eagles' great defenses of recent years were Chuck Bednarik, Tom Brookshier, and Leo Sugar. Two competent defenders still with the team were defensive back Irv Cross and defensive tackle Ed Khayat. Timmy Brown and Ted Dean could give defenses problems when they carried the ball, and the Eagles' receiving corps was still one of the best in the NFL. The big question was how effectively Hill would be able to get them the ball. The oddsmakers did not think much of his chances, making the Bears a 13-point favorite.[56]

The lineups:

Eagles	Pos.	Bears
Ron Goodwin	LE	Angelo Coia
Dave Graham	LT	Herman Lee
Ed Blaine	LG	Ted Karras
Jim Schrader	C	Mike Pyle
Pete Case	RG	Bob Wetoska
J.D. Smith	RT	Steve Barnett
Pete Retzlaff	RE	Mike Ditka
King Hill	QB	Bill Wade
Timmy Brown	LH	Ron Bull
Tom McDonald	RH	Johnny Morris
Ted Dean	FB	Rick Casares

The Bears prevailed in their most boring victory to date, 16–7. Defensive tackle Earl Leggett recovered a fumble on the Eagles' 39-yard line but the Bears offense could not move the ball much further, so Roger Leclerc kicked a 45-yard field goal for an early 3–0 lead. They got the ball back quickly after Hill's offense went three-and-out, and Johnny Morris returned the Eagles' punt 13 yards to set up the offense on the Eagles' 33. Wade hit Marconi on a screen pass in the right flat, and thanks to pancake blocks by Bob Wetoska and Mike Pyle, it was good for 22 yards. Marconi, who replaced Casares, a late scratch due to a leg issue, then made a short four-yard gain on an end sweep. This play proved costly to the Bears. Ronnie Bull and Ted Karras were ahead of Marconi, leading the convoy. When Bull hesitated Karras could not stop and ran up his back, Karras' knee jarring the back of Bull's helmet. Halas immediately took Bull out and put in Willie Galimore. Wade liked how well the first short pass to Marconi worked so he called it again. This time Galimore put a devastating block on Eagles defensive back Don Burroughs; the only Eagle still with a shot at him was Jimmy Carr, whom Marconi overpowered at the goal line to give the Bears a 10–0 advantage. Later in the second period Hill connected with Tommy McDonald in the corner of the end zone, throwing a floater just out of Bennie McRae's reach, to make it 10–7 at halftime.

The Bears' ball-control offense worked perfectly in the third period, when Philadelphia only had two offensive possessions and six plays. After an 80-yard, 17-play drive Galimore went off-tackle from the seven, avoiding the grasp of defensive tackle (and former Bear) John Mellekas and then side-stepping the oft-victimized Carr to juke in for the touchdown. When Jencks' extra-point kick hit the upright—his first miss in 22 attempts—the score was settled, 16–7.

After the game fans were trying to figure out if the Bears were more mediocre than the Eagles were inept. Philadelphia fumbled four times and lost the ball twice. Hill had a terrible time with the Bears' pass rush but a worse time of it with the Bears' secondary. Caroline, Petitbon, Taylor, and Whitsell all had interceptions, and on several occasions the overwhelmed Hill threw into multiple coverage. Caroline's interception came at the end of the game, as the Eagles' pass blocking deteriorated and Doug Atkins knocked Hill out completely with a brutal sack. Hill had to be carted off the field and taken to nearby Illinois Masonic Hospital. Needless to say, King's homecoming to Chicago could not have gone worse. The Bears outgained the Eagles, 366 yards to 214, as Wade completed 20 of 35 passes with one interception and one touchdown, while Hill's statistics were 10 of 24 with one touchdown and three interceptions (an earlier pick by the Bears was thrown by running back Timmy Brown).

The Bears themselves were unimpressed with their win. Mike Ditka called it a poor offensive showing and nobody should expect to win with 16 points. Mike Pyle added that the Eagles defensive line was improved. Stan Jones complimented the quickness of Timmy Brown.[57] Nobody mentioned that the Bears missed three field goals and one extra point. With success in the kicking game the score would have been 27–7, which would not have been a "lousy" victory. Others minimized the Eagles' strengths and talked about the Bears' accomplishments. Wade that the Eagles were better than most people thought, but said the game plan worked "admirably." Johnny Morris, with seven catches for 95 yards, mentioned that he was being loosely defended all game.[58] It was evident that Hill was confounded by the Bears' nickel back coverage, yielding three interceptions throughout the game. The NFL was learning that it was one thing to see Allen's defensive schemes on film but something else entirely for a quarterback to know what to do with them when he is under pressure and has to make split-second decisions.

Both teams had concerns about serious injuries to key players.[59] Ronnie Bull and King Hill were admitted to nearby Illinois Masonic Hospital for observation after the game. Bull suffered a head injury when the Bears were running a Joe Marconi sweep around end and Hill was carted off after a brutal sack by Doug Atkins—who told the press that he did not think he hit Hill hard enough to hurt him. Both Bull and Hill were released from the hospital on Monday, October 28, and were expected to play November 3.

The public's interest in Bears games was becoming very intense, and the Eagles home game was not on network television in the Chicago area or on a closed circuit broadcast to theaters. Consequently, fans looked for tickets anywhere they could. The sellers' market resulted in the arrests of eight individuals for scalping tickets. Arrested by plainclothes Chicago police for offering to sell tickets in excess of their printed value were the following individuals: Walter T. Bear, 28, 14 East Ontario, Chicago; Bert Hahn, 56, 672 Western, Lake Forest; Richard Eshoo, 30, 4412 South Paulina, Chicago; Frank Lubell, 35, 1128 West Diversey, Chicago; Thomas Gower, 55, 409 North Banker, Effingham, Illinois; Howard Hankin, 17, 6216 North Whipple, Chicago; Gary Martin, 341 West 16th, Chicago Heights; and Frank Emole, 17, 71 West 24th, Chicago Heights. Bear was fined $25 but the fine was rescinded after he got a lecture from the judge. All the others also got off easy, with lectures or stern warnings. The plainclothes detail was under the supervision of Chicago Lt. Edward M. Mowen of the Town Hall district, 850 West Addison, two blocks east of Wrigley Field.[60]

In other games the Rams topped the visiting 49ers, 28–21; the Redskins could do nothing with their guests from St. Louis and lost, 21–7;

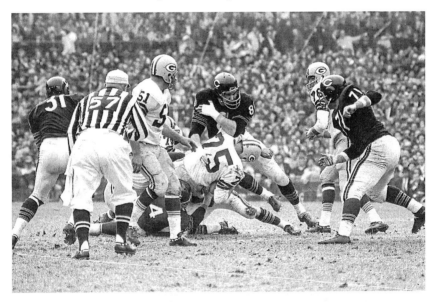

Massive Doug Atkins (81) head slaps Forrest Gregg (75) while Earl Leggett (71) comes up to join the party and Jim Ringo (51) and Bob Skoronski (76) watch helplessly. Joe Fortunato is #31. Head slaps became illegal in 1977.

Detroit easily handled Minnesota, 28–10; Pittsburgh hosted Dallas and won, 27–21, in a game closer than most expected; and Green Bay, playing at Baltimore, kept pace with the Bears, winning 34–20. The biggest game of the week was in Cleveland, a showdown between the Browns and the Giants. The Browns won their matchup in Yankee Stadium two week earlier, 36–24, but the Giants smothered the Browns' running game while Y.A. Tittle completed 21 of 31 passes for a surprisingly easy 33–6 victory for the visitors. The Giants' offense racked up 402 yards, 182 on the ground and 220 in the air, while their defense allowed Cleveland but 63 yards rushing and 114 yards passing. The first-place Browns were no longer undefeated and the Giants were only behind them by one game.

As October drew to a close the end of the seventh week marked the halfway point in the 1963 NFL season. The Bears, Browns, and Cardinals were doing better than many had expected. The Giants and Packers were excelling at their expected levels, while Dallas and Detroit were the biggest disappointments of the season thus far.

The standings at the halfway point:

Western Division		*Eastern Division*	
Chicago	6–1	Cleveland	6–1
Green Bay	6–1	New York	5–2
Baltimore	3–4	St. Louis	5–2
Detroit	3–4	Pittsburgh	4–2–1
Minnesota	2–5	Philadelphia	4–2–1
Los Angeles	2–5	Washington	2–5
San Francisco	1–6	Dallas	1–6

8

November

*Declaring Their Dominance,
Surviving a Tragedy*

With the coming of November, Bears fans were ecstatic about the team's nearly peerless showing in the first half of the season. With three home games and a Thanksgiving weekend trip to Pittsburgh on the schedule, most fans thought, with a victory over Green Bay in the middle of the month, they might be able to coast into the Western Division title. Many thought the big Green Bay game was the only potential November obstacle, since the rest the month consisted of matchups with Baltimore, Los Angeles, and away at Pittsburgh. This was an easier schedule than the Packers. Thanks to the annual Thanksgiving Day game in Detroit, Green Bay had five games in one month: Pittsburgh, Minnesota, at Chicago, San Francisco, and at Detroit. Between the November 17 Bears matchup and the Thanksgiving game at Detroit the Packers had three games in 12 days, and two of them on the road, a brutal test for any team. Not only that, but the Packers would be without Bart Starr until the end of the month. Plenty of reasons for optimism, right?

Maybe right, but veteran Bear personnel knew better. Halas spent a lot of time mentally looking over his shoulder and seeing how resourceful his worthy opponents in the Northland were. They took note of the fact that Lombardi claimed veteran former Bear Zeke Bratkowski to back up John Roach at quarterback.[1] Until Bratkowski reached Wisconsin the Packers were actually without a backup quarterback, since Paul Hornung was on an indefinite suspension. He marveled at how rookie Lionel Aldridge seamlessly filled in on defense, replacing the traded Bill Quinlan. Also, were they not supposed to be weaker on offense with Hornung on an indefinite leave? Jerry Kramer had no problems kicking, Tom Moore was one of the leading running backs in the NFL, and when he was out with an injury, reserve Elijah Pitts—whom the Packers discovered at tiny Philander Smith College in Arkansas—gained more than 150 yards.[2] The Bears' best hope was having good health before the Packer game, earning a victory in that crucial contest, and hoping the Packers stubbed their toe on their tough November schedule.

The worries that Green Bay presented had to be set aside, since the Bears' first opponent, Baltimore, was a tougher opponent than they were in early October. Since the Bears' 10–3 victory over them on October 5 in Wrigley Field, the Colts beat the 49ers and Lions and acquitted themselves fairly well at the end of October in a loss to the Packers, a game that was closer than the 34–20 score. Another concern for the Chicagoans as they traveled east was the revenge factor; in 1962 the Bears decimated the Colts, 57–0. In that game Wade and Bukich passed for 407 yards with Charlie Bivins, Ronnie Bull, Rick Casares, and Joe Marconi running for another 98, while the Bears' defense allowed the Colts only 118 yards. The Bears recorded four sacks and handcuffed Johnny Unitas to such an extent that his passer rating for the afternoon was only 38.7. The Chicagoans also remembered that their victory over the Colts at Wrigley Field on October 6 was the toughest triumph of the year, and in the upcoming game, both Raymond Berry and Jimmy Orr, two of the premier pass receivers in the NFL, would be playing full time.

They would be needed; with four losses, a defeat at the hands of the Bears would be Baltimore's fifth loss, completely eliminating them from contention for anything.

The lineups:

Colts	*Pos.*	*Bears*
Raymond Berry	LE	Angelo Coia
Bob Vogel	LT	Herman Lee
Jim Parker	LG	Ted Karras
Dick Szymanski	C	Mike Pyle
Alex Sandusky	RG	Bob Wetoska
George Preas	RT	Steve Barnett
John Mackey	RE	Mike Ditka
Johnny Unitas	QB	Bill Wade
Tom Matte	LH	Ronnie Bull
Jimmy Orr	RH	Johnny Morris
J.W. Lockett	FB	Rick Casares

A crowd of 60,065 jammed into Memorial Stadium soon realized that this, indeed, would not be the Colts' year. The Bears won their sixth consecutive game against them, 17–7, outclassing their hosts in every aspect of the game. Things got bad early for Baltimore. They opened the game with a great drive, going from their 25 to the Bear 28, but Jim Martin missed a field goal attempt from the 35. Things went further downhill from there. They had the Bears pinned back at their own 15 early in the game when

Wade went back to pass and was surprised to find Colts defensive back Andy Nelson breathing down his neck, thanks to a well-executed corner-back blitz. Wade was able to dance away from him and get a desperation safety-valve pass to Marconi, who was open in the left flat. Wade led Marconi perfectly; he had a full head of steam upon catching the ball. A convoy of blockers, led by Herman Lee and Ronnie Bull, joined in to escort him, and Marconi reached the Colts' 22-yard line before he was finally tackled by defensive back Jim Welch. More proof that those that live by the blitz can die by the blitz: if Nelson had stayed in the defensive backfield Marconi would have never had 63 yards of daylight. A nice run by Casares got the Bears close and Wade snuck the ball over for the first score. Bull came out after the first period and was replaced by Willie Galimore. The Bears offense was ultra-conservative in the first half, and Unitas had no success against the Bears defense, so the half ended 7–0.

Early in the third quarter Unitas dropped back from his own 28 and saw Raymond Berry around the 35-yard line. In his eagerness to get Berry the ball he did not notice how closely Joe Fortunato, Bill George, and Bennie McRae were to Berry. Fortunato picked the ball off and got down to the Colts' 25. Two running plays by Bivins and Casares got them down to the 17, where Baltimore stiffened. On fourth and one, the Colts were expecting another Wade sneak, but instead he tossed a beautiful floater to Casares in the flat, who cruised into the end zone unchallenged.

Unitas finally got the Baltimore offense in gear with the game's most efficient drive, 70 yards in seven plays. Lenny Moore showed he still had the moves, confounding Bear tacklers with a 25-yard scamper to the end zone at the end of the drive and suddenly it seemed like a game, Bears 14, Colts 7. As the third period ended, Unitas flubbed a pitch-out to Moore and Larry Morris recovered. The Colts' last-ditch drive died out at the Bears' 25. Wade engineered a well-planned 14-play drive to kill the clock. With only 90 seconds left Leclerc kicked his only field goal of the game. Final score: Bears, 17, Colts 7.

While many Chicagoans who watched the televised game may have felt a little cheated that their team could muster only 17 points against a foe they hung 57 on in Baltimore a year ago, Halas was not the least bit disappointed. He formulated a game plan "on the basis of ball control and that worked … [we] ruled out passes in the waning moments of the first half rather than risk an interception."[3] The idea was to have Wade keep the ball on the ground, eat up as much clock as possible, and keep the ball out of Unitas' hands, especially in front of the 60,000 rabid Colts fans. Wade only threw 12 passes but completed nine of them, ending the game with a passer rating of 136.1. Morris and Ditka combined for only three receptions, and Casares, Galimore, and Marconi combined for six. The game plan also included a very conservative but successful running game, with Galimore and Bivins replacing Bull for most of the game and combining for 73 yards on 16 carries. Thanks in large part to the Bears' defense, Wade outplayed Unitas, who completed only 11 of 18 and was sacked five times. The vaunted Colts long game was stifled; Unitas' longest completion was for only 26 yards. The Bears had six games left, and five of them were at home. With Los Angeles coming to the Northside the following week, the Packer showdown in Chicago loomed very large.

In other week eight games Dallas hung another home loss on the Redskins, 35–20; Minnesota won its third game of the year at home, beating the Rams, 21–13; and Detroit scored at will in the fourth quarter at Kezar Stadium and beat the hapless 49ers, 45–7. In the more meaningful games the Cardinals' defense could not stop Y.A. Tittle, and the Giants won their big showdown game in St. Louis, 38–21; Cleveland stayed on top of the Eastern Division by winning in Philadelphia, 23–17, as fullback Jim Brown riddled the weak Eagles defense for 223 rushing yards; and Green Bay, on the strength of Jim Taylor's and Tom Moore's combined 229 yards on the ground, beat Pittsburgh in a game played in Milwaukee, 33–14. Cleveland remained a game up on the Giants in the east and the Bears and Packers remained tied for first place in the west.

Halas did his best to keep his charges fired up and invested in the upcoming Rams game, fearing a letdown based on overconfidence and also the team looking ahead one week to the Packer contest.[4] Since the wipeout they had given the Rams three weeks ago in the Coliseum, Rams head coach Harlan Svare had settled on a quarterback and observed the defense getting better. The Rams were fairly successful after their huge loss to the Bears, beating Minnesota and San Francisco in home games and losing their one road matchup in the Twin Cities. With Bratkowski off to Green Bay, Roman Gabriel—the Rams' out-sized, first-round draft pick out of North Carolina State—had the starting quarterback job all to himself. While he was short on experience, his size (6'5", 220) allowed him to see over lineman and be difficult to take down when he ran or was in danger of being sacked. Svare utilized a system with alternating offensive guards coming in and delivering the play call to save the young Gabriel from a task he was not ready to undertake.[5] Their defensive play was much improved as well; Deacon Jones, Lamar Lundy, Rosey Grier, and rookie Merlin Olsen were starting to jell, and six-year veteran Jack Pardee was established as one of the most consistent linebackers in the NFL. To prevent Wade from having his way all afternoon with his two favorite downfield receivers, Svare told the press that eight-year veteran (and three-time Pro-Bowler) Linden Crow would cover Ditka and Ed Meador, a former Arkansas Tech wonder boy who was becoming one of the leaders on the

Rams defense, would cover Johnny Morris. In spite of the Rams' improvement the oddsmakers were not the least bit impressed; the Bears were 17-point favorites.

The Bears' defense got a big boost a few days before the game when the Bears were able to activate defensive end Ed O'Bradovich.[6] The former University of Illinois star was one of the most pleasant surprises of the 1962 season. In the 13 games he started in that first year he recovered five fumbles, got four sacks, made 62 tackles, and assisted on 26 others. The official word from the team was that O'Bradovich was suffering from a viral infection, strep throat, and a stomach disorder.[7] The untold situation, kept out of the media, was more serious. O'Bradovich was not even invited to training camp, four months before his activation. "They took an EKG and I couldn't pass the physical," the 23-year-old explained. "Dr. Brown, the head internist, wouldn't let me play. I told him I had an irregular cardiogram all my life."[8] O'Bradovich's first-year performance was good enough to rank him seventh in the Rookie of the Year balloting; based on his first season, his return was very welcomed.

The Rams activated linebacker Ken Kirk for the game but also announced that their two first-string running backs, Dick Bass and Jon Arnett, were doubtful to play.

The lineups:

Rams	Pos.	Bears
Carroll Dale	LE	Angelo Coia
Joe Carollo	LT	Herman Lee
Charlie Cowan	LG	Ted Karras
Art Hunter	C	Mike Pyle
Joe Scibelli	RG	Bob Wetoska
Frank Varichionne	RT	Steve Barnett
Red Phillips	RE	Mike Ditka
Roman Gabriel	QB	Bill Wade
Art Perkins	LH	Willie Galimore
Pervis Atkins	RH	Johnny Morris
Ben Wilson	FB	Rick Casares

Bill Wade had the offense on the march early in the first period, but the drive stalled after two holding penalties were called. Roger Leclerc's 30-yard field goal attempt was good to give them an early lead. The Rams were unsuccessful running or throwing the ball in the first quarter but the Bears' offense stalled as well. After several failed offensive drives in the second period Halas got impulsive and took Wade out in favor of Rudy Bukich. The Bears got close to the Rams' end zone again in the third period, but their improved red-zone defense held, and the Chicagoans had to settle for a 16-yard field goal by Leclerc: Bears 6, Rams 0 at the start of the fourth period. Later in the fourth the Bears had a chance to put it away with another Leclerc field goal, but the kick was blocked by linebacker Jack Pardee, giving the Rams one last chance, starting at the Bears' 40. With less than one minute left Gabriel had a difficult time with the Bears' pass rush, and his last two hurried throws were thwarted by Richie Petitbon and Roosevelt Taylor.

The Bears escaped with their lives, 6–0. The Rams' vastly improved defense confounded Wade and Bukich almost as much as the Bears' defense confounded young Gabriel. The Rams offense crossed the 50-yard line only twice during the entire game. Rookie defense tackle Johnny Johnson did a great job filling in for Stan Jones, who left the game with a pulled muscle. In nine games the Bears had now surrendered only 10 touchdowns with only three of them on running plays. The Rams second-string running backs, Ben Wilson and Art Perkins, subbing for Bass and Arnett, gained only 50 yards on 23 carries. To get something going Svare did put a hobbled Arnett in for two rushes; he ended the day with minus four rushing yards. Gabriel completed only seven of 23 passes and was sacked five times. All totaled, the Bears defense deserved the shutout. They also won because Bivins, Casares, Galimore, and Marconi gained 105 yards on 31 carries and caught two passes for a net gain of another 42 yards. Wade completed only 12 of 30 pass attempts, but Bukich was four for four (albeit for only 30 yards). The ball-control offense, designed to eat up the clock and keep the peerless Bear defense fresh, was reaching a pinnacle of success. Bears fans were coming to grips with the fact that this was not a team that was going to dominate every game and that after years of being doormats the Rams were developing a very competent defensive corps themselves.

In other week-nine games the Colts outlasted the fading Lions, 24–21; the Cardinals stayed near the top of the Eastern Division by beating the Redskins, 24–20; the Giants overwhelmed the weak Eagles, 42–14; and Pittsburgh surprised Cleveland, 9–7. The Packers kept pace with the Bears, easily handling the Vikings, 28–7, and the cellar-dwelling 49ers beat the Cowboys, 31–24. What mattered the most to Chicagoans at the end of week 10, however, was that Green Bay was coming to town, and the Bears were 9–1 for the first time since November 21, 1948.

With week nine's results the Eastern Division suddenly had a pennant race. With Cleveland losing to Pittsburgh the lead was now tied between New York and the Browns. St. Louis did themselves a big favor with their victory, remaining only one game behind the division leaders, and Pittsburgh, now at 5–3–1 when ties did not count, was only one game behind the leaders in the loss column.

The stage was set for the biggest football game in Chicago in many

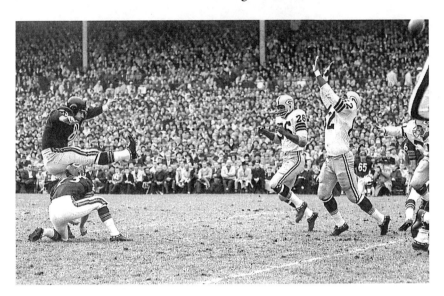

Roger Leclerc was the NFL's fourth most accurate field goal kicker in 1963. Dave Whitsell holds while Herb Adderley (26) and Lionel Aldridge (62) rush in too late to block it. Tom Bettis (65) watches from the sidelines. Note the 26 lucky spectators with field-level folding seats along the sidelines, one of the many great features of Wrigley Field as an NFL venue.

years, and the biggest sports event in the city since October 1959 when the White Sox opened the World Series on the South Side with the Dodgers. It seemed like everyone in the Chicago area wanted to see the Packers-Bears game, but because of the NFL's television blackout rule and the fact that there was no closed-circuit theater coverage, a ticket to the game was required. It created a field day for scalpers. In spite of the stern warnings the Bears had about ticket gouging, scalpers were selling tickets up to 13 times face value, with a $5 grandstand ducat going for as much as $65.[9] Ads in the classified sections of the newspapers appeared, with some prices as high as $100 for the $5 seats in the upper deck.[10] The *Chicago Tribune* printed information about where one could go outside the blackout area and watch the game on one of the 116 CBS national television stations that would be carrying it. It involved a fair amount of travelling. Fans would have to trek to Milwaukee to the north; Rockford, Illinois, to the west; and South Bend, Indiana, to the east.[11] WGN Radio, which broadcast the Bears games with Jack Brickhouse and Irv Kupcinet, announced that four Midwest stations would be picking up their feed and carrying the broadcasts: WKMI in Kalamazoo, Michigan; WSGW in Saginaw, Michigan; WWBC in Bay City, Michigan; and KRSI in Minneapolis–St. Paul.[12]

Even the railroads got into the act. The Santa Fe Railroad was running a special train to Galesburg, Illinois, out of Chicago's Dearborn Station. A 10-coach special would leave at 9:00 a.m. and get to Galesburg in time for customers to get to the Custer Hotel, where television sets would be set up for 440 viewers. The 366-mile round trip cost $10 and was sold out Monday morning, November 11, six days before the game.[13] Another railway excursion to the north was not yet sold out. The Milwaukee Road was running a limited express from Chicago's Union Station to Fontana, Wisconsin, 72 miles away on the shores of Lake Geneva, where the Abbey Resort's three restaurants and four convention centers would be televising the game. The cost for the round trip and facility entrance was $7.80. This venue even featured halftime entertainment; a high school band complete with majorettes would perform after the second quarter.[14]

The Bears had an offer for their rabid followers on Tuesday morning, November 12. A block-long line started outside the Bears' main office in Chicago's Loop at 4:30 a.m., three and a half hours before the office would open to sell 1,500 standing room tickets in the lower-deck grandstand area, with a limit of four to a customer. The tickets, at $2.50, were gone in 40 minutes.[15]

As was his custom during the season every Monday, on November 11, Halas spoke at the *Chicago American*'s Quarterback Club luncheon at the Morrison Hotel in the Loop. On this date he brought offensive line coach Chuck Mather, Richie Petitbon, Mike Ditka, and Bill Wade. Halas was asked, due to the huge demand for tickets, if he ever considered moving the games to Soldier Field. He responded by saying that since there are only 18,000 seats between the goal lines at Soldier Field—compared to around 33,000 at Wrigley Field—he would not want to face any of his season ticket holders who did not get one of those seats, and there would be thousands of them.[16] He also pointed out that the Bears season-opening victory over the Packers could well work against his team in the upcoming contest, with the Packers looking for revenge, wanting to prove the Bears' win in Green Bay was an aberration.

While big games often make or break a player's career, the same can be said for coaches. George Allen and Jim Dooley, Halas' right-hand men, were beginning to be seen as just important to the team's success as the players themselves. Jim Dooley ceaselessly pored over the films of the Packers' defense to prepare the Bears' offense for the big contest. For example, his meticulous film study revealed that linebacker Ray Nitschke would shuffle his feet before the ball was hiked when he intended to blitz and that defensive back Willie Wood would turn a certain way if he were to rush the line or drop back into pass defense.[17] "Dooley had a brilliant mind for the game," Bill Wade claimed. "He was the best I've ever been around analyzing film."[18] Angelo Coia echoed Wade's sentiments: "I thought Jim Dooley was as smart a coach as we had."[19]

Defensive coordinator George Allen operated the same way. All season he had extensive notes on the offensive tendencies of Bears opponents that he would morph into virtual term papers, starting with small cards that he would organize to formulate the defensive game plan to the smallest detail, that Bear defenders would use to their advantage throughout the game.[20] The careers of both men in large part were shaped by their diligence and innovation in the 1963 season.

By Wednesday, four days before the big contest, Halas was up to his old tricks. The *Chicago Tribune* printed a photo of the Bears practicing in the north end zone of Wrigley Field with one uniformed guard in the bleachers and another in the grandstand close by.[21] Both of the men were gazing through binoculars, looking north, at the apartment buildings on the north side of Waveland Avenue. Halas had a habit of being paranoid about spies at various times throughout his coaching career. He once told linebacker Larry Morris, who was holding a licked finger in the air to check the wind direction, to put his hand down; the opposition might see it and be inadvertently tipped off about the wind direction. The old owner-coach then cautioned everyone present that no one under any circumstances would be allowed inside for the rest of the week. The reason: "We'll be too busy."[22]

Meanwhile in Green Bay, Lombardi was taking an opposite tack. The Packers had open practices in the field outside City Stadium, which was their usual practice site, open for anyone to see. "Unless the fans turn out to be a nuisance, we'll continue our regular policy of practicing out in the open. So far this season, it hasn't bothered us," explained the innovative master.[23] Very soon, however, privacy became the priority; he closed all practices to the public and the press the following day.[24]

The Packers, undefeated since their opening day loss to the Bears, knew what was at stake in this game. In spite of injuries, and Hornung's absence during the eight-game winning streak, following their loss to the Bears the Packers scored 265 points while yielding only 116; their average margin of victory in this span was 33 to 14. Defensively and offensively the Bears and Packers led the NFL in 20 of 48 categories. The Bears led the league in points allowed (82 in nine games, just over only nine points per game) and total yards allowed (1982, 220 per game). The Packers led the NFL in first downs allowed, only 117, to the Bears' 121. The Packers had grabbed 20 of 28 enemy fumbles and intercepted 19 passes. The Bears lead the NFL in interceptions (32) and had recovered 11 of 22 enemy fumbles.[25]

The Bears, in spite of their mediocre scoring totals the last few games, led all teams in passing. Wade and Bukich had completed 161 tosses for an NFL-best 59.9 percent completion rate. The tandem also had eight interceptions, fewer than any other team. Phil Handler's offensive linemen deserved some of the credit; the line had given up the fewest yards to sacks, only 100, among all 14 teams.[26] The Packers' Tom Moore had played brilliantly replacing Hornung, and when Moore was out with injuries, Elijah Pitts proved to be a more than capable replacement. John Roach, while throwing more interceptions than touchdown passes, did not embarrass himself in victories over St. Louis, Baltimore, Pittsburgh, or Minnesota. To fortify the quarterback position, former Bear veteran Zeke Bratkowski came from Los Angeles to back up Roach.

Bear president Mugs Halas expressed concern about Bratkowski possibly playing against his old team. "Some of Zeke's better games as a Ram were against us," he explained.[27] His father the Papa Bear did not comment about this. Lombardi wanted to give Halas something else to think about so he issued a statement saying that there was a good chance that Bart Starr would be able to play.[28] If that were the case, Starr would be suiting up exactly four weeks after a bone break in his hand, which was very unlikely to happen.

Lombardi was pleased with his team at this point in the season but unable to enjoy it as much as he should due to some personal difficulties. He was putting tremendous pressure on himself to win a third consecutive title, something done only twice before in the NFL, by the 1929–1931 Packers and the 1922–1924 Canton/Cleveland Bulldogs. Physically he was not feeling like himself.[29] The team offices were moved from downtown to a new addition of City Stadium, and he now had to climb a flight of stairs to reach his office, leaving him short of breath. He decided to quit smoking, a habit he was ashamed of, thinking of it as an indication of personal weakness and a bad example for children. Dizzy spells convinced him to finally give up the habit. It would be hard to do; Lombardi went through three cartons of Salems (more than four packs a day) per week.[30] Smoking was ingrained in pro football culture at that time, to the point that players and coaches routinely smoked during halftime of the games. Paul Hornung claimed Lombardi calmed himself with four cigarettes at every half.[31] His coaching staff continued to smoke (defensive coordinator Phil Bengston favored non-filtered Camels) making it even harder for Lombardi to quit.[32] The team's biggest star, Paul Hornung, did testimonials for Marlboro cigarettes; the manufacturer, Philip Morris, supplied free cartons to him throughout the season, which he shared with his teammates. Hornung himself admitted to smoking five packs a day in his playing days, commenting in his autobiography that at least he was not a hypocrite.[33] Lombardi paid a price for quitting, gaining 20 pounds, but never smoked again.[34]

Lombardi scheduled the Packers' Saturday practice in Green Bay instead of Chicago. The team flew to Chicago on a chartered United Airlines plane to avoid distractions and keep some level of privacy.[35] This was the first time the Packers ever flew to Chicago; in previous years they used the Chicago Northwestern Railroad.[36] They checked into their usual Chicago home, the Drake Hotel, three miles south of Wrigley Field on Lake Shore Drive, on Saturday afternoon. The last time the Bears and Packers were 8–1 and locked in a first-place tie was 22 years before, on December 14, 1941, one week after Pearl Harbor. On that date, in a divisional round playoff game, the Bears handled the Packers, 33–14, in front of a sold-out Wrigley Field with 43,425 in attendance. They went on the following week to beat Steve Owen's New York Giants, 37–9. Would history repeat itself?

The lineups:

Packers	Pos.	Bears
Max McGee	LE	Bo Farrington
Bob Skoronski	LT	Herman Lee
Fuzzy Thurston	LG	Ted Karras
Jim Ringo	C	Mike Pyle
Jerry Kramer	RG	Jim Cadile
Forrest Gregg	RT	Bob Wetoska
Ron Kramer	RE	Mike Ditka
John Roach	QB	Bill Wade
Tom Moore	LH	Willie Galimore
Boyd Dowler	RH	Johnny Morris
Jim Taylor	FB	Joe Marconi

As a last-ditch goodwill offering to their crazed fans the Bears released 900 additional standing room tickets in the back of the left field bleachers, underneath the centerfield scoreboard, and along the left field catwalk, selling for $2.50 each, available Sunday at 9:00 a.m. The line at the bleacher box office at the corner of Sheffield and Waveland started forming at 2:45 a.m.[37] Willie Galimore started in Ronnie Bull's place due to Bull's foot being injured. The Bears anticipated good things with two breakaway speed backs starting the game. Wetoska moved to right tackle and Jim Cadile, who impressed line coach Phil Handler with his recent play, started at right guard. The Packers started the week as six-point favorites, largely due to the Bears' lack of offense the last few weeks, but the line was four at the start of the game. Bart Starr not starting at quarterback, the gamblers figured, would make the game a little closer.

Bob Jencks kicked off to start the game and J.C. Caroline cut Herb Adderley down at the ankles with a surprising tackle, setting the Packers up at their 16-yard line. Caroline and Adderley were known to socialize off the field, and Caroline had heard from a mutual friend that Adderley was boasting that he would run a kickoff back for a touchdown. "It wasn't

Charlie Bivins (49) returns a kickoff against the Packers. Herman Lee (70) blocks Lionel Aldridge (67) while Ray Nitschke (66) and Willie Wood (24) close in. Steve Barnett (73), Earl Leggett (71), and Ronnie Bull (29) watch from the sidelines. Jess Whittenton is #47 for the Packers.

going to happen against me," Caroline said years later.[38] It was a brilliant play by Caroline and seemed to set the tone for what was to follow, the Packers' worst loss in over two years. Historians had to go back more than 31 games, to November 5, 1961, to find a worse Green Bay defeat.

The Packers' opening salvos were two running plays by Jim Taylor that went nowhere, thanks to the Bears defensive line. Roach avoided a heavy pass rush and completed a short pass to Max McGee, good enough for a first down at their 29. The Packers did not get much further and punter Jerry Norton shanked the kick, giving the Bears good field position at their own 40. After they were unable to contain Marconi and Galimore or prevent a completion from Wade to Ditka the Packers stiffened up, and the Bears' drive ended with a field goal by Roger Leclerc. History repeated itself before the first quarter ended. Roach could not rally the Packers offense, Norton came in to punt, and once again he did not come through, this second poor kick giving the Bears the ball around their 40-yard line once again. Leclerc kicked his second field goal, this one from the 46: Bears 6, Packers 0.

On the ensuing kickoff Adderley had a head of steam when he was blindsided at the 33 by Bo Farrington. Adderley's fumble was recovered by Leclerc at the Green Bay 36; after two rushes the Bears were at the 27.

Wade called a pitchout to the left for Galimore, who caught the lateral but saw how clogged his route was with Packer defenders. He quickly cut sharply, seeing an opening between end and tackle, used his quick acceleration to best advantage, and scored. This meant more than the Bears suddenly being up 13–0. Galimore, recovering from two knee surgeries and on the shelf at the start of the season, suddenly ran one in like he used to. A badly needed weapon missing in the Bears' offense—a breakaway running back—had reappeared.

Neither offense produced anything else in the first half. The Bears received the kickoff to start the third quarter and put together a drive consisting of short passes and line rushes. They ate up the clock in fine fashion and finished with Leclerc's third field goal, putting the Packers now three scores behind, 16–0. The fuming Lombardi took Roach out and put Zeke Bratkowski in at quarterback. His last appearance in Wrigley Field was almost three years previously, December 4, 1960, when a desperate George Halas put him after yanking Ed Brown in a one-sided 41–13 loss to these same Green Bay Packers.

Bratkowski had the Packers driving into Bears territory in the fourth quarter when he aimed a pass for Max McGee, who appeared to be open, down the left sideline. Bratkowski got hasty and his feet got happy when he saw Ed O'Bradovich closing in on him on the right side. Preoccupied with O'Bradovich's rush, he did not notice that Roosevelt Taylor, arguably the fastest man on the field, had him dead to rights on a safety blitz. He hurried the pass McGee's way, not paying attention to Davey Whitsell, who was laying low, giving McGee some room to maneuver. When the ball was in the air, Whitsell made his break, tipped the pass away from a very surprised McGee, and made an acrobatic interception. The Bears took over but had limited success moving the ball, settling for another field goal, this one from 42 yards out, by Leclerc; it was now Bears 19, Packers 0, and the obvious outcome of the game very predictable.

A similar situation occurred a few minutes later for Bears fans, when Bratkowski dropped back and once again saw what appeared to be an open Boyd Dowler. Bratkowski to his credit stayed in the pocket long enough to get off a good throw even though Joe Fortunato, after tricking the Packers' pass blockers with a delayed red dog, was an arm's length away. Showing his world-class hurdler's speed Bennie McRae closed in on McGee and intercepted the ball in full stride, putting the crowd in a frenzy with his patented kick-step sprint. Packers running back Earl Gros knocked him out at the four, and the huge throng at Wrigley went delirious. Soon after Wade ran it in on a quarterback sweep from five yards out.

Bewildered by the turn of events and frustrated by their consistent failure, the Packers started to turn on each other, screaming and cursing at each other. Defensive end Willie Davis and linebacker Dan Currie verbally went at it; defensive back Willie Wood chewed out the entire defensive line; Nitschke was screaming and swearing at everyone; and all of them were targeting rookie linebacker David Robinson.[39] The offense tallied a touchdown after Bratkowski was finally able to make a 64-yard completion to McGee, who only caught three passes all game. As the gun went off the Bears were the new big dog in the NFL, proving it with a surprisingly convincing 26–7 conquest of the NFL's reigning dynasty.

Packer followers had to go back 31 games, to November 5, 1961, to find a worse Green Bay defeat. At that time the Colts handed them a 45–21 drubbing, six weeks before the Packers went on to beat New York for the NFL championship. It was a victory for the Bears in every sense of the word. Wade outplayed both Roach and Bratkowski, with his legs and his arm, while only throwing 14 passes. Galimore showed the NFL he was back, gaining 79 yards on 14 rushes, and treating the world to a 27-yard touchdown run with his patented moves so artfully executed a photo of it ended up on the cover of the following week's *Sports Illustrated*. Bivins, Casares, and Marconi combined for 111 yards on 33 attempts, and

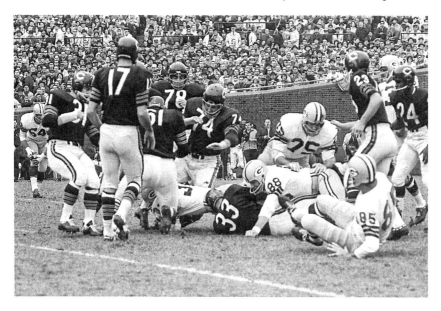

The Packers' Jim Taylor (31, on ground) experiences the hardships presented by the greatest defense of the pre–Super Bowl era, while Max McGee (85), Ron Kramer (88), and Forrest Gregg (75) try their best. Participating in this typical Bear gang-tackle are Joe Fortunato (31), Richie Petitbon (17), Bill George (61), Stan Jones (78), Bob Kilcullen (74), and Larry Morris (33), while Dave Whitsell (23) and Roosevelt Taylor (24) stand at the ready.

even a banged-up Ronnie Bull got in long enough to make four runs for 30 yards.

As efficient and effective as the offense was, it was a rare occurrence in the 1960s to see a defense smother Green Bay as effectively as the Bears did on this day. George Allen had the Packer offense scouted so thoroughly that at one point Larry Morris called a fake audible, using the same verbiage the Packers used in one of their own audibles for an alternate blocking scheme. The Packers' line picked it up, thinking that the voice was one of their own; the result was right tackle Forrest Gregg ran smack dab into center Jim Ringo, allowing the Bears' Stan Jones to stick Tom Moore with an eight-yard loss. The Bears' defense intercepted Roach twice and Bratkowski three times. Taylor had two picks, while McRae, Petitbon, and Whitsell had one each. Lombardi and his staff had yet to solve the Bears' five pass defender nickel defense. Rick Casares knew Bratkowski's weakness and saw it coming. "When we were in college—I at Florida, Zeke at Georgia—we always knew we could rush him, and he'd put it up in the air for interceptions."[40] The Bears held Jim Taylor and Tom Moore to a paltry 73 yards on 19 carries; the punishing Taylor, who often had his way running against the Bears, managed only 23 yards on seven tries. Mike Ditka explained that he had never sensed a team so unified and disciplined before the game. "In the Los Angeles game, we had a lot of suggestions made in the huddle; [against the Packers] you heard only one guy talking, and that was Bill Wade."[41] Wade simply said, "We beat the Packers at their own game."[42] Lombardi had no alibis, saying only that his team was beaten in every phase of the game.

Lombardi's mild response with the media was different than his response with his team. Defensive coordinator Phil Bengston mentioned to him in a spirit of consolation that the team was flat through the whole game. Packers broadcaster Ray Scott said when Lombardi heard that "he turned on Bengston like a tiger, yelling, 'How could you be flat for a game like this?'"[43] During the Packers' bus ride back to O'Hare Airport, a glum Lombardi never said a word. Once the chartered plane took off, he told his wife, Marie, who traveled with him for all road games, that he was outcoached, unable to answer the innovative schemes that Allen, Dooley, Handler, and Stydahar threw at his team all afternoon. He vowed to rectify the situation in 1964. Knowing how down his team was, Lombardi started walking the aisle of the aircraft, patting each player on the back and allowing the beer to be passed out. "They're down enough already," he explained to one of his coaches.[44]

While both sides respected each other, there was no love lost between the teams, and some hard feelings and retribution existed as well. A frustrated and humiliated Ray Nitschke could not handle his team's predicament in the fourth quarter any longer and intentionally went low on Rick Casares while another Packer defender was hitting him high. Nitschke didn't settle for simply getting him down. "[He] drove off to the side and grabbed Casares' ankle and broke it. It was a really dirty tackle," Paul Hornung claimed.[45]

The Casares injury at the hands of Nitschke was an intriguing sidelight of the game, a brutal encounter between two individuals many thought to be the most fearless and intimidating players in the NFL. Mike Ditka claimed that Casares was the toughest individual he ever played with, that not even the gargantuan Doug Atkins would cross him.[46] Casares was born in Tampa; when he was seven, his father was killed in a gang war, and his mother sent him to live with an aunt and uncle in Paterson, New Jersey. At 15 he forged the birth information on an application for the New Jersey Golden Gloves tournament and, in spite of his tender age, got to the championship match. He returned to Tampa and was introduced to sports by his teachers at Thomas Jefferson High as a way to keep him in school; as a freshman he was 6'1" and 190 pounds. He excelled at football, basketball, baseball and track and field; the Florida High School Athletic Association named him one of the 33 all-time greatest Florida football players of the last 100 years.

Casares earned a scholarship to the University of Florida in Gainesville. He was a highly-decorated 210-pound running back in the SEC, earning Honorable Mention All-American honors, and he also captained the basketball team his junior year. Casares earned second-team All-SEC honors in basketball his last year at Gainesville but did not compete after his junior year, when he was drafted into the Army. In the 1954 NFL draft Halas picked Casares in the second round, the 18th player picked. He was offered $20,000 to play in the CFL by the Toronto Argonauts, a figure the penurious Halas would never match. In spite of the huge offer from Canada, Casares chose to play in the NFL and settle for the $10,000 Halas paid him to play in the 1955 season.

He excelled from the start of his NFL career, earning All-Pro honors his first year—which featured an 81-yard run from scrimmage against the Baltimore Colts—and taking the NFL rushing crown in 1956 after gaining an astounding 1,126 yards on 235 carries, a yardage total just 20 yards shy of the NFL single-season record. His performance was a big reason the Bears reached the championship game in 1956, and Casares became a major sports figure in Chicago. Much to his coaches' chagrin, the handsome, swarthy fullback was in Chicago's society pages and gossip columns almost as much as he was in the sports section. Casares took to Chicago's sybaritic scene like a moth to a candle, spending time with Chicagoland's most eligible and glamorous young women and enjoying Chicago's nightlife on a regular basis. His cavorting with Bobby Layne and Paul Hornung raised some concerns; Casares was one of the first individuals interrogated during the gambling scandal that led to Hornung's and Alex Karras' suspension. He invested heavily in a bowling complex in the growing suburban area northwest of Chicago, capitalizing on his status throughout the 1950s as one of Chicago's three most prominent pro athletes, along with Ernie Banks and Minnie Miñoso. Halas had a love-hate relationship with his great ball carrier, awed by what Casares could do on the field but dismayed by his off-field behavior.[47]

Ray Nitschke had a similar hardscrabble childhood. His father died in an automobile accident when he was four, and his mother died of a blood clot when he was 13. His two older brothers—Robert, eight years older, and Richard, four years his senior—would raise the young adolescent together. Nitschke was constantly getting into fights in his tough-guy hometown, Maywood, Illinois; Paul Hornung pointed out that if it were not for football, Nitschke would have ended up in a penitentiary.[48] "I took it out on everybody else," Nitschke explained to author David Maraniss. "A day didn't go by that I didn't belt some other kid in the neighborhood. I was like that right through high school and college and even after I joined the Packers. Didn't take anything from anybody."[49] As a freshman at rough Proviso High School in Chicago's football-elite Suburban League he was playing fullback, but academic difficulties and poor grades cost him his eligibility his sophomore year, something he was embarrassed about for the rest of his life. He was eligible his junior year and played quarterback and safety; one young Maywood resident who watched and admired his gridiron accomplishments was a youthful Ed O'Bradovich.[50] Nitschke starred at basketball and baseball, pitching so well that the St. Louis Browns offered him a $3,000 signing bonus after high school.[51] Nitschke, however, was intent on playing football, had many scholarship offers, and decided to go to the University of Illinois with dreams of quarterbacking the Illini in the Rose Bowl.

A poor student not enjoying college academics, Nitschke drank, smoked, and fought to cope with his frustrations.[52] He was moved to fullback, and with single-platoon football being the norm, he played linebacker on defense. At the end of his senior year, his ability to cover ground and his sure tackling prompted Cleveland Browns coach Paul Brown to call him the best linebacker in college football. All his life Nitschke dreamed about playing for his hometown Chicago Bears, but when the NFL draft occurred in 1957, he was taken in the third round by the Packers.

The truculent attitude continued. He once got pistol-whipped in Chicago.[53] Enjoying a Harlem nightclub with Emlen Tunnell and a group of players, he started smarting off when another gentleman came up to him and said, "Hey, white boy, sit down and shut up or your ass will be out the door." The speaker turned out to be Wilt Chamberlain, and Nitschke quickly behaved.[54] After the 1961 championship game his brothers Robert and Richard picked a fight with Packers Dan Currie and Bill Quinlan—and paid a humiliating price for it.[55]

However, once Lombardi arrived in Green Bay in 1959, Nitschke found the father figure he was missing his entire life. Lombardi got the credit for channeling Nitschke's aggression and rage into the proper channels to make him an eventual Hall of Fame defender. Another calming influence was his wife, Jackie Fourchette, whom he met when she was waitressing in Green Bay.[56]

Perhaps it was inevitable that these two great and tenacious athletes would at some point lock horns. Casares, who many felt was the most fearless player in the NFL, the one player that nobody in the league ever wished to cross, did not say a word about Nitschke's transgression. He would get his revenge four months later, in a restaurant in Wisconsin.[57]

The other games in week 10 did not matter as much to Chicagoans as they had in previous weeks. The Colts got past the Vikings, 37–34, scoring a touchdown on the last five seconds, and the Rams surprised the Lions, 28–21. In the east the Giants completely outclassed the 49ers, 48–14, and moved into a tie for first place because the Browns lost to the Cardinals, 20–14. The Cowboys beat the Eagles, 27–20, and the Steelers stayed in contention for the eastern title with a 34–28 victory over the Redskins. The Steelers were now 4–1 in their last five games and very eager to host the Bears on Sunday, November 24.

It was a good week in the courtroom for one of the Bears' coaches as well. Sid Luckman was facing a $39,895 penalty for non-payment of state sales taxes at his automobile dealership, Sid Luckman Motors, from 1951 to 1953. The lawsuit was instituted by William G. Clark, the Illinois attorney general, but Judge William V. Brothers ruled that even though the business owed the taxes, Luckman himself could not be held personally liable.[58] Luckman was spared any hometown embarrassment when the story only ran in the *New York Times*.

Halas was still basking in the glow of the victory over the Packers days after the final whistle. He mentioned that he never saw a team as completely inspired as his charges were in the Packer game.[59] Focusing entirely on the Forbes Field matchup against the Steelers, he pointed out that the Steelers' defense was less scheme-oriented than the Packers and instead they went after opponents with "reckless abandon."[60] He expressed worry about Steelers quarterback Ed Brown's accuracy with long passes but professed no concern that Brown, as a former Bear, would have knowledge of their defense, since it had changed so much since he was traded. He also warned the media the Steelers' coach Buddy Parker had one of the keenest minds in pro football and that the Bears' biggest problem would be getting the players "up" enough two weeks in a row.[61]

Ed Brown, traded in 1962 to the Steelers in exchange for a first-round draft pick, admitted to wanting to win this upcoming game with his old team with a special intensity.[62] Brown put in eight loyal years on the north side with the Bears and played a big part in their Western Division championship in 1956, leading the entire NFL in passing. Brown was close to Rick Casares, who was extremely critical of Halas when he dispatched Brown to the Steelers. "Ed Brown was the best in the league, and we loved him," said Casares, "he was our man."[63] In spite of Brown's achievements in 1956 Halas soured on him when the Bears lost their first three games in 1957. His solution was to have a quarterback roulette the rest of the season, the infamous "Three B's" phenomenon, rotating George Blanda, Zeke Bratkowski, and Brown. By the end of the 1950s Halas was tired of Brown's late-night carousing and traded him to Pittsburgh. He got off to an erratic start with the Steelers in 1962, and Parker responded by leaving Bobby Layne as the first-string quarterback. Layne retired before the 1963 season started, and Brown was the Steelers' quarterback from the outset. Layne took over as a quarterback consultant, part-time coach. He was Parker's telephone observer in the press box and met with Brown in the locker room during every halftime.[64] Brown, having a very good year, was a big reason the Steelers were still in the Eastern Division race.

Parker surprised the media by being adamant that the Steelers could win the game. Saying the Bears running game and not their defense brought them to victory over the Packers, Parker emphasized that if his team did not give the ball away—the Packers lost two fumbles and threw five interceptions—and they could contain the Bears rushing, they would win.[65]

With Casares unavailable for the rest of the season the Bears had a big hole in their backfield that needed filling. The Bears announced that halfback Billy Martin, out since August after breaking his leg against Baltimore in the preseason game in New Orleans, was being activated to take Casares' place on the roster.[66] The former University of Minnesota star would be used behind Bull and Galimore at left halfback; Charlie Bivins, the previous third-stringer in that position, became the second-string fullback, behind Joe Marconi.

Knowing that any chance for a title would be determined by the matchup with the Bears, Steelers coach Buddy Parker moved the team's practices from South Park to Forbes Field. "The Bears probably have more spies than the Russians," he said, "we can limit the number of persons watching us."[67] He also told the press that the Pittsburgh front office received a telegram signed by 1,000 Packer fans which read, "Beat the Bears."[68]

Friday, November 22, when the Bears were packing up to fly to Pittsburgh, the team and the rest of the nation got word that President Kennedy was assassinated in Dallas. The event virtually paralyzed all activities and events in the country. Stores and movie theaters were closed, concerts, high school events and AFL games were postponed. Everything came to a halt. Then came one of the biggest surprises of all: NFL commissioner Pete Rozelle announced that the week 11 games of November 24 would go on as planned.[69]

Rozelle wrestled with the issue while he waited to hear from Kennedy's press secretary Pierre Salinger, whom he had known since college. Salinger was out of the country—en route by plane to Asia but rerouted back to Washington after word of the assassination—and very difficult to contact. When finally reached by phone Salinger told Rozelle to not cancel any of the games. "Jack would have wanted you to play."[70] That was all Rozelle needed to hear.

The young commissioner faced outrage from all corners after this decision. Most of the NFL players and coaches did not want any part of it; Frank McNamee, owner of the Philadelphia Eagles, said he would miss his first home game in 15 years. Philadelphia's mayor James Tate tried unsuccessfully to get a court order to stop the Eagles' home game against Washington from occurring. CBS refused to honor its broadcast contract and declared its intention to not air any NFL games anywhere in the country. The *New York Times* wrote, "For that exercise in tasteless stupidity there is neither excuse nor defense, as nothing could illustrate more clearly than the banal, empty phrases with which Rozelle sought to justify the decision."[71]

So with heavy hearts and preoccupied minds, the Steelers and Bears readied for their battle at Forbes Field. The two teams had little history between them, in spite of the closeness of George Halas to their founder Arthur Rooney. Since the Steelers' first season in 1933 there had only been 12 games between the two teams and the Bears had won 11 of them. On November 30, 1958, the Steelers won convincingly, 24–10, for their only success. The most recent game was at Wrigley Field on December 6, 1959, with the Bears winning, 27–21. Over the last four seasons the Steelers were 26–24–2, showing a huge improvement in 1962, when they finished second to the Giants and went 9–5, just like the Bears.

The Steelers started the season with a banged-up defense, but they were very settled offensively and defensively for the tiff with the Bears. Defensively they were over the tragic loss of Big Daddy Liscomb, thanks to the steller play of linebacker Myron Pottios, lineman John Reger, and the greatest athlete ever born in Prienzing, Bavaria, the legendary Ernie Stautner. Defensive tackle Joe Krupa shored up the left side of the line. The eight-year veteran was a Chicago native who prepped at Weber Catholic,[72] a perennial football power in Chicago's famed Catholic League, facing off against the Bears' Tom Bettis when Weber would lock horns with St. Mel's. On offense Brown had the luxury of handing off to the pride of Waterproof, Louisiana, future Hall of Famer John Henry Johnson. Johnson gained 1,141 yards in 1962, second best in the NFL, and he was one of the most feared rushers in the league. His backfield mate was Dick Hoak, at 5'11" and 195 pounds, three inches shorter and 35 pounds lighter than Johnson, shifty and quick. Brown's passing targets were all above average. Gary Ballman, Preston Carpenter, Buddy Dial, and Red Mack were effective receivers; Dial was a Pro-Bowler who caught 50 passes in 1962 and was on a pace to top that in this current season. Ballman also was a special teams' weapon, with two kickoffs returned for touchdowns against Green Bay and Washington.

The lineups:

Bears	Pos.	Steelers
Bo Farrington	LE	Gary Ballman
Herman Lee	LT	Dan James
Ted Karras	LG	Mike Sandusky
Mike Pyle	C	Buzz Nutter
Jim Cadile	RG	Ray Lemek
Bob Wetoska	RT	Charles Bradshaw
Mike Ditka	RE	Preston Carpenter
Bill Wade	QB	Ed Brown
Willie Galimore	LH	Dick Hoak
Johnny Morris	RH	Buddy Dial
Joe Marconi	FB	John Henry Johnson

The game turned out to be a harrowing, nerve-wracking experience for the Bears, who got almost more than they bargained for against a desperate Steeler team. In front of the largest Forbes Field crowd all season, 36,465, the Steelers moved within one game of first place in the NFL Eastern Division by settling for a 17–17 tie.[73]

The Bears surprised the Steelers' defense in the first quarter by abandoning their ball-control offense. Wade dropped back and hit Bo Farrington, who had beaten defensive backs Dick Haley and Clendon Thomas with a late burst of speed. Farrington was dragged down at the one-yard line, and Wade called for a sweep by Galimore around the right end. The shifty speedster saw an opening off tackle when defensive end Fred Atkinson overcommitted. He cut sharply inside, where Glen Glass had him dead to rights, but Glass fell for Galimore's head fake and missed the tackle while Galimore dived into the end zone, just inside the right upright. Galimore was hit very hard at the goal line by linebacker Andy Russell but his momentum carried him in for the score. Bears 7, Steelers 0, with the 58-yard pass play to Farrington giving the Steelers something to think about.

Early in the second period, the next time Wade had the ball he tried to pick on Haley but paid a heavy price for it. Haley, who was Mike Ditka's collegiate teammate at Pitt, intercepted a wayward Wade offering at the Pittsburgh 45 and ran it back all the way to the Bears' 10-yard line. Dick Hoak slashed into the end zone a few plays later from the six, knotting the game up at 7–7. The Bears got the ball and put a nice drive together, eating the clock with a mix of runs and passes. At the 14-yard line Wade dropped back while Ditka was running a short down-and-out toward the right side of the end zone. Ditka had been double-teamed, but he was a step ahead of Haley after his cut and well behind Russell. He dove for the catch and was ruled down at the one yard line. Ronnie Bull ran it in from there, easily avoiding linebacker Myron Pottios who had taken the wrong angle, putting the Bears ahead, 14–7.

Just as Wade thought of Haley, Steeler quarterback Ed Brown started thinking about Davey Whitsell. Brown knew Whitsell was the slowest member of the Bears' stellar defensive backfield and also that he like to gamble sometimes in quest of an interception. He hit Buddy Dial, the dangerous Steeler receiver, after Whitsell was playing him deep, respectful of Dial's shiftiness and speed. This set the Steelers up at the Bears' 31. The half was coming to a close, so Brown went into his bag of tricks, setting up his offense in a spread formation, resembling a deep shotgun set. The Bears' pass rush was often collapsing his pocket, so this formation gave him much more time to pass. Instead of looking for Dial or Ballman downfield he sent reserve halfback Roy Curry, a speedy rookie out of Jackson State, deep downfield on the right sideline. No Bears linebacker picked him up, Bennie McRae made a desperate sprint and just missed intercepting the pass, and Curry danced around Whitsell to get into the end zone. The half ended in a 14–14 tie. Curry's first pass reception of his career—which also would turn out to be the only one—came in his team's most important game of the year.

The Steelers' offense was able to drive on the Bears in the third period but two field goal attempts by Lou Michaels, from the 29- and 34-yard lines, were no good. The fourth period started in a tie. With the Bears deep in their own territory, Wade called for a pass out in the left flat, oblivious to the fact that no Bear was near it and it went right to Steeler linebacker John Reger. Reger could have walked in for a touchdown, but, miraculously for the Bears, he dropped the ball. The Bears punted and Ed Brown engineered a drive that stalled close to the Bears' goal line. Lou Michaels, zero for two in the second half, finally kicked through the uprights, the go-ahead field goal making the score 17–14. For the first time in 18 quarters of football—going back to October 20, their loss in San Francisco—the Bears were behind in the score.

Disaster almost occurred on the kickoff when Michaels' kick was fumbled by Charlie Bivins and recovered by the Steelers' John Burrell. Luckily for the Bears, the refs suspiciously called the Steelers offside on the kick, and on the do-over Bull caught the kickoff successfully. Wade called for two long pass plays, both of which were unsuccessful, and on both Ditka had run long pass patterns. He came back to the huddle and told Wade that he was too gassed to run another long pattern but said he would try a hook about 10 yards out and then try to run for a first down.[74] Since it was third and 20, the Bears' options were limited. Wade hit Ditka at the 30, eight yards past the line of scrimmage. He spun around and avoided a diving tackle attempt by Clendon Thomas. At the 35 he pulled his foot out of linebacker John Reger's grasp, and at the 40 he was simultaneously hit by defensive backs Willie Daniel, Glen Glass, and linebacker Myron Pottios. The three Steelers all hit Ditka high, but he kept his legs churning and broke away from their grasp. The big tight end managed a slight burst of acceleration away from that trio, and some Bears were behind him sealing off the backside, but as an exhausted Ditka tired, Clendon Thomas—the first Steeler to hit him on the play—caught him from behind at the 15. The most spectacular run the NFL experienced in years put the Bears in a position to tie the game. Ditka lay on the turf, Christ-like, for what seemed like an eternity. On the next play Bo Farrington dropped a pass in the end zone.[75] The Bear offense could only get down to the nine, and Leclerc tied the game with an 18-yard field goal.

The Steelers got the ball and Dick Hoak got loose on a run around end, with nobody near him. Inexplicably, referee Norm Schachter ended the play, calling the ball dead. At Forbes Field, the opposing team's benches were on the same sideline. After the call was made Ernie Stautner, Joe Krupa, Myron Pottios, and John Henry Johnson started swearing at Halas, charging that he had paid off the officials to rig the game. Fortunately for the Papa Bear 900 pounds of enraged Steelers calmed down before they could get to him. Final score: Bears 17, Steelers 17.

"We played like a bunch of jackasses," said linebacker Larry Morris after the game. "We got some bad breaks," added Doug Atkins. "We ran into a team that wanted very, very badly to win," said a measured Bill Wade.[76] "We'll settle for the tie; needless to say, we would have rather won," rationalized George Halas. "But we're still ahead of Green Bay. Our future is still in our hands. I'm glad we're going home to finish out the season in

Wrigley Field," he continued. Commotion set in soon after. A Pittsburgh writer entered the locker room and immediately confronted Halas, yelling at him that he had paid the officials, a reference to the aborted run by Hoak in the fourth quarter. When he did not calm down, Ditka and two other Bears grabbed him and rudely escorted him out of the locker room.[77] The Bears flew back to Chicago, lucky to still be alive, perhaps in more ways than one.

In other week 11 games, the most depressing Sunday in the NFL's history, the Vikings beat the Lions, 34–31, ruining their season even further; the Redskins won their third game of the year, beating the Eagles 13–10 to move ahead of them in the Eastern Division; and the Rams beat the visiting Colts by one point, 17–16. In the more important games the Packers recovered from their loss to the Bears by crushing the 49ers, 28–10. The Packers had just four days to prepare for their Thanksgiving matchup in Detroit, giving the Bears some hope for a little more breathing room in the standings. The Browns stayed in the thick of the Eastern Division title race by handling the Cowboys, 27–17, and the Cardinals stayed abreast of the lead as well with a 24–17 upset in Yankee Stadium over the hosting Giants. While the Bears stayed ahead in the west, the Browns, Cardinals, and Giants were all tied for first at 8–3. Just one game behind them—and tied with them in the loss column—were the now significant Pittsburgh Steelers. In the end, Rozelle may have been correct letting the games go on. Many felt a need to escape through football. Almost 67,000 fans came to Yankee Stadium, and there were sellouts in Philadelphia, for a weak team, and in Milwaukee, for the world's champions.

While the Bears readied themselves for the Vikings, commissioner Pete Rozelle announced that if the Packers and Bears tied for the title, a playoff game would be played on December 22 between the two teams in Green Bay. In the Eastern Division, with three teams in first and another just a game behind, the NFL office presented 10 different playoff scenarios based upon what things looked like after week 14, on December 15. There were four versions of triple tie playoffs and six combinations of possible two-way ties. If there were a triple tie, the December 29 championship game, which would be in either Chicago or Green Bay, would be moved to Sunday, January 5, with the playoff games scheduled for Sunday, December 22, and Sunday, December 29. Based on the schedule, with New York playing Pittsburgh and St. Louis still having to play Cleveland, a four-way tie was mathematically not possible.

Week 12 started on Thanksgiving Day, with the Packers traveling to Tiger Stadium for their annual holiday matchup with the Lions. The Lions entered the game at a dismal 3–7, but records usually meant nothing for this holiday affair, and they gave the visiting Packers more than they could handle, tying them at the end, 13–13. The Lions opened the scoring with a second period field goal but Elijah Pitts answered that with a three-yard touchdown run. The score stayed at 6–3 because Jerry Kramer's extra point was blocked by Detroit's John Gordy. Wayne Walker kicked his second field goal before the half, so the third period started at 6–6. Lombardi was thrilled to have Bart Starr back for the game but dismayed that he lost his defensive quarterback for the rest of the season: Ray Nitschke suffered a broken arm.

At the start of the fourth period Jerry Kramer missed a chip-shot 10-yard field goal attempt that would prove disastrous for Green Bay. The Packers finally mounted a drive in the fourth period which ended with Starr hitting Ron Kramer for a seven-yard touchdown pass for a 13–6 lead. Bruce Compton had replaced an injured Night Train Lane, and when Starr saw Compton on Kramer, he acted quickly. The game ended when quarterback Earl Morrall led the Lions on a long, time-consuming 78-yard drive consisting of 17 plays. It ended when Nick Pietrosante lumbered in from the one-yard line and Wayne Walker kicked the extra point to end the game in a 13–13 tie. Kramer's missed field goal turned out to be the biggest and most costly Packer gaffe of the season. The Lions' impenetrable rush defense was the difference. Starr, Taylor and Pitts totaled 31 yards in 21 attempts. There was no love lost between the two foes, and Lions linebacker Joe Schmidt summed it up perfectly: "We just sent them to Miami [site of the NFL's playoff bowl game for second-place finishers], where they belong."[78] November came to a close, three games left in the season. At the dawn of December, the only standings that mattered were as follows:

West Division	*East Division*
Chicago 9–1–1	New York 8–3
Green Bay 9–2–1	St. Louis 8–3
Cleveland 8–3	Pittsburgh 6–3–2

9

December

Earning It the Hard Way

Since ties neither benefited nor damaged NFL teams in 1963, the Bears started the final month of the season very pleased with their situation. With a record of 9-1-1, they had a winning percentage of .900. If they tied their last three games, they would still be at .900, and the Western Division title would be theirs, because it was impossible for the Packers to catch them. When the Packers tied the Lions on Thanksgiving Day, their fate was sealed. If they had beaten Detroit and were to win out their last two games—against San Francisco and Los Angeles—they would finish at 12-2, an .857 winning percentage, still behind the Bears' .900 mark. By only tying Detroit their best record could be 11-2-1, at .846. Three ties and the Bears are in; three wins and the Bears are in; one Bear loss with two Packer victories, and the Bears travel to Green Bay for a playoff game December 22 to determine the Western Division champion. The Bears' fate was entirely in their hands, and Green Bay was hoping for some assistance from either 4-7 Minnesota, 2-9 San Francisco, or 4-7-1 Detroit. The Bears' remaining opponents were 10-23, a .303 winning percentage. These same opponents' road record was an even more dismal 3-13 (.230). The Bears would have to stub their toe to a significant extent to lose one of these contests and give the Packers a chance at a playoff game.

While the Vikings were 4-7 they were a much improved team compared to where they were September 22, when the Bears notched one of their easiest victories of the year, 28-7, in Bloomington, Minnesota. The Vikings scored 34 points in each of their last two games, one a 37–34 loss to Baltimore and the other a 34–31 victory over Detroit. Their quarterback, the diminutive Fran Tarkenton, was giving NFL defenses fits with his quick feet and mostly accurate passes. The agility and quick cutting skills young Tarkenton possessed made him the best scrambling quarterback in football, and he had three very good receivers—rookie Paul Flatley, Jerry Reichow, and Gordy Smith—to help him out. Tarkenton's performances were so good that he was the third-ranked passer in the NFL leading up to the Bears game. Setting up the Vikings aerial attack on the ground was halfback Tommy Mason and former Bear fullback Bill Brown. At the 11-week mark of the 1963 season the only backs with more yards from scrimmage than Mason were the two "Jim's," Brown of Cleveland and Taylor of Green Bay. Bill Brown, who grew up near Chicago in Mendota, Illinois, played for the Fighting Illini. He was drafted by the Bears but left unprotected when the Vikings entered the league and was always ready for some revenge against Halas. Viking head coach Norm Van Brocklin, however, would start Tom Wilson at fullback against the Bears.[1] Wilson got the starting nod after averaging almost four yards per rush in the second half of the Vikings victory over Detroit one week before. If Tarkenton were able to avoid the Bears' pass rush and keep a clear head trying to figure out the Bears' swarming pass defense schemes, he would be a major problem at Wrigley Field on December 1.

Perhaps to shore up the spirits of his men, who were still reeling like the rest of the country over the Kennedy assassination and also their disappointing tie in Pittsburgh, Halas played up the fact that their three remaining games were in Chicago. "We may have an advantage playing our last three games at home," he told the media.[2] "Playing before home town fans could be a tremendous asset. The latest example was the Green Bay game," he continued, stating the obvious. "Those fans helped beat the Packers. They helped tremendously."[3] These declarations were actually a good way to deflect pressure from his players. Nobody was talking about the offense's weaknesses; they had managed only eight touchdowns in their last five games. Jim Dooley's emphasis on error-free ball-control schemes kept the defense off the field and the team in the victory column, but the margin for error was precariously thin, and now that it was December there well might be some games where the Bears would not just be playing against a gridiron opponent but also fighting adverse weather. An encouraging development for the Viking game was the fact that both Ronnie Bull and Johnny Morris would be at 100 percent.[4]

The lineups:

Vikings	Pos.	Bears
Paul Flatley	LE	Bo Farrington
Grady Alderman	LT	Herman Lee
Gerry Huth	LG	Ted Karras
Mick Tinglehoff	C	Mike Pyle
Larry Bowie	RG	Jim Cadile
Erroll Linden	RT	Bob Wetoska
Gordy Smith	RE	Mike Ditka
Fran Tarkenton	QB	Bill Wade

Vikings	Pos.	Bears
Tommy Mason	LH	Ronnie Bull
Jerry Reichow	RH	Johnny Morris
Tom Wilson	FB	Joe Marconi

A crowd of 47,249 braved a frigid 23-degree air temperature and a 13-degree wind chill but found no warmth in the Bears' first half performance. On the third play of the game Wade fumbled after a rough tackle by the Vikings defensive tackle Paul Dickson, giving Tarkenton great field position early in the game. The Bears' defense stiffened, however, and Minnesota settled for a 16-yard field goal: Minnesota 3, Chicago 0. The Bears' defense quickly settled the score, however, when Doug Atkins completely leveled fullback Bill Brown. Brown fumbled and was knocked out of the game. The Bears offense took over but could not move the ball. They also settled for a 16-yard field goal to tie the score.

Vikings head coach Norm Van Brocklin's defensive strategy successfully stifled the Bears for the rest of the half. Like the Steelers, Van Brocklin always had either two backs or a back and the tight end stay in to pass block and stave off the Bears' pass rush. This meant only three receivers going out, but Tarkenton's maneuverability added to the scheme's effectiveness. The only problem was the Bears linebackers were agile and not easily fooled; Tarkenton soon paid the price. Executing a scramble around end, the diminutive quarterback was knocked senseless by a host of Bear defenders and replaced by the one of the heroes of the College All-Star game four months earlier, Ron Vander Kelen. This was the only high point for the Bears in the second quarter. Their offense went nowhere, with many dropped passes and four fumbles. Special teams, a strength all season, also played poorly. Billy Butler ran a Bobby Joe Green punt back 16 yards to the Viking 42. Vander Kelen then masterminded a six play, 58-yard drive that ended with fullback Tommy Wilson going in from the two. Minnesota's 10–3 advantage soon grew even bigger. Tommy Mason outwitted the Bears punting unit next, taking Green's punt on the 19 and running it back 28 yards to the Vikings 47. Vander Kelen dropped back to pass and did not notice Larry Morris' red dog until the last moment. Morris got ahold of his foot but the tall quarterback shook loose, scrambling to his right, and spotted Gordy Smith all by himself 10 yards downfield. Vander Kelen hit him with a perfect pass, and Smith raced down the sideline, evading a diving tackle by Petitbon and beating McRae into the end zone. The cold, huge crowd at Wrigley was library-silent. A championship seemed to be slipping away, with the Bears behind, 17–3, as the first half came to a close.

Doug Atkins' oppositionality and George Halas' obstinance ruined the Bears' halftime.[5] Roger Leclerc remarked that one of Halas' arbitrary rules was no Cokes at the half. As the team lumbered into the locker room Atkins grabbed a Coke bottle, and Halas came over and insisted that Atkins hand it over. "Atkins then puts it behind his back and taunts him, saying,

'You can't have it.' They argued back and forth and finally Halas says, 'Doug, look, this is silly. Take one more sip and give me the Coke back.' Just then the referee came in and notified the team that there was two minutes left before the second half begins. The entire halftime was taken up with the two of them arguing."[6] The most important halftime of the season turned out to be the least fruitful.

Perhaps it was a good thing that the players did not have to listen to their elderly coach at the break, for they looked like a team that took it upon themselves to shape up in the second half. On the kickoff J.C. Caroline upended Billy Butler so hard he lost the ball and Ed O'Bradovich recovered for the Bears. This good fortune did not last long, however, as Galimore soon fumbled on a tough hit by left linebacker Roy Winston. Joe Fortunato picked off a Vander Kelen offering, and a modest Bear drive ended with Roger Leclerc missing a field goal. The Bears got the ball back quickly and Wade went to work. On third and two at the Vikings 41-yard line, Minnesota's defensive line and linebackers were congealed in the middle, looking for Wade to sneak for the first down. Wade head-faked a run and then fired a flare pass to Marconi; the Vikings defense was so unprepared for a pass play that he made it all the way down to the Vikings' 13. Ted Karras' earth-moving block then got Galimore to the four, where Wade ran it in: 17–10 Vikings, with momentum changing.

The fourth quarter was nerve-wracking for all the Bears fans. As the clock ticked down no scoring took place, but the Bears were dominating the game. The Vikings never crossed mid-field in the second half and were held to on 25 offensive plays including their punts. After a failed Viking drive the Bears got down to the Vikings' 31. A piling-on penalty assessed to Viking linebacker Bill Jobko turned into a 20-yard gain for the Bears, whereupon Wade threw a flare pass to Marconi from eight yards out and the versatile fullback rambled in for the tying score.

With the game tied the Bears were back where they wanted to be, avoiding a loss. The Viking offense sputtered through the last moments of the game and Wade led one more drive, which stalled at the Vikings 28. Instead of lining up for a 35-yard field goal which could have won the game, Halas called for a running play to kill more of the clock. Ronnie Bull swept around the right end and was immediately met by Winston. To keep the play alive, he lateralled back to Wade who safely caught the ball but was thrown down for a 10-yard loss by defensive end Jim Marshall. So instead of a three-point lead with a chance to kick off deep into Viking territory, the game was still tied but the Vikings were starting at their own 38. The old coach breathed a sigh of relief when the gun went off: 17–17, Vikings and Bears in a tie, Bears securely in first place—for another week.

The huge crowd booed Halas as he trudged down the west sideline toward the door in the left field corner that went to the locker room. "We're still on top," he told the press after the game.[7] "They [the Vikings] played a better game than the Packers did two weeks ago," he went on to explain. "We started slowly but came to life in the second half. I feel a lot better about this tie than I did about the one with the Steelers."[8]

While the reporters focused on Halas, players started to mention who was really responsible for bailing this contest out—Bill Wade. Ditka proposed that Wade get the game ball and others agreed. "He called a great game today by sticking to the stuff we knew would work," said veteran lineman Bob Wetoska.[9] Another player who wished to remain anonymous then added, "This [today] was Billy Wade's offense. A great majority of the time we were running what Wade wanted us to run."[10] The mild-mannered, gentlemanly team leader took no credit, as usual, pointing out that there was no way you could beat the Bears' defense except with luck. The locker room knew, however, that Wade was relying on his uncanny football intuition to change plays that were sent in, adjust to defensive shifts, and find defensive weaknesses he could exploit. Wade went along with the ball-control game plans the coaching staff laid out but was very confident in his own football acumen. Dooley and Halas knew this and respected him too much to place limits on him. NFL followers were too busy oohing and aahing about Charley Johnson's accuracy, Fran Tarkenton's footwork, Y.A. Tittle's success, and Johnny Unitas' play calling to notice that Wade could duplicate those qualities when he needed to, but this year what he needed was error-free execution and clock-eating drives. Having the best record of any quarterback in the NFL in 1963 up to this point in the season proved what a master he was.

Vander Kelen said he was in awe of the Bears defense but insisted he was not frightened.[11] This was his third big game in less than a year, counting the Rose Bowl and College All-Star game, and he wanted to make the most of the opportunity. He pointed out that the Bears' double-teaming of Paul Flatley minimized the Vikings offensive effectiveness. "The Bears got charged up [in the second half] and we couldn't cope with them," Van Brocklin concluded.[12]

In other games, the visiting Rams beat the 49ers, 21–17, and the Colts won on the road in Washington, 36–20, with Johnny Unitas throwing for 355 yards against a weak Redskin defense. The remaining three games, remarkably, all had playoff implications.

Visiting Cleveland put a huge crimp in St. Louis' title plans with a

24–10 victory. Charley Johnson could complete only nine of 26 passes and was sacked four times, two factors which sealed the Cards' fate. New York won a difficult matchup with lowly Dallas, 34–27, with the win leaving them tied with Cleveland for first place. Pittsburgh stayed in contention with New York and Cleveland by tying Philadelphia, 20–20, coming back from deficits of 17–3 and 20–10.

Four tie games in an eight-day span—which had never happened before in the NFL—meant that six teams were still in contention with only two weeks left in the season. This was the kind of season league officials dreamed about. If the Bears were to win or tie their last two games, they would be in. If the Packers were to win their remaining two games and the Bears were to lose one of their two contests, they would host a play-off game in Green Bay three days before Christmas. Both Cleveland and New York had one easy game and one difficult game left on their schedules. Cleveland's two matchups were on the road, in Detroit—difficult—and Washington—easy. New York had two home games, hosting a weak Washington team and then facing a contender to whom they already lost, Pittsburgh.

Pittsburgh's schedule was tougher. They had to travel to Dallas and then close out the season in Yankee Stadium against the Giants. If the Giants and Steelers both were to win in week 13 their end-of-season matchup could determine the division championship. If Cleveland stumbled in either of its last two games, a Giants loss to the Steelers in that scenario would leave the Giants at 10–4 and the Steelers at 8–3–3. The Steelers would then take the crown, by .013, as both the Browns and the Giants would be 10–4, .714, and the Steelers would be 8–3–3, .727. If Cleveland and New York were to end the season in a tie, a playoff game would be played Sunday, December 22, in Cleveland.

The NFL draft was held on Tuesday, December 2, in Chicago's Loop at the Sheraton-Chicago Hotel. The Bears, with the best record in the NFL, would draft last, while the 49ers at 2–10 would draft first. The first player picked was split end Dave Parks of Texas Tech, a surprise, with the likes of Nebraska's tackle Bob Brown, Arizona State's Charley Taylor, and Ohio State's Paul Warfield available. The Bears took tackle Dick Evey from Tennessee with their first pick. This draft was a fruitful one, with 10 eventual Hall of Famers taken among the 280 players selected. Bobby Brown, Charley Taylor, Carl Eller, Paul Warfield, Mel Renfro, Paul Krause, Dave Wilcox, Bob Hayes (seventh round), Leroy Kelly (eighth round), and Roger Staubach (10th round, 129th player taken), all Hall of Famers, made this a particularly notable draft. Prior to this draft, only five players drafted in the eighth round or later became Hall of Fame inductees, going back to the first NFL draft in 1936. The list includes Wayne Millner, eighth round,

1936; Danny Fortmann, ninth round, 1936; Tony Canadeo, ninth round, 1941; Don Maynard, ninth round, 1957; and Jackie Smith, 10th round, 1962.

Before their Wrigley Field contest with the 49ers on December 8, the Bears settled an issue they had with NFL headquarters. Pete Rozelle and his staff were concerned about an NFL championship game being held at Wrigley Field. The reason they gave was that Wrigley Field had no lights, while Soldier Field did, but many assumed this issue was a smokescreen for the real issue, Wrigley Field's diminutive capacity of 49,000.[13] Soldier Field could accommodate anywhere between 75,000 and 100,000 fans, albeit with more than half of them with substandard viewing. Doubling the revenue of the expected gate at Wrigley Field was not a matter the NFL took lightly.

This would not be the first time that concerns about Wrigley Field for important contests came up. The 1918 World Series between the Boston Red Sox and Chicago Cubs was moved from Wrigley Field to Comiskey Park because of Comiskey's larger capacity. If not having lights was the real issue, Rozelle himself would have come up with the solution that Halas proposed.

"Under no circumstances will the playoff for the championship be shifted out of Wrigley Field," declared Halas.[14] Out of respect to NFL headquarters, he then said he gave serious consideration to Rozelle's concerns about the lack of lights being a huge complication if the game needed a sudden-death overtime. Halas' solution was to move the opening kickoff from 1:05 p.m. Central Standard Time to 12:05. He did not mention the stadium capacity issue, the fact that Soldier Field had only 18,000 seats between the sidelines, or that he had 34,000 season ticket holders with seats between the goal lines, and about 16,000 of them would be furious to have inferior seats in the larger lakefront site. George Strickler in the *Chicago Tribune* also pointed out that there should be some sentiment involved, since the game would be the 30th anniversary of the first NFL championship playoff, played at Wrigley with Red Grange saving the day (and the championship) against the Giants.[15] Halas also announced pricing for the playoff game if the Bears won the division: upper and lower box seats, east outfield stands, $12.50 each; upper and lower grandstand seating, $10; left field and center field bleachers, $6.

The Packers wasted no time informing their fans about upcoming playoffs, including in their press release some information showing them jumping the gun. On Friday, December 6, with a two-game West Coast swing still in front of the team, Green Bay's front office started accepting ticket orders not only for a potential divisional playoff game against the Bears but also for the NFL world championship game.[16] Ticket pricing was the same as for regular season Packers games, $6, $5.25, and $3.75. There was no public comment but the Bears did some in-house grumbling about this display of overconfidence by their intense rivals.[17]

A more immediate concern taking up most of the Bears' attention was playing San Francisco, the only team that defeated them, on Sunday, December 8. Since their victory over the Bears October 20 the 49ers had done very little to distinguish themselves, going 1–5 and scoring 100 points while giving up 194, a margin of 32–17 per game. On paper, the only 49er to worry about in the upcoming contest was Abe Woodson, especially in light of some successful punt returns the Vikings had against the Bears in the previous week's tie game.

Woodson was a kick return specialist who had few peers. A native of Chicago's West Side, Woodson prepped at Austin High School, a Chicago Public League football factory through the mid–20th century. When he was the 15th pick in the 1957 NFL draft, Woodson was the 11th Austin High graduate to play in the NFL. One of Woodson's admirers was the Bears' Ronnie Bull. "I just had a mutual admiration for Woodson. He always gave his best all the time. He was an outstanding kick returner and he was willing to do it, too."[18]

The defense got some very bad news on the eve of the game when trainer Ed Rozy announced that defensive tackle Earl Leggett was unable to play due to chipped knee cartilage that was causing his knee to randomly lock up on him. The injury happened in the Viking game, and Halas said that the problem had not responded to treatment.[19] To fill the void Allen and Halas called up rookie Johnny Johnson from the taxi squad. Johnson impressed line coach Joe Stydahar during the preseason. The Indiana University star, who prepped just east of Chicago in Hobart, Indiana, filled in for an injured Stan Jones in the big Packer game three weeks earlier and did well. Taking Leggett's roster spot would be the healed-up veteran, Fred Williams, out since the first Viking game with a separated shoulder which had been surgically repaired. Leggett's absence was the source of some anxiety; with him and Jones plugging the middle of the defensive line only six rushing touchdowns had been scored against the Bears thus far in the season. Williams would be rusty after 10 weeks, coming off surgery, and Johnson, in spite of his good showing so far, was still an inexperienced rookie.

After a short practice and meeting on Saturday, December 7, the Bears gathered around their televisions to watch the Packers-Rams game on the West Coast. Since the Rams were 5–2 in their last seven games—a vast improvement, thanks to a stiffening defensive line and an improving Roman Gabriel—and the fact that the Packers lost Ray Nitschke to a broken arm, there was a glimmer of hope that the defending champions, who had not played in nine days, might go down to defeat. With the Rams ahead 14–10 at halftime things looked promising, indeed.

However, Bart Starr, Max McGee, and Jimmy Taylor did what they did best in the second half, leading the Packers to three touchdowns, and the game ended in a 31–14 Green Bay victory. Taylor rushed for 113 yards on 17 carries, with one touchdown and a 40-yard gain his highlights; he out-rushed the entire Rams offense by 19 yards. McGee caught seven passes for 103 yards and scored three touchdowns, while the Packers defense, minus Nitschke, intercepted Gabriel three times and got six sacks. The Pack-ers hustled out of Los Angeles to settle into Palo Alto, their West Coast encampment, in time to watch the 49ers play the Bears.[20]

An anxious crowd of 46,994 ignored overcast skies and a cold wind, filling Wrigley Field with an air of both hopefulness and dread, expect-ing a victory but remembering the last two weeks and the debacle in San Francisco two months ago. They felt a little better the first time the 49ers had the ball. Fred Williams and Larry Morris ganged up on running back Don Lisbon, forcing him to fumble, and Ed O'Bradovich recovered at the Bears' 49-yard line. On the first play from scrimmage Wade handed off to Galimore, who was heading around left end when he made one of his patented full-speed cuts and accelerated off tackle. Two 49ers lineback-ers, Mike Dowdle and Ed Pine, could do nothing to stop him, and Bears guard Roger Davis eliminated defensive end Dan Colchico from the play. Galimore was at full speed, outrunning defensive back Abe Woodson for a 51-yard touchdown sprint that put the Bears ahead to stay. Later in the first period Marconi cut upfield after taking a handoff from Wade and broke through for a 19-yard score. The Bears were ahead by two touchdowns for the first time in three weeks.

Bear nemesis J.D. Smith managed to score from three yards out after the Bears muffed a kicking play with a bad snap from center. Due to inju-ries Larry Morris was the kick snapper on this day, with no better than mixed results. While the lead was only 14–7 at halftime, there was little concern among the Bear faithful. With the 49ers' lack of a running game and LaMar McHan's subpar performance at quarterback, the 49ers did not resemble the only team to have beaten the Bears.

Doug Atkins ended the day for McHan in the third quarter with a massive blow that knocked him out of the game. Bob Waters, a small col-lege (Presbyterian) product with limited game experience, replaced him and could do nothing. Wade finished a drive in the third quarter with a three-yard TD run, and in the fourth quarter Roosevelt Taylor intercepted a Waters offering and ran it back 30 yards for the last score of the game. In a heavy snowfall that started in the third quarter, the Bears sealed it, 27–7.

The Bears not only needed to shore up their kick return defense but also had to factor in the threat that the 49ers' Abe Woodson posed. To throw off Woodson's timing they decided to let Roger Leclerc instead of

Bob Jencks execute the kickoffs. Leclerc's kicks were quicker line drives than Jencks' kicks, hopefully causing more disruptions for Woodson. Leclerc offered only bounding squib kicks; Woodson was limited to only one punt and one kickoff return throughout the entire game, fumbling punts on two other occasions, a very un–Woodson-like performance. Richie Petitbon had two interceptions, Dave Whitsell added another, and Roosevelt Taylor's pickoff went for a touchdown. The 49ers also fumbled four times. Optimists noted that the Bears were back to being the team they were three weeks earlier, when they manhandled the Packers, and they looked more than ready for the Lions. Pessimists pointed out that they had just played the 49ers, who the Packers would get to pick on next week, so they better be ready for the Lions—especially in light of what the Lions did earlier on this day.

Week 13 finished with the Colts crushing the Vikings, 41–10; the Cardinals easily handling the Eagles, 38–14; the Steelers keeping in contention with a squeaker over the Cowboys, 24–19; the Giants, as expected, pounding the Redskins, 44–14; and in perhaps the biggest surprise of the 1963 NFL season, the Lions crushing the championship hopes out of the Browns, 38–10, and eliminating them from Eastern Division contention. The Browns' loss meant that week 14's matchup between Pittsburgh and New York in Yankee Stadium would decide the Eastern Division champion. If the Giants won or tied, the title would be theirs, since they would finish either 11–3 or 10–3–1. If the Steelers wonn they would finish at 8–3–3, a .727 winning percentage, better than the Giants' .714 if they finished 10–4. For Bears fans, overshadowing the drama in the Eastern Division race was the fact that their heroes' upcoming opponent tied the Packers 10 days before and had just thrashed the Browns. It would take one of their best efforts of the year for the Bears to win the West.

The Packers, settled into their Palo Alto digs in preparation of their game with San Francisco, had plenty of opinions about the Bears victory. Vince Lombardi said he was not surprised about the game. He watched the first three quarters and then assembled his coaching staff and started working on the game plan for the Saturday, December 14, matchup. Tackle Forrest Gregg was optimistic: "I still feel we'll win the title. The Bears have to play Detroit, and let me tell you, the Lions are capable of beating anybody when they put their minds to it. I just hope they didn't shoot the works against Cleveland." Bart Starr declared that he still felt the Packers had a chance, but they had to concern themselves with the 49ers. Tackle Norm Masters felt it was up to the Lions' offense, not their defense, to win the game. "If Earl Morrall plays a good game, the Lions will beat the Bears."[21]

Some Packers felt the opposite. Center Jim Ringo said, "The Bears are getting tougher by the week, they're a solid football team, and they can smell that championship money. It's one of the world's loveliest aromas."[22] Veteran lineman Dave Hanner talked about what made the Bears so much better in 1963 than in previous years.[23] He broke it down to three factors: the team effort on defense, improved offensive line blocking, and fullback Joe Marconi. "Defensively, the Bears are playing as a unit for the first time in several years. That's the big change between their 1963 defense and two years ago. They still stunt, but there's a pattern to it this year; it's organized."[24] He went on to say that "the presence of Marconi after Casares was hurt has helped a lot; he's given the line confidence, and they are blocking well on both pass protection and in opening the holes for runners." Hanner praised Mike Ditka as being virtually unstoppable but then was optimistic about the Packers' chances if there was a playoff game for the division. "I'd love it. I just can't believe we would lose to then three times in a row."[25]

Detroit coach George Wilson took questions from the media and declared, "We are a much better team than we were back in September when the Bears beat us. Much of the improvement is due to experience. We're getting better pass protection and our blocking on the offensive line has improved. Also we had some injuries [when we lost to them]."[26]

The play of fullback Nick Pietrosante was seen as a big factor in the Lions' greatly improved third down efficiency. In their first six games the Lions had 73 third downs and converted successfully for a first down only 12 times, a poor 16 percent efficiency rating. In their last seven games they reached third down 98 times and made it 52 times, 53 percent of the time, one of the best in the NFL. This performance was in stark contrast to what the Bears' last two opponents, San Francisco and Minnesota, had been achieving.

With Chicago's temperatures not reaching 20 degrees for a high and snow flurries swirling around unpredictably, Halas moved the practices indoors, to the Chicago Polo Armory on Chicago Avenue near Northwestern University's downtown campus. The team would gather inside the armory for three practices, both to practice more efficiently out of the cold and also to rest Wrigley Field's turf in the bad weather. The field was expected to be in decent playing condition if there was not a prolonged deep freeze.[27] With the mid–December sun approaching its lowest angle of the year in the southern sky, the north half of Wrigley Field—left and left-center field, or the north end zone to the 50-yard line—received sunshine from about 11:00 a.m. until 3:00 p.m. The south part of the field—the infield up to the first base side box seats, or the 50-yard line to the south end zone—was constantly in shadow and prone to prematurely freeze. With inclement winter weather providing two distinct characteristics to the field, everything from footwear to defensive and offensive schemes had to be accounted for. The Bears braved the cold on Thursday, December 14, and had the groundskeepers remove the tarp on the north end of the field so they could practice outdoors.[28]

With the season winding to a close the NFL office announced the All-Pro selections along with certain other honors. George Halas was named Coach of the Year, riding the wave of innovation and success for which George Allen and Jim Dooley were largely responsible. Six players were named All-Pro: Doug Atkins, Mike Ditka, Joe Fortunato, Bill George, Richie Petitbon, and Roosevelt Taylor. Lions quarterback Earl Morrall was not daunted by the selection, claiming the Lions would be ready and that they "have an edge" on the Bears.[29] "We're not going to give them a gift," said Morrall, referring to turnovers. "We played a tough game against Cleveland and we can do it again."[30] Morrall was having the best season of his life up to this point. He had 23 touchdown passes in the first 13 games of 1963, while throwing only 37 in his previous seven years in the league. The game December 15 would be his ninth time facing the Bears in his career, and historically things had not gone well for the Muskegon, Michigan, native. Morrall had one win and eight losses in his previous Bears encounters, completing 65 of 146 passes for a 44.5 percent completion rate. He had thrown only four touchdown passes against them and had eight passes intercepted. His passer rating was 69.0 in the Lions-Packers Thanksgiving Day tie on November 28 and 100 in the upset of Cleveland, a game in which he threw two touchdown passes. Based on his history against the Bears it was unlikely that Morrall himself could dominate their defense; not even Bart Starr or Johnny Unitas were able to do so in 1963.

The Bears went to bed on the eve of their final game knowing that the Packers, tied with the 49ers at halftime, pulled out a 21–17 victory, thanks largely to the peerless passing duo of Bart Starr to Boyd Dowler. What they did not realize was that during the night a tragedy with national implications occurred in Detroit, and it could have a huge impact on the game.

The Lions' much-heralded defensive back, Night Train Lane, became blues singer Dinah Washington's seventh husband when they wed in July 1963. Lane was toward the end of his Hall of Fame career, and Washington was earning $150,000 a year from her recordings and appearances. Their apartment at 4002 West Buena Vista Street, close to Lane's El Taco restaurant, became a headquarters for the elite in Detroit's Black society.[31]

On the night of Friday, December 13, Lane drove to the Detroit Metropolitan Airport to pick up Washington's two teenage sons from previous marriages, George Jenkins and Robert Grayson. The young men were returning home from New England prep schools. The four of them had a quiet night at home, bags packed for the trip to Chicago the next day for the Sunday Bears-Lions game. At 3:45 a.m. noise from the off-air television station's signal woke up Lane, and he found Washington motionless, lying on the floor.

Lane called the family doctor, B.C. Ross, who could not revive her and pronounced her deceased 65 minutes later. The police report said that Ross believed "subject had ingested an unknown type of pill. There was an unlabeled bottle containing about 50 orange and blue pills on a nightstand near the bed."[32] Everyone was convinced that the overdose was accidental. Washington had a big engagement after the new year on the West Coast and was deliberately trying to lose as much weight as she could before the engagement. The autopsy revealed that she had more than double the safe amount of amobarbital and secobarbital in her blood.[33]

Lane, shocked and stupefied, did not accompany the Lions to Chicago.[34] Suddenly the Lions' vaunted defensive secondary was without its two future Hall of Famers: Yale Lary, injured while tackling Cleveland end Rich Kreitling the week before, and Lane. The Lions were looking at playing the Bears with second-year men in their defensive secondary, Tom Hall and Larry Vargo. Hall played at Minnesota and was taken in the seventh round of the 1962 draft by the Lions. He had played in every game since he was drafted but one and had seen a fair amount of action in the Lions' defensive backfield in 1963, intercepting three passes. Vargo, taken in the 11th round of the same draft after playing at Detroit's Mercy College, had only one start to his name prior to this Bears contest. The tragic passing of Dinah Washington left the Lions' defense in a weakened condition.[35]

The lineups:

Lions	Pos.	Bears
Gail Cogdill	LE	Bo Farrington
Daryl Sanders	LT	Herman Lee
Dan LaRose	LG	Ted Karras
Bob Whitlow	C	Mike Pyle
John Gordy	RG	Jim Cadile
Bob Scholtz	RT	Bob Wetoska
Jim Gibbons	RE	Mike Ditka
Earl Morrall	QB	Bill Wade
Tom Watkins	LH	Ronnie Bull
Nick Pietrosante	FB	Joe Marconi
Terry Barr	RH	Johnny Morris

The weather prevented a sellout, in spite of the tremendous importance of the Lions game. With the temperature below 15 degrees and a stiff north wind creating a wind chill around zero, the chance to stay comfortable was more important than watching the Bears clinch their first title in seven years. As was their custom throughout the season the Bears lost the coin toss and kicked off to start the game. The Lions got no further than their own 30-yard line on their first possession which ended in a punt, fielded by the Bears' Billy Martin at the Bears' 30. Martin sprinted upfield, then cut to the left where Bob Wetoska cleared the sideline with a great block. He now had nothing but a clear field in front of him and reached the end zone easily with his great speed. Bears fans went wild—just think, a special teams touchdown to start the big game—just as the linesman brought the ball back to the 50, where Martin's foot had touched out of bounds. Wade was able to move the offense deep into Lions territory, where their defense stiffened and Roger Leclerc came in and kicked a 20-yard field goal. Morrall came back out with the Lions' offense. Effectively mixing passes and runs, the Lions moved from their own 37 to the Bears eight-yard line. With first and goal from the eight, Morrall ill-advisedly called a pass play into the end zone, which Roosevelt Taylor sniffed out perfectly. He intercepted the pass and got all the way out to the 22-yard line. A few possessions later Wade saw Johnny Morris streaking down the west sideline and fired the ball his direction. Wade did not see Larry Vargo, subbing for the injured Yale Lary, intentionally laying back. Vargo made his break to the ball, caught it in full stride, and raced to the end zone, a rare and costly pick-six mistake by the Bears' quarterback. The half ended, Lions 7, Bears 3; the cold weather was suddenly much more uncomfortable for the huge throng in the stands.

Both defenses dominated the start of the third quarter. On the Bears' third possession they reached midfield when Wade called on Morris to go down and in after reaching the 35. Night Train Lane's substitute, Hall, was giving Morris all kinds of room throughout the game, knowing that he could never match Morris' speed. After Morris' cut, Hall, who was already out of position, slipped on the frozen turf, losing yet another step. Morris found his top gear, in spite of the hardened surface, and effortlessly reached the end zone. Bears fans were ecstatic, and the weather suddenly did not matter so much: Bears 10, Lions 7 after Bob Jencks' extra point. Three minutes later Wade engineered another drive into the Lions' territory. With 30 seconds left in the third quarter Ditka got behind Hall, snaring Wade's second touchdown pass of the day for a 17–7 Bears advantage. For the first time since November 25, 1962—20 games ago—the Bears had scored two touchdowns in a third quarter.

The Lions' lost season, however, would not end quite so meekly. Early in the fourth quarter they started possession at their own 29-yard line. On the strength of tough rushes by Nick Pietrosante and Bobby Watkins, coupled with some savvy passing by Morrall, the Lions pulled off a perfectly executed 71-yard drive. The big play was a 20-yard completion to Terry

Barr. Barr was in front of Bennie McRae at the 20, with Roosevelt Taylor closing in on his left side. Both McRae's and Barr's hands got the ball at the same time, but Barr's momentum helped him swing the ball away from McRae for a crucial reception. Morrall next called a delay, handing off to Tommy Watkins, who rumbled all the way to the four-yard line. The Lions scored from the four when Morrall crossed up the Bear defense with a quick pass to Terry Barr, who had two steps to the inside on an extremely frustrated McRae. After Wayne Walker's extra point, with the long shadows creeping northward in Wrigley Field, the Lions crept uncomfortably close to the Bears, 17–14.

The Lions got the ball back with 3:22 left in the game. With the ball on their own 34 Morrall called the same halfback delay to Watkins that worked so well before their last touchdown; this time it worked even better. Linebacker Larry Morris was suckered into thinking Morrall was going to pass. Even though he was in the Lions' backfield as Morrall handed off, he had already overcommitted and could do nothing. Middle linebacker Bill George was screened off by two Lion blockers and Watkins was off with a full head of steam. Unable to out-race Taylor or McRae, the two Bear defenders finally got him down at the Bears' 35. Morrall then hit Gail Cogdill in the left flat, moving the ball to the 27. Deciding to go for broke, Morrall dropped back on the next play looking for Cogdill, who was hurrying to the middle of the goal line. He panicked when he saw Atkins getting past offensive tackle Daryl Sanders, hurrying his throw, which landed harmlessly in the end zone, a good five yards past Cogdill and the Bear defenders.

On the next play he saw Barr make his cut at the 15-yard line in front of McRae. He fired a low pass toward Barr, which McRae broke up, treating Barr rather rudely in the process. It was now fourth down, 10 to go, from the Lions' 27, and Morrall's pass to Barr was deflected by the Bears' Ed O'Bradovich. The Bears took over on downs, and everyone in frigid Wrigley Field sensed a championship; only 53 seconds remained in the game. However…

It was not going to happen just yet. After three running plays the Bears were just short of a first down and had to punt. Morrall lined up his offense at his own 36-yard line. He hit Barr with a pass in the flat at the 42, where McRae picked him up, carried him back two yards, and then violently threw him to the turf; somehow Barr managed to hold on to the ball. The Lions had time for one more play. Morrall took the snap and dropped back. Atkins was bull-rushing from the right side, and in spite of being double-teamed he was able to collapse the pocket, causing Morrall to hurry his throw. He saw Gail Cogdill, who looked open, near the left sideline at the 42. Dave Whitsell had been playing him a little deeper than usual but made his break as soon as he saw the ball in the air. He got in front of the waiting and very surprised Cogdill while in full sprint. Watkins and Morrall, the only Lions in pursuit, were eight yards behind him when he reached the end zone. Whitsell jubilantly threw the ball into the left field bleachers, after which Ed O'Bradovich lifted him in the air with a bear hug while the rest of the Bears' defenders joined them in the end zone. On a more personal level it once again matched two of the greatest athletes in western Michigan's history against each other: Earl Morrall, the big-city Muskegon wonder boy from Michigan State, and Dave Whitsell, the pride of tiny Hart, Michigan, an Indiana alum whose collegiate star never shone as brightly as Morrall's. Whitsell would go on to finish a fine 12-year career with 46 interceptions, four of which were touchdowns, but none would ever be bigger than this one, his sixth interception of the season and the first touchdown of his career. The Bears ended the season with an NFL-best 36 pickoffs, the most in the NFL since the Detroit Lions' 38 10 years earlier.

The Bears outgained the Lions, 321 to 221 yards, and in spite of throwing two interceptions, Wade outplayed the red-hot Morrall. Wade hit on 14 of 29 passes for 235 yards, two touchdowns, was sacked twice, and threw two interceptions. Morrall completed 12 of 24 passes for only 122 yards, including one touchdown toss. He was sacked three times and threw two interceptions, the one to Whitsell perhaps the most significant interception of the 1963 NFL season. The Lions gave the Bears all they could handle and never backed down. They also had a lot to say after the game.

Head coach George Wilson reminded the press that in spite of the loss he and his wife would be attending the annual Bears alumni reunion dinner that Halas sponsored every year at the end of the season. Wilson told the press, "[The Bears' Johnny] Morris and our men who did not play in the secondary made the difference. If we would have had Yale Lary and Night Train Lane, I think it would have been a different game."[36] Morris caught eight passes for 171 yards, outgaining the entire Lions passing offense by 49 yards. Wilson claimed the inexperience of Larry Vargo and Tom Hall, who replaced Lary and Lane, made a huge difference in the game. While this line of thinking undoubtedly made him feel better about the loss, it was an inaccurate observation. In the first Bears-Lions game, when the Lions had a more complete roster, Morris caught eight passes, one of which was a touchdown in which he spun Lane around like a top.

Tom Hall had a lot to tell the press about the game. He was coming off the best game of his career the week before, when his brilliant punt return and an interception helped seal the Browns' fate and ensure the Lions' big upset victory. "I was on Morris all day," he lamented, "that's the first time I played against him. He bolts out very fast; you have to respect his speed

The Bears had one of the best pass defenses in NFL history in 1963. Diminutive safety Roosevelt Taylor (24) uses his 41-inch vertical leap with the cagey Dave Whitsell (23) providing reinforcement. Taylor led the NFL with nine interceptions in 1963, and Whitsell's clutch interception in the final game of the season sealed the Bears' title. Max McGee (85) watches helplessly while Bill George (61, partially obscured by McGee), Forrest Gregg (75), and Jim Taylor (31) watch. Bears on the sidelines are Halas (dark suit and sunglasses), Pyle (50), Bivins (49), Glueck (43), Marconi (34), Johnny Johnson (76), Bob Jencks (80), Barnett (73), Rick Casares (35), and Bobby Joe Green (88).

and give him room. Sometimes he stops fast, and that's pretty tough to cover."[37] He pointed out that he slipped on Morris' seemingly easy touchdown and had trouble with the frozen parts of the field.

"You also have to respect their running game," Hall went on to explain. "You have to be ready to contain their sweeps, which holds [your position] and then their passing game becomes more effective."[38]

Rookie offensive tackle Daryl Sanders, whose last game in Chicago was an upset over the Packers in Soldier Field's College All-Star game in August, was respectful of the victorious Bears, saying they were the best he faced all year. "I'd have to give the Bears a little edge over the Packers; they were tough today. They changed defenses every time we called signals. Because of that you have to be thinking—it changes your blocks. Morrall called more audibles than usual today, and we also lost three plays because of the crowd noise."[39]

The game and the season left a bitter taste in the mouth of one Lion star, wide receiver Gail Cogdill, the 1960 NFL Rookie of the Year. He only caught two passes for 16 yards. "Morrall threw to me about three times today," he complained. "That's the way it's been all year. They know I'm burned up about this and they don't do anything about it."[40] When asked about the Bears' defense, he sarcastically said, "I didn't have a chance to tell." He also complained about Morrall's performance on the last play of the game. As the intended receiver on Whitsell's historic interception, he complained, "I was waiting for Morrall to pump fake [and draw Whitsell up], before going down field, because I knew Whitsell was there. But instead he threw it immediately."[41]

In their jubilant post-game locker room the Bears learned that in two weeks they would be meeting the New York Giants. In the biggest showdown game of the year, a contest the winner of which would wear the Eastern Division crown, the Giants thrilled a packed Yankee Stadium with a convincing 33–17 victory over the Pittsburgh Steelers. The game boiled down to Y.A. Tittle solving the mystery of the Steelers' tough defense better than Ed Brown could figure out what Giant defenders were doing. In spite of gaining 191 yards on the ground—104 of them by the irrepressible John Henry Johnson—the Steelers were behind 16-0 before Lou Michaels kicked a field goal in the second quarter to put them on the board. Brown, who completed only 13 of 33 passes, threw three interceptions—to Erich Barnes, Jim Lynch, and Jimmy Patton—which greatly hampered his chances. Tittle threw 17 completions in 26 attempts for 308 yards and three touchdowns. One completion was an impossible grab late in the game by Frank Gifford which sealed the Steelers' fate. Brown, in his third game in the Bronx, remained winless. As a starter for the Bears in their division-winning 1956 campaign he engineered a 17–17 tie during the season over Thanksgiving weekend, but a month later he was at the helm for the Bears in their 47–7 defeat in the title game. For the most part the Bears seemed pleased to be facing the New Yorkers for all the marbles and were not the least bit intimidated. "Old Mr. Tittle is going to have two bald heads when we get through with him," boasted the truculent young Bear defensive end, Ed O'Bradovich.[42] Such bravado out of the mouth of comparative youth could be excused on this day; the Bears deserved their well-earned title, and, indeed, they did it the hard way.

10

December

The Irrepressible Force Meets
the Immovable Object

The NFL world was ecstatic about many aspects of the 1963 season. The league successfully weathered two of its biggest storms in many years, a gambling scandal by two of its stars and a drug-related death of another one. The 14-team league had six teams vying for a championship in the season's 13th week and still had four in the running on the final day of the season. Attendance at games continued to grow and the media contracts, whether local radio coverage or national television exposure, continued to be more lucrative. Lastly, in many quarters the feeling was the best game of the year would be the last one, when an irrepressible force—the New York Giants' offense—would go head to head with an immovable object—the Chicago Bears' defense. It was also perfectly okay with the NFL office and the television networks that the two contestants were from the largest metropolitan areas of the country.

The NFL had come a long way in the 30 years since the first Giants-Bears title match on December 17, 1933. At that time Giants owner Timothy Mara, Sr., gave away two Giants tickets with every ton of coal purchased from his coal company.[1] The sea-change of interest from 30 years earlier had made the NFL the most popular and prosperous professional sports organization in the world.

The early prognostications had the Bears' impenetrable defense stifling Y.A. Tittle and the Giants' chances, even though it seemed illogical that a team as good as New York could lose three consecutive championship games. The Bears having the home-field advantage had something to do with this; revenge for the humiliating loss they suffered at the hands of the Giants in 1956 did also. The *Chicago Daily Defender* was one of the first newspapers to go out on a limb and predict that the Bears and Giants would be the contestants in the championship game, and it mentioned not just the Bears' defense but also the revenge factor in picking them to win.[2]

Buddy Parker, whose Steelers lost out on the Eastern Division championship by losing in New York while the Bears were beating the Lions, was not impressed enough by the Giants to think the championship would be theirs.[3] Giants halfback Phil King offered his own take on the championship game. When asked if he preferred to see the Bears instead of the Packers, who had conquered his team the last two years in the big matchup, King deadpanned, "I'd prefer to play the 49ers."[4]

While the Bears met the challenges presented by all the quality teams they faced during the 1963 season with the possible exception of Pittsburgh, the Giants would present special challenges to them, with skills in certain areas of the game that the Bears had not seen all season.

Tittle threw an incredible 36 touchdowns in 14 games with only 14 interceptions. He completed a league-best 60.8 percent of his passes, and nobody in 1963 surpassed his passer rating of 104.8. He had a bevy of well-above-average receivers: the veteran Frank Gifford, All-Pro Del Shofner, Aaron Thomas, and Joe Walton. While some Bears thought Gifford was getting old, past his prime, and overrated, he made big third-down catches all season, including an incredible one-hand back-breaker against the Steelers that helped clinch the crown. Also, in some games the imposing Shofner seemed unstoppable, especially so when Tittle was clicking with his accuracy, which was usually the case. Tittle's short game included very effective swing passes and screens to his running backs. In the running game Joe Morrison and Phil King had been every bit as effective over the season as Joe Marconi and Ronnie Bull. Eddie Dove, whom the Giants got in mid-season, was the fifth best punt returner in the NFL in 1963.

Their defense, while not as effective and intimidating as the Bears', was on a par with what the Bears faced against Green Bay and Detroit, and during 1963 Giant defenders had a knack for shutting down the opposition in the most critical games. The for-all-the-marbles last game of the season they had with the Pittsburgh Steelers was a case in point. Steeler quarterback Ed Brown, no stranger to big games, was sacked once and intercepted twice. Brown was harassed by the Giants' pass rush all game, and his rhythm and timing were off, as he overthrew and underthrew receivers throughout the game. Brown, who led the NFL in fourth-quarter comebacks and game-winning drives in 1963, was confounded by the Giants' defense throughout the critical contest. At the same time the Giants' receivers were giving the Steelers secondary absolute fits. Gifford caught five passes for 94 yards, and Shofner three for 110 in two quarters. Shofner had his way with Steelers defensive back Willie Daniel for an artistic touchdown early in the game and then embarrassed him a second time to set the Giants up on the Steelers' 14. The frustrated Daniel slammed Shofner to the frozen turf so hard that Shofner did not play in the second half.

The matchup between the two, however, demonstrated how seemingly unfair it was to have to cover a receiver like Shofner, with his silky-smooth moves and a 6'3" frame; stretched out completely Daniel was 5'11". With the current Bears defensive configuration, Dave Whitsell would cover Shofner; unfortunately for the Bears he was the same height as Daniel.

The Giants, however, did have some chinks in their armor, and Allen and Dooley had almost two weeks to study them. The Giants offensive line was prone to giving up sacks. Pittsburgh registered seven sacks in their big win against them September 22 and got three more in week 14. Cleveland sacked Tittle five times when they beat the Giants in Yankee Stadium on October 13. While Pittsburgh and Cleveland both had excellent defensive lines and linebackers, they did not compare to the same seven Bears defenders, and neither team had a secondary nearly as fast as the Bears' quintet of Caroline, McRae, Petitbon, Taylor, and Whitsell. Also, the Giants' defense could be formidable, but skilled, experienced running backs had big days against them, in particular the Browns' Jim Brown, the Steelers' John Henry Johnson, and the Cardinals' Bill Triplett. Against the Bears the Giants would have to stop Bull and Marconi, both above-average all year, and also try to stop one of the top two scatbacks in the NFL, Willie Galimore. Just as the Giants presented special problems for the Bears, the Bears were perfectly capable of giving the Giants headaches like they had not seen all season.

Meanwhile, Halas gave the Bears three days off after the Sunday, December 15, victory. He celebrated with fellow Bear alumni in the annual Bear reunion dinner held at the end of every season at the Edgewater Beach Hotel.[5] It was a great venue for him if he decided to party too hard, since he lived on the two upper floors of the southeast tower of the Edgewater Beach Cooperative Apartments, the grand old pink edifice at the end of Chicago's Lake Shore Drive. After the Detroit game the fawning by the Chicago media over Halas got a little over the top, giving him credit for practically everything while ignoring the brilliantly innovative schemes of George Allen and Jim Dooley, the film breakdowns by Paddy Driscoll, or the line tutelage of Phil Handler and Jumbo Joe Stydahar. David Condon in his "In the Wake of the News" column in the *Chicago Tribune* offered his readers an hour-by-hour description of what he described as Halas' "rigorous" schedule during the football season, taking such liberties with the facts to claim that "the players generally bundle up as though they were accompanying Admiral Byrd to the South Pole. Halas keeps warm on his own energy."[6]

Of Chicago's five major daily newspapers, two rarely found fault with Halas, one was neutral, and two were praiseworthy when needed but severely critical when warranted. The morning *Chicago Daily Tribune* and afternoon *Chicago American* were published by Don Maxwell, a longtime intimate of Halas who went out of his way to ensure favorable press for the Bears. The *Chicago Daily Defender*, one of the most influential Black newspapers in the country at that time, showed a fair amount of Bears boosterism but never shied away from being critical when it was warranted. The morning *Sun-Times* and the afternoon *Daily News* offered perhaps the most impartial and comprehensive coverage of all the papers. Both were quick to criticize when they felt it was justified and never bashful about pointing out the team's troubles. Halas had a particular distrust of one legendary Chicago sports columnist, Bill Gleason. Gleason was a South Side Irishman who, like many of his neighbors, was an ardent Chicago Cardinals fan since his childhood and had a knack for seeing through Halas' occasional smokescreens and frequent bluster.

The amount of influence Halas had on Chicago journalism came to light in a disagreement Halas had with a young sports journalist during the 1963 season. Halas had a skewed view of the fourth estate and its mission in society. He felt that local journalists should be cheerleaders for his team, supportive and not critical.[7] Gleason was one of his harshest critics, and over the 1960 Christmas holidays at the end of a disappointing 5–6–1 Bears season, Gleason wrote that Halas should give Chicagoans a gift by resigning as head coach. His paper, the *American*, was the afternoon counterpart of the *Tribune* and part of Maxwell's responsibilities. To keep Gleason further away from Halas, Maxwell had Gleason taken off the Bears beat and made him a columnist. He gave the daily Bears coverage to a young reporter who grew up a Bears fan, Ed Stone.

Stone loved the team, but some of Gleason's skepticism toward its founder had rubbed off on him, and he refused to be a "cheerleader" or only write favorable information. In 1963 Stone's skepticism of Halas reached the breaking point after the October 20 Bears loss in San Francisco. Stone wrote that Halas "choked" at halftime when he gave up on Wade and replaced him with Bukich, who threw two interceptions and earned a passer rating of 35.0 in his worst outing of the season. While the Bears were down 17–7 at halftime, Wade had completed 15 of 20 passes. Halas voiced his indignation at the *Tribune*'s highest levels, and Stone was removed from the Bears beat. He was relegated to office work, rewriting the copy of his colleagues who covered the team.[8] Halas, however, had not heard the end of this. Gleason, who could be as cunning as Halas, was furious about Stone's plight, and he planned his revenge for the eve of the championship game.

The NFL and the Bears front office announced that a limited public sale of tickets for the championship game would occur Monday, December 23, at the Bears ticket office at 173 West Madison in Chicago's Loop.[9]

No public sale of tickets would be sold at Wrigley Field or handled by mail order. It was not known how many tickets would be available to the public because of the complicated formula the NFL had for distributing playoff tickets. The other 12 teams were each allocated 50 tickets, as was the NFL's publicity department and commissioner Rozelle's office staff. Added to the 34,000 season ticket holders who were receiving their tickets in the mail, that left about 13,000 seats. However, per NFL rules, the visiting Giants were entitled to 20 percent of those, or 2,600 tickets, lowering the amount that the public could buy to around 10,000. There would be a limit of two tickets per customer; lower deck box seats ($12.50) and lower deck grandstand ($10) would be sold first. When seats were gone the team would release the sale of standing room tickets in the grandstand ($6) and in the bleachers ($4).[10]

With millions of Chicagoans wanting to watch the game, such a limited number of tickets available, and the game being blacked out on Chicago-area television, Bear fans got some relief a few days later when the NFL announced an agreement with Theatre Network Television, Inc., for an unprecedented, closed circuit theater-network television showing of the game in real time at three large Chicago venues.[11] The Chicago Amphitheatre, located in the Chicago Stockyard district, would have 11,500 seats available; the lakefront's modern, three-year-old McCormick Place convention center would have 6,000; and the antiquated (1899) Chicago Coliseum at 1513 South Wabash, south of the Loop and just west of Soldier Field, had seating for 8,000. This meant that more than 25,000 fans would be able to see the game, live, after shelling out between $4 and $7.50 for admission. The NFL was thrilled with this new source of revenue. If sales were good it was a guaranteed cash cow, generating possibly $150,000, with the only expense being three very short-term rentals. Since the league's contract with CBS called for $4,650,000 for the broadcasting of 98 regular season games—less than $50,000 per contest—this closed-circuit arrangement was three times more lucrative. The NFL also announced that it might investigate closed-circuit arrangements for regular season games in the future.[12] After worrying that Wrigley Field's capacity might be too small to satiate the league financially, Rozelle could now lick his lips, knowing that there could conceivably be 72,000 paying customers for the big game.

To further hype the Bears and Giants during the two weeks before the contest, United Press International (UPI) announced its All-Pro team. UPI had a selection committee of 42 sports writers, three from each NFL city, that voted on the individuals.[13] Fifteen of the 22 players were from three teams, the Bears, Giants, and Packers. Doug Atkins, Mike Ditka, Joe Fortunato, Bill George, and Richie Petitbon were the Bears selected.

There was some surprise that Larry Morris and Roosevelt Taylor were not; they received second team honors. The Giants on the squad were Y.A. Tittle, Del Shofner, offensive tackle Roosevelt Brown, defensive end Jim Katcavage, and defensive back Dick Lynch. Offensive linemen Forrest Gregg, Jerry Kramer, and Jim Ringo, along with linebackers Henry Jordan and Bill Forester, were the five Green Bay selections.

This lineup of the NFL's top performers meant that two All-Pros, Doug Atkins and Roosevelt Brown, would be going head to head in the title game. It also meant that the All-Pro quarterback, Tittle, would be looking across the line of scrimmage at four first-team All-Pro defenders and two more who were named to the second team.

The press picked up on the upcoming Atkins-Brown embroglio.[14] Emlen Tunnell, the Hall of Fame defensive back working as one of the Giants' chief scouts, said, "They've got to block Atkins, or Tittle will be in for a very rough afternoon, and he's not easy to get out of there. For his size, he is very agile. He jumps and hurdles and if he's not on top of the passer, he's so close it's nerve wracking."[15] Tunnell was referring to Atkins' legendary ability to actually hurdle over offensive linemen when the mood struck him. At Tennessee Atkins could do a standing broad jump of 6'7"—almost the span of his height.[16] "Rosey [Brown] took pretty good care of Atkins last year," Tunnell went on, referring to the late-season 26–24 win the Giants had over the Bears at Wrigley Field, the game in which they clinched the Eastern Division crown. "[But] Atkins is playing better this year, he's always been a great player, but he hasn't always been this consistently great."[17] Tunnell went on to praise the Bears' linebacking trio of Morris, George, and Fortunato as the best he had ever seen, with size, mobility, and experience, and incorrectly identified George as the captain, not knowing that Halas named Fortunato to lead at the start of the '63 season. Tunnell mentioned that having Morris set up behind Atkins had wreaked havoc on opponent's passing game, with Morris often using Atkins as a screen while executing a double-blitz. He referred to the maneuver as a "tractor-trailer" act, which, when coupled with the speed of the Bears' secondary, presented a myriad of difficulties for a quarterback.[18] Another stunt Atkins was famous for when he could not reach the quarterback was either picking up or hurling the lineman trying to block him *backward*, into the quarterback, while he was attempting to throw. With all this unsolicited praise for an opponent, it seemed difficult to tell if Tunnell was speaking for himself or for his team. Obviously so much praise could never be used as bulletin board material, but it also could have been put out to make the Bears complacent.

The Bears themselves were saying nothing about their opponent. Allen and Dooley were working relentlessly to detect the Giants' keys and tendencies that could help the Bears. Halas privately expressed his personal concerns about Dave Whitsell to Whitsell himself. The Indiana alum had the unenviable task of covering perennial All-Pro Del Shofner; Whitsell was lighter than Shofner and a good four inches shorter. Halas met with Whitsell and for some reason told him he might not play, since he was not sure how well he could do against Shofner.[19]

A change like this would make very little sense. Whitsell, with six interceptions during the season, one of which sealed the victory over the Eagles and another which ensured the Western Division championship, had been covering receivers taller than he was all year with a great deal of success. Throughout his career Whitsell's accomplishments did not necessarily come from shut-down, blanket coverage as much as from the head games he played so successfully with opposing quarterbacks. He excelled at giving a receiver just enough space for the quarterback to think that he was open and then come close to the ball with timing that was uncannily accurate, breaking up the pass or—as in six instances in 1963—intercepting it. Halas' revelation to Whitsell said more about how worried he was about the Giants than Whitsell's capabilities.

In fairness to Halas, however, Shofner was always a concern to everyone. While Frank Gifford enjoyed a longer tenure as a fixture in the Giants receiving corps, and often got the lion's share of the publicity with his clutch catches, Shofner had become the darling of the Giants' offense. William N. Wallace wrote a virtual paean about him in the Monday, December 23, *New York Times*.[20] Shofner had lots of time to contribute to the article; he was not practicing so that his bruised ribs, which came courtesy of a brutal frustration tackle by the Steelers' Willie Daniel, could heal. Wallace waxed poetic about how Shofner married Carol Seley (daughter of the Los Angeles Rams' co-owner Harold Seley), how the two of them set up an off-season home in San Gabriel, California, and how during the football season they lived in the historic Grand Concourse Hotel—Babe Ruth's home back in the day—within walking distance of Yankee Stadium. Frank Gifford, Mickey Mantle, Roger Maris and a bevy of other famous athletes called the Grand Concourse home, in-season. Shofner said that he looked forward to the championship game challenge and added, "I like best a pass defender who's going to cover me tight, like two, three yards away. When they stick that close, they let me play them, instead of the other way around." He went on to talk about what he liked to do with sticky, close-up defenders: "On deep pass patterns they have to run backward. If we start even, I know I can run faster forward than they can backward. Plus, when he's all over me, he's got to go with my moves." Washington cornerback Claude Crabb said, "Shofner's a weaver. If he has a pattern of any kind, it's his weaving motion as he leaves the scrimmage line. It drives you crazy watching him dip in and out … he's so fast, that if you make the wrong move, you can't recover." Shofner did single out two defenders as giving him the most trouble, Jesse Whittenton of the Packers and Jimmy Hill—who was just as tall as Shofner—of the Cardinals.[21] Tittle claimed that Shofner was the best receiver that he had ever thrown to, a heady claim considering that the list included individuals like Gifford and R.C. Owens.[22] While they did not play against each other in high school, both Tittle and Shofner hailed from the same area in east Texas. Tittle was from Marshall and Shofner from the much smaller town of Center. The combination rated among the best passing duos in the NFL, on a par with Bart Starr and Boyd Dowler, Bill Wade and Mike Ditka, or Charley Johnson and Bobby Joe Conrad.

Soon after the All-Pro announcement, the NFL publicized the rosters for the Pro Bowl game. The contest would be held two weeks after the championship game, January 12, 1964, in the Memorial Coliseum in Los Angeles. Along with the All-Pro nominees, four additional Bears were on the roster: Joe Marconi, Mike Pyle, Roosevelt Taylor, and Bill Wade.[23]

Wade's inclusion could not have been more just or come at a better time. In the evening of the Bears' big victory over the Lions, NBC aired a special titled *The Making of a Pro*. The program glorified the New York Giants and also featured sections on top NFL quarterbacks. Wade, the choreographer of a championship offense that lost only one game, was totally ignored in the program, not mentioned once.[24]

While the television show producers and certain members of the media may have preferred to ignore Wade's effectiveness, on Thursday, December 20, Giants coach Allie Sherman did the exact opposite. He verbalized his respect for the Bears' offense, saying, "They have two good quarterbacks in Wade and Bukich. Wade has quick wrists and is tall enough to see over charging linemen, while Bukich has the strongest arm in football for the long bomb."[25] Sherman obviously had taken note of Wade's talents at "finesse passing," the soft, short tosses just out of linemen's reach and the pin-point accurate swing passes, and his talent for the quick strike over the middle on a button hook or slant route. These were perfect skills to make a ball-control offense work effectively. At this stage of his career, Bukich's ability to throw long was perhaps only matched by two others, Roman Gabriel of the Rams and Ed Brown of the Steelers. "Rudy the Rifle" used to boast that he could stand on second base at Wrigley Field and throw the ball out of the stadium onto Waveland Avenue if he wished, a distance of some 115 yards, 20 feet above the ground.

Sherman did not stop in his praise with just the Bears' quarterbacks. He warned of the running speed of Willie Galimore and Ronnie Bull as well as the effectiveness of Mike Ditka. "They move the ball and can hurt you if you're not on your toes at all times."[26]

Some of the Bears took advantage of the pre-championship-game interim to cash in on their newly-earned fame. Willie Galimore was booked for two appearances at Wieboldt's Department Stores, their South Side store at 63rd and Halsted in Chicago and their four-story outlet in Evanston.[27] Galimore's association with the event was not with the department store itself but through an agreement he had with S & H Green Stamps.[28] Some of his teammates also enjoyed the benefits of doing testimonials and endorsements throughout the season. Ditka and Marconi were spokesmen for builders of a west suburban subdivision. Ronnie Bull was featured in the ads for Uptown Federal Savings. J.C. Caroline pushed the products of Berkshire Papers, Inc. Members of the coaching staff were prominent in endorsements appearing in print advertising as well. Joe Stydahar, Sid Luckman, trainer Ed Rozy—endorsing Desenex foot powder—all used their NFL association and notoriety to profit from advertisements.[29] Thanks to Halas, this lucrative source of side income became the source of anger and concern among the players after the championship game was over.[30]

A source of more immediate concern was the weather Chicago was experiencing, which did not bode well for the title game. On Tuesday night, December 17, Chicago experienced a major snowfall in the midst of one of the longest cold snaps in the city's history. December 17 was the sixth consecutive day of below-zero temperatures, and it would be five more days before the temperature would stay above zero for 24 hours.[31] The condition of Wrigley Field's turf, even though the game was nine days away, became a major worry. Late Decembers always had the southern half of the field in shadows, with the deep cold increasingly solidifying the frozen turf every day. Unless there was a major thaw for many consecutive days before December 29, the condition of the field would be a huge factor in the game.

Looking back in the history of the Bears and Giants in championship games, Halas was all too familiar with how cold weather could affect the outcome, usually leaving his team the worse for it. Every technology known at the time to keep the field playable was put in place.[32] An army of workers were hired at three times the minimum wage, earning $29 a day,[33] to blanket the field, end zones, and sidelines with a thick layer of hay. The pay rate was justifiable given the arduous physical labor in such a wind-swept and frigid environment. A collection of jet engines mounted on special carts blew hot exhaust air under the tarp to keep the field thawed. Twelve kerosene-operated blowers, six for each team's sideline, were readied to keep players' feet warm. Trainer Ed Rozy amassed a collection of six different types of footwear, ranging from basketball sneakers to West German soccer shoes, for the players to try for the best traction.[34]

Quarterback Bill Wade immediately settled on a pair of Chuck Taylor high-top basketball shoes. While the subzero cold snap was predicted to abate, whatever warming trend might occur the week before the game was not supposed to be nearly enough to restore the field.

The weather mattered very little, however, in the minds of NFL fans intent on seeing the game. The *Christian Science Monitor* reported that as of Friday, December 20, all the east stands—the portable bleacher seating in right and center field—and the entire upper deck were sold out.[35] These facts did not dissuade those intent on seeing the game. A line formed in front of the Bears' Loop office at 173 West Madison Avenue at 7 p.m. Sunday, a full 14 hours before the ticket office would open.[36] The line at one point had 500 people, and 4,000 tickets were purchased in three hours. Everyone who had waited overnight, the *Chicago Tribune* reported, had tickets by 11:00 a.m. Halas was ecstatic about the turnout for tickets, in light of the terrible weather. He claimed the demand was the greatest he had seen since Red Grange's Wrigley Field debut in 1925.[37] Of the 25,000 seats available for closed circuit television viewing, only 9,000 were left. The most desirable venue, McCormick Place, was virtually sold out, with remaining seats available in the reserved sections of the International Amphitheatre and the Coliseum.

As if taking a cue from David Condon's affectionate and exaggerated tribute to George Halas in his "Wake of the News" column, columnist Dick Young in the *New York Daily News* wrote one of the most absurd sports columns of the year, reprinted in the *Chicago Tribune* with the title "Big Wind Blows in from East."[38] Young embarrassed himself by claiming that the Giants' superiority in innumerable non-playing issues dictated a sure New York victory. "The Giants work harder at winning," he claimed. "They will win with superior preparation—hard work—in the brains department. For every hour on the playing field, they put in three or four hours with books, movies, and lectures."[39] Young's inexperience with modern NFL franchises was becoming glaringly evident. The Giants go into a game with "a plan," he went on to explain. "With an offense plan and a defense plan. They don't pick the plan out of thin air; they come by it slowly, arduously, after hours and days of painstaking analysis of the opponent and themselves." This naivety was followed by a common theme in the New York media: Y.A. Tittle worship. "You should see Tittle studying," Young cooed. "He sits in his locker, half undressed, his play book resting on his crossed knees, eyeglasses perched on the tip of his nose, pencil in hand. That is his weapon five days a week, a pencil. What he does with a pencil is every bit as vital as what he does with the football, and as he sits doing his homework he looks not like the superb quarterback but like Ichabod Crane."[40] If he had gone any further, his copy editor may have discarded it for being too homoerotic. Young's article ended with a similar description on defensive end Andy Robustelli's player/coaching accomplishments and how precise and thorough he was.

Even though the game featured the teams of the country's two biggest cities and media markets, the press in both Chicago and New York were showing a glaring partiality and "homerism" that appeared very biased and provincial. Condon's worship of Halas, possibly ordered by his boss, publisher Don Maxwell, had embarrassing exaggerations and descriptions, giving no credit to the innovators who brought the Bears to such great success. Young's missive, placing the Giants at a higher level of sophistication and thoroughness than their 13 rivals, either willfully ignored basic facts about the NFL of that era or intentionally misled his readers.

Two newspapers not involved in misleading their readers about the championship matchup were the *Chicago Daily Defender* and the *Christian Science Monitor*. In November, when there were six teams in the hunt for an opportunity in the NFL title game, the *Defender* predicted that by the end of week 14 it would be the Bears and the Giants. Their columnist Al Monroe, in his "So They Say" column on December 26, predicted a relatively low-scoring game with the Bears prevailing by a margin between three and six points. His reasoning was that the Bear coaching staff would come up with a way to slow down Tittle's passing attack and that in spite of how well balanced the Giants might be rushing the ball and playing defense their "main forte" was relying on Tittle's passing. The Bears intercepted 36 passes that season—the same number of touchdowns Tittle threw—and had a more ferocious pass rush than Tittle had faced all season. Without mentioning anything about the weather, Monroe picked the Bears to avenge their 1956 loss.[41]

The *Christian Science Monitor*, while not making a prediction on the game, wrote up the observation and viewpoints of the only coach who had success against both teams during the 1963 season, Buddy Parker of the Pittsburgh Steelers. Parker's Steelers beat the Giants badly early in September, tied the Bears over the Thanksgiving weekend, and lost to the Giants in a game which decided the NFL Eastern Division title in week 14. Parker said the Bears have "one of the best sets of deep backs I've ever seen; the best pass rusher in the business [Atkins], and probably the best linebacking unit in the league, with two first team all-pros [Fortunato and George] and one second team all-pro [Morris]. That's why I think the Giants may have more trouble with the Bears than they had with the Green Bay Packers the last two years."[42] He went on to say that the Bears rushing game must be effective, since the Giants tough defensive unit "gets better when you're forced to pass. [Also] ... one thing that I'd consider is that Tittle has never been able to win the big game in the past. Of course, Wade hasn't either, but this is first shot."[43] An advantage Wade had over Tittle, throughout his career, was his running ability. Tittle preferred to stay in the pocket, but Wade had always been comfortable running with the ball and was often successful, especially in short yardage situations.

Parker was a very respected NFL figure with eight years of playing experience and 15 years of head coaching responsibilities for three different teams. He won an NFL championship as a player once and as a head coach twice. Four teams—the Baltimore Colts, Philadelphia Eagles, San Francisco 49ers, and Parker's Pittsburgh Steelers—played both the Bears and the Giants in 1963, and Parker did better than any of them, going 1–1 against the Giants and tying the Bears, so he was basing his opinion both on his vast experience and also some very recent competitions. Like Monroe in the *Defender*, Parker did not account for the weather. In the 1960s, with no indoor stadiums and all fields being natural grass playing surfaces, a team sometimes had to overcome two foes to win, their opponent and Mother Nature. Horrible field conditions would give the Giants, with their potent passing game, a big advantage, unless it was wet, which would affect both quarterbacks' grip. The Giants' receivers knew where they would be going, and the Bears' pass rushers would need good footing just to get going. Since the Giants had the superior passing game to start with, they would benefit the most in extremely frigid conditions.

An individual who could easily negate that Giants advantage, whom they did not play against in their narrow victory at Wrigley Field in 1962, was defensive tackle Stan Jones. Jones, a four-time Pro Bowl selection as an offensive lineman, made the switch to defensive tackle under the design of George Allen and the tutelage of Jumbo Joe Stydahar. His play at this new position was a big reason the Bears defense was the best in the NFL. "The first time I saw him in training camp, I knew Stan would fill the position easily. But I wasn't prepared for his mobility. He can catch plays going away from him to either direction. Against Detroit last Sunday, he made eight unassisted tackles. I rate Jones and Earl Leggett as the outstanding tackles in the league this year," Stydahar said.[44] Defensive captain Joe Fortunato echoed the sentiments of Jones' defensive line coach. "Stan did a surprising job of learning all the defenses in a hurry. He has tremendous strength, and along with that, he can go with the ball real well because he's so quick."[45] Jones' strength came from a lifetime of extremely disciplined weight training. He was one of the first NFL players to use weights year-round and the hard work certainly paid off. During the season he religiously trained at the Irving Park Y.M.C.A., not far from Wrigley Field. The Giants had not engaged with Jones as a defensive tackle, and those who had played against him in 1963 figured that the New Yorkers would be in for an unpleasant surprise.

Another reason the Giants might want to be wary about Jones was his memory. Seventeen players who were to take the field on December 29 played in the 47–7 championship rout in Yankee Stadium on December 30, 1956, and Jones was one of them. The Bears seemed ill-prepared in that contest compared to their hosts, and the bitter memory still lingered with more players than just Jones. The following individuals remembered it well: Doug Atkins, who played injured in the game; J.C. Caroline, who played both ways; Rick Casares, who led the NFL in rushing in 1956 but was held to 43 yards in the championship matchup, in part due to the spy/monster defensive scheme the Giants used on him with Sam Huff; and defenders Joe Fortunato, Bill George, and Fred Williams, their defensive unit going the entire game without a sack or an interception. The Giants who basked in championship glory that cold afternoon still with the team were Roosevelt Brown, Don Chandler, Frank Gifford, Sam Huff, Jim Katcavage, Dick Modzelewski, Jimmy Patton, Jack Stroud, Andy Robustelli, and Alex Webster. Casares, out with a broken ankle courtesy of Ray Nitschke, would not be able to settle any scores with Huff on December 29; the other six could and had every intention of doing so.

Like the Bears, the Giants had no practices or meetings on Christmas Eve or Christmas Day. After the holidays coach Allie Sherman disclosed that three injured Giants would be ready to play against the Bears.[46] Linebacker Sam Huff's injured ankle no longer bothered him, Del Shofner's bruised ribs had healed to the point where he could play, and running back Alex Webster, whose back and legs limited him for the last month, said he was good to go. The Bears, who were remarkably free of injuries all season, had everyone but Casares and the recently injured Earl Leggett available.

After the Christmas weekend the Giants scheduled a padded practice with no contact and the Bears had a day of full pads with tackling dummies and blocking sleds but no physical contact. Halas did not want the players "to lose the feel of jarring contact because of the time lag with the last game being December 15."[47]

On December 26, the championship game still had tickets available, thanks in large part to the brutally cold weather Chicagoans were suffering through. Sixteen hundred tickets were still available six days before the game; one reason was the opportunity to see the game indoors on closed-circuit theater television. The weather was also on the minds of the players, but Doug Atkins paid it no mind. "What's the difference about the weather?" Atkins asked a reporter.[48] "We know it's going to be cold for sure, and you know that if the field is frozen or at all wet, it's going to help both offensive teams and hurt the defenses."[49]

Quarterback coach Sid Luckman blithely ignored the weather and mentioned that he thought the Bears offense might "break loose and play the kind of ball it is capable of playing."[50] Starting quarterback Bill Wade did not issue such a prediction but did express the quiet air of confidence that had become his trademark over the years. He was asked about any trepidation facing Sam Huff, the Giants' publicity-driven intimidator, and played it coy. "Sam's a big, active fellow. You never know exactly where he's going to show up."[51] He went on to quietly point out that he had a pretty good "book" on Huff—just like Huff probably did on him. Halas was also asked about the Giants and had nothing but kind remarks. "It's a very resourceful team, directed by a brainy, hard working coaching staff. I don't want to make any comparisons, but the Giants are at least as formidable as Green Bay."[52] With the polite pregame banter both teams had for each other, they could have simply wallpapered over their bulletin boards; it was obvious there would be no controversial press clippings that could be used as bulletin board material before this game.

The Giants' chartered flight arrived in Chicago at 6:25 Friday evening, and the team was immediately bussed to the Edgewater Beach Hotel, their headquarters for the championship weekend. Sherman announced that tight end Joe Walton was too injured to start and Aaron Thomas would replace him, although Walton would see some playing time.[53] Halas was asked about the change and was so careful not to offer any bulletin board material, but in the process he inadvertently made what could be "locker material" for Walton. "That's bad," Halas said of Walton not starting. "Thomas is better than Walton."[54] It was not known if Walton pasted this inadvertent slight in his locker or if the veteran gave it any mind. Based on the 1963 season, however, the Giants would not miss much of anything if Thomas played more than Walton.

Thomas was a 6'3", 205-pound pass receiver who had seen action at split end, tight end, and flanker during his time with the Giants. In the 1963 season he played a variety of receiver positions in all 14 games and started in five of them, making 22 catches and three touchdowns. His longest reception was for 55 yards. He was San Francisco's fourth-round draft pick after graduating from Oregon State and was in his third year as a pro. Thomas had no catches in his previous two championship games against the Packers.

Walton was smaller than Thomas at 5'11", 202 pounds, and he had been a reliable fixture in the Giants' offense ever since his second year with the team in 1958. In 1963 he missed two games due to injury and started at tight end in 11 contests, making 26 catches, six of which went for touchdowns, his longest for 43 yards. Walton was a highly-regarded end when he graduated from Pittsburgh in 1957 and was taken in the second round by the Washington Redskins. While he was shut out in the 1961 championship game, he acquitted himself very well in frigid Yankee Stadium the following year, catching five passes for 75 yards in the Giants' losing cause. In that game no receiver on either team matched Walton's 75 yards, and only Del Shofner caught as many passes. Halas was obviously blowing smoke with his assessment of the Giants' tight end situation, and his defensive coordinator George Allen was counting his blessings that the leading receiver in last year's championship game's artic weather would be seeing limited duty.

To preserve Wrigley Field's turf Halas hired charter buses Friday, December 27, to take his players—and hired security men with binoculars—to a northern section of Lincoln Park, between the Wilson and Lawrence exits on Lake Shore Drive, for a frigid outdoor practice. The security men scoped the area at Halas' orders, looking for "spies."[55] The makeshift field, in the expansive Montrose Harbor area, was very empty with adverse weather conditions—20 degrees with a light snow falling. Halas did not commit to a Saturday practice, saying that it would be dependent upon the weather conditions. For some reason Halas could not come clean with the media regarding the condition of the field for the game. He said the turf was going to be perfect but paradoxically added that sneakers would be the footwear of the day. The Giants were scheduled for a workout at Wrigley Field on Saturday, a workout that might be moved to another location depending on the condition of the turf.[56]

Commissioner Pete Rozelle came to Chicago and held a press conference in the Loop at the Sheraton-Chicago Hotel. He announced that Norm Schachter would referee the game, with Ralph Morcroft umpiring, Dan Tehan acting as head linesman, Ralph Vandenberg as back judge, and Fred Swearingen as field judge.[57] This would be a stroll down memory lane of sorts for Tehan, who was the head linesman in the very first NFL title game in 1933, which the Bears won in Wrigley Field.

Rozelle also mentioned that an additional 6,000 seats were made available at McCormick Place's closed-circuit television venue, raising the total number of individuals who could watch the contest indoors to 31,000. Rozelle could not conceal his joy when he discussed title game revenue with the media. He gushed that the gate could be a record $1.5 million, breaking it down as follows: Wrigley Field sellout, $500,000; NBC television broadcasting rights, $926,000; film rights, $25,000; and local (Chicago and New York) radio, $10,000. Not included in these totals was an additional $25,000 to $50,000 expected from the closed-circuit revenue. As of Thursday, December 26, 20,000 of the 31,000 closed circuit seats had been sold.[58]

Even more impressive than the total revenues were the net revenue totals Rozelle was expecting. Net proceeds, he explained, could be as much as half of the total revenue, $750,000.[59] He mentioned that 88 percent of the ticket revenue, $440,000, would be profit; 41 percent, close to $383,000, would be the NFL's take from the NBC revenue; and as much as 24 percent of the closed-circuit revenue—$50,000—could be the league's. If that were the case, the windfall for TNT's innovative theater broadcasts could mean as much as $160,000 in revenue for them on a single day.[60] It was no wonder the NFL was so intrigued with the closed-circuit format.

Both the Bears and the Giants got abbreviated workouts in at Wrigley Field on Saturday. Halas had the north end of the field uncovered as the Bears tested footwear and ran some plays, giving way to the Giants at noon, which would be their first steps on Wrigley Field turf in 13 months.[61] The Giants were pleased with the condition of the turf, with most of them opting for their traditional football spikes, including Tittle, who declared that he would wear his usual high-top football shoe. Halfback Phil King, like the Bears' Bill Wade, opted for rubber-bottomed basketball shoes, while fullback Alex Webster was pleased with the way he was able to cut in his spikes. Both teams were relieved at the Sunday weather forecast that came out—temperatures in the 20s with no precipitation.[62]

The oddsmakers, who earlier in the week made the Giants a one-point favorite, closed their books on Saturday afternoon calling the game a toss-up. The unpredictability of the weather and the Bears' home-field advantage seemed to wipe out the New Yorkers' slim one-point advantage.[63] Arthur Daley in his "Sport of the Times" column went with the Giants, solely because of Y.A. Tittle's arm. Daley went into great detail about the superstitions Tittle had before every game. The long laces in his high-top shoes, considered his good-luck charms, had not been changed in many years, but instead simply knotted together in many places where they had broken. Nobody but Del Shofner could help him pull his jersey over his shoulder pads. On the bus to the stadium Shofner, Webster, Morrison and Tittle himself had to sit in the same seats in the back of the bus on every trip. On Sunday morning, December 29, there would be a short three-mile bus trip south down Sheridan Road from the Edgewater Beach to Wrigley Field. The Giants would have a lot more on their minds on that brief journey than where they were sitting.

Columnist Bill Gleason got his revenge against Papa Bear Halas before the game. Still burned about colleague Ed Stone's treatment by the Bears coach, Gleason called a longtime acquaintance of his, the legendary columnist George Frazier, writing at the time for the *Boston Herald*. Frazier, a graduate of Boston Latin and Harvard, was a highly respected individual, considered a columnist's columnist. Gleason introduced Stone to Frazier, who was in Chicago for the championship game. They both told

Frazier about Halas' treatment of Stone and the press in general, and he eagerly used it as fodder for a Sunday column that turned out to be a screed about Halas. In the piece titled "A Monster of the Midway," Frazier zeroed in on Halas' darker side and his coziness with *Tribune* czar Don Maxwell. He ended the diatribe referring to both as enemies of "Freedom of the Press."[64]

11

December

The Nation Witnesses a Classic

On the eve of his 12th championship game, George Halas learned yet again how, in the contemporary Manhattan-based Rozelle era of the National Football League, his clout and influence was not what it once was. The NFL office, in New York City since Rozelle took over, was staffed by ardent followers of pro football. Given the venue, a vast number were fans of New York's team, which just happened to be playing Halas' Bears on Sunday. Conspiracy theorists reasoned that that was the reason Joe Kuharich, supervisor of NFL officials, had his office inform Halas that his habit of roaming the sideline at will to constantly remind NFL officials "how they are doing" would not be allowed anymore.[1] The Bears founder learned that his team would be penalized 15 yards if he did not stay within the two 40-yard lines, which was mandated by NFL rules.

With the NFL championship being held in Wrigley Field for the first time in 30 years, it came as a surprise that game was not sold out. The weather in Chicago had been so cold that at the end of the day on Saturday tickets were still available at the Bears box office for the game.[2] In spite of the weather this would not have been the case if the closed-circuit venues had not been established, with more than 20,000 already paying for the privilege to see the game in indoor comfort. The forecast the day before the game was that the weather would be dry and sunny, somewhere between 15 and 20 degrees, much like it was for the Detroit game two weeks before. On Sunday morning everyone sensed that it would be much colder than that.

While the oddsmakers were declaring the game a toss-up, if pressure and expectations could influence the outcome, the Giants were at a disadvantage. As the season started only the Bears believed in themselves. The rest of the NFL world saw them as an above-average but aging team, usually picked no higher than fourth in the Western Division, expected to finish behind Green Bay, Detroit, and even Baltimore.[3] Yet they won 11 games and lost only one, and six of those victories came against those same three teams who were supposed to finish ahead of them.

The Bears earned their chance at the NFL title, and indeed were happy to be there, but the burden and weight of expectation was not one of their concerns. It was a different story for New York.

Not only were the two biggest cities matching up but also two of the three most successful franchises in the NFL. Going back to 1920 and including the 1963 season, Green Bay had won eight titles and appeared in 10 championship games; the Bears had won seven crowns and appeared in 12 title matches; and the Giants had four championships to their name and appearances in 15 title games. This was the Giants' fifth appearance in a championship game in the last six years and their sixth in the last eight. But for all their successes, the elephant in the room for the New Yorkers was their inability to win a title game. The pressure was on the Gotham squad this time to finally produce. They had lost their previous four championship games, in 1958 and '59 to Baltimore and in '61 and '62 to Green Bay. Regardless how much favorable press coverage their young coach, Allie Sherman, generated in the media capital of the country, and in spite of this being his third consecutive championship game, his teams had yet to score either on offense or defense. The Giants' only points thus far had come on a blocked punt against the Packers in 1962. Was playing in the Eastern Division, and not having to face a steady diet of the defenses of Chicago, Detroit, Green Bay, and (in 1963, at least) Los Angeles a reason for his success? Sherman's much-ballyhooed and fawned-over quarterback, Y.A. Tittle, could do nothing against the Packers' defense in his title game play on either occasion and had a reputation of not being able to win the "big one"; many thought he was running out of time. Only three NFL players—Lou Groza of Cleveland, Leo Nomellini of San Francisco, and Ernie Stautner of Pittsburgh—were older than Tittle, and only one player, Cleveland's Jim Brown, was earning more than his $36,000 annual salary.[4] If Tittle failed against another stout defense, was he worth it? Sunday morning, as they checked out of the Edgewater Beach, the Giants had more on their minds than where to sit on the bus.

When their buses did arrive at the corner of Addison and Sheffield, near the southeast entrance of Wrigley Field closest to their small visitor's locker room just above the first base dugout, the Giants got a taste of Halas' hospitality. In spite of the single-digit temperature outside he had the hot water turned off in the Giants' locker room.[5] Over the decades Papa Bear was famous for his dirty tricks, and this certainly was one of the more devious ones. Once the Giants took the field they were subjected to what all visiting teams, football and baseball, endured: boos, catcalls, and epithets from a throng of Chicago fans in uncomfortably close proximity. The tiny visitors' locker room was about 18 steps up from field level, and a steel staircase, exposed to the public on both sides, had to be descended to get to the field. As the Giants' entourage went down the steps, they learned first-hand what little regard Bears fans had for them and how unpopular they were.

The lineups:

Giants Defense

Name	Position	Height/ Weight	Yrs	College
Dick Lynch	R. Cornerback	6'1" 198	6	Notre Dame
Jim Patton	Free Safety	5'11" 183	9	Mississippi
Tom Scott	R. Linebacker	6'2" 218	11	Virginia
Andy Robustelli	Right End	6'1" 230	13	Arnold
John LoVetere	R. Tackle	6'4" 280	5	Compton
Sam Huff	Middle L.B.	6'1" 230	8	W. Virginia
D. Modzelewski	Left Tackle	6'0" 250	11	Maryland
Jim Katcavage	Left End	6'3" 237	8	Dayton
Jerry Hillebrand	L. Linebacker	6'3" 240	1	Colorado
Dick Pesonen	Strong Safety	6'0" 190	4	Minn. Duluth
Erich Barnes	L. Cornerback	6'3" 198	6	Purdue
Eddie Dove	Kick Returner	6'2" 181	5	Colorado
Hugh McElhenny	Kick Returner	6'1" 195	12	Washington

Bears Offense

Name	Position	Height/ Weight	Yrs	College
Bo Farrington	Left End	6'3" 217	4	Prairie View
Herman Lee	Left Tackle	6'3" 247	7	Florida A&M
Ted Karras	Left Guard	6'1" 243	6	Indiana
Mike Pyle	Center	6'3" 245	3	Yale
Jim Cadile	Right Guard	6'3" 240	2	San Jose (Cal.)
Bob Wetoska	Right Tackle	6'3" 240	4	Notre Dame
Mike Ditka	Tight End	6'3" 230	3	Pittsburgh
Billy Wade	Quarterback	6'2" 205	10	Vanderbilt
Willie Galimore	Halfback	6'0" 187	7	Florida A&M
Joe Marconi	Fullback	6'2" 225	8	West Virginia
Johnny Morris	Flanker	5'10" 180	6	Santa Barbara
Bob Joe Green	Punter	5'11" 175	4	Florida
Roger Leclerc	Kicker	6'3" 235	4	Trinity

The Giants' defense presented more challenges to the Bears' offense than any defense they had seen in 1963, with the possible exception of Green Bay's. Wetoska and Cadile on the Bears' right side would have their hands full with Katcavage and Modzelewski; Katcavage had 20.5 sacks during the season and Modzelewski had four. Johnny Morris would be covered most of the game by former Bear Erich Barnes, who had something to prove to Halas. Barnes was five inches taller and almost 20 pounds heavier than Morris, and he was known as an intimidator when the mood hit him. The Giants, however, had to deal with Ditka. It was felt that strong safety Dick Pesonen, 40 pounds lighter and three inches shorter, would have his hands full covering and tackling Ditka, one of the hardest pass catchers in the league to bring down. The left linebacker, Jerry Hillebrand, was replacing the injured Bill Winter from St. Olaf College, who played well enough in 1962 to garner some Defensive Rookie of the Year attention. Winter's absence with Ditka across the line was an advantage for the Bears, even though Hillebrand had been filling in capably. Dick Lynch would give up size and speed covering Bo Farrington, along with Farrington's frequent replacement, Angelo Coia. Both Coia and Farrington had exceptional speed, but Lynch, one of the best cornerbacks in the NFL, tied Roosevelt Taylor for the most interceptions in 1963. The Giants also had not seen a running back with Galimore's acceleration, shiftiness, or speed all season. With Wade, the Giants were facing an intelligent signal caller who would undoubtedly play head games with them on snap counts, cadence, and audibling at the line. Given Wade's height they could not count on knocking down passes at the line of scrimmage, and Wade's talent at running the ball always had to be respected. Leclerc's field goal percentage of 56.5 percent was fourth best in the NFL in 1963. He was six for eight inside the 20-yard line, two for two from the 20 to the 29, three for five from the 30 to the 39, and two for eight past the 40. Leclerc had a knack for making field goals in the clutch; he made key kicks in two games against the Packers and made the crucial field goal in the fourth quarter to tie the score at the end of the game with the Steelers.

Giants Offense

Name	Position	Height/ Weight	Yrs	College
Del Shofner	Left End	6'3", 186	7	Baylor
Roosevelt Brown	Left Tackle	6'3", 255	11	Morgan State
Darrell Dess	Left Guard	6'0", 243	6	N. Carolina
Greg Larson	Center	6'3", 250	3	Minnesota
Bookie Bolin	Right Guard	6'2", 240	2	Mississippi
Jack Stroud	Right Tackle	6'1", 235	11	Tennessee
Aaron Thomas	Tight End	6'3", 210	3	Oregon State
Y.A. Tittle	Quarterback	6'0", 192	16	LSU
Phil King	Halfback	6'4", 223	6	Vanderbilt
Joe Morrison	Fullback	6'1", 210	5	Cincinnati
Frank Gifford	Flanker	6'0", 197	11	USC
Don Chandler	Punter and Kicker	6'2", 215	8	Florida

Bears Defense

Name	Position	Height/Weight	Yrs	College
Dave Whitsell	R. Cornerback	5'11", 189	6	Indiana
Roosevelt Taylor	Free Safety	5'10", 185	3	Grambling St.
Larry Morris	R. Linebacker	6'2", 226	8	Georgia
Doug Atkins	Right End	6'8", 270	11	Tennessee
Fred Williams	Right Tackle	6'4", 249	12	Arkansas
Bill George	Middle L.B.	6'2", 237	12	Wake Forest
Stan Jones	Left Tackle	6'1", 252	10	Maryland
Ed O'Bradovich	Left End	6'3", 255	2	Illinois
Joe Fortunato	L. Linebacker	6'1", 225	9	Mississippi St.
Richie Petitbon	Strong Safety	6'3", 206	5	Tulane
Bennie McRae	L. Cornerback	6'0", 180	2	Michigan
Ronnie Bull	Kick Returner	6'0", 200	2	Baylor
Billy Martin	Kick Returner	5'11", 197	2	Minnesota

The entire subtext for the championship game involved these two groups of athletes. The Bears had not seen an offense like the Giants all year, and the Giants had never played a defense like the Bears all year. Could the Bears stifle the Giants' peerless passing attack, and could the smaller Giants offensive line handle the Bears' dominating front seven? The Bears defensive front had a penchant for collapsing the pocket, Atkins and George in particular, and Tittle was not known for his mobility. Fortunato was the Bears' defensive captain, and Morris not only was quick but was also one of the hardest hitting linebackers in the NFL. Halas was concerned about the Giants' passing, concerned enough to tell Whitsell he might not want him to play against the sometimes-unstoppable Shofner. Whitsell gave up size to the tall Texan, and dealing with his moves on an iffy field could be an added nightmare. Also, Whitsell's technique of laying low to sucker quarterbacks into throwing ill-advisedly might not work so well with a savvy veteran like Tittle. While Halas handled the issue poorly, the concern about Whitsell stopping Shofner was indeed legitimate. Gifford would be facing Bennie McRae, which perhaps was the most even matchup in the game. While the two of them were about the same size, McRae was much faster than Gifford, a great leaper, and a fearless, hard tackler. Gifford, after his devastating skull fracture after Chuck Bednarik's crushing tackle in 1961, would sometimes shy away after hard hits, but he was still one of the most clutch receivers in the NFL—as he had been for years—and in spite of his age, he had a knack for getting open against much more athletic defenders. Gifford exuded a quiet confidence that was reassuring to his teammates but often came off as arrogant to his opponents. One of his catch phrases was "We always win."[6] Aaron Thomas, replacing starting tight end Joe Walton, was the same size as Richie Petit-bon, but he did not pose much of a challenge to the Bears' strong safety.

The lightning-fast Roosevelt Taylor, who with nine pickoffs shared the NFL's interception title with the Giants' Dick Lynch, was better than any safety Tittle had seen all year. Also better than any group Tittle had faced was the Bears' linebacking trio, which some students of the game were calling the best in NFL history. Another factor not in the Giants' favor was the young mastermind choreographing the moves of this unique group of athletes. George Allen, the Bears' defensive coordinator, was earning a reputation as the NFL's new defensive genius. Arthur Daley in his game-day column "Sports of the Times" still thought Tittle was the key. "If YAT [Tittle] can start off hot, this could get lop-sided just as did the second game with the Browns, forcing the opposition to play his kind of game. And Tittle is the master of the quick score."[7] Tittle finished the season with 36 touchdown passes; the same number of interceptions the Bears' defense had. This, indeed, was going to be a game.

Right before the kickoff two Giants and four Bears met at midfield for the ceremonial coin toss and to exchange handshakes.[8] Veterans Jack Stroud and Andy Robustelli represented the Giants while Mike Ditka, Joe Fortunato, Larry Morris, and Mike Pyle came out for the Bears. Robustelli and Morris exchanged arm waves to each other as the brief meeting ended. Don Chandler kicked off to start the game, with Billy Martin and Ron-nie Bull deep at the south end of the field, the bright, blinding sun at their backs. Martin felt blessed and special, standing in Wrigley Field's shad-ows with tens of thousands of rabid fans cheering him on. A native Chica-goan and proud product of Wendell Phillips High School's Chicago Public League football program, he had been fielding kicks at Chicago's Hansen Stadium and Normal Field just six years earlier; this was a local boy who indeed made good. He bobbled the ball in the end zone and ran it out, and the Giants' Dick Lynch made a textbook diving tackle to nail him at the 10.

Wade came out and set his offense, handing off to Galimore on the first play of the game. Galimore was nailed after gaining only two yards. Wade handed to Marconi next. Marconi tried the middle, gaining about three yards to make it third and five at the 15. Wade dropped back on third down, drew the Giants' front line toward him in a rush, and then took off, getting up to the 23-yard line for a first down. Knowing the Giants had not seen a lot of quick scatbacks Wade called Galimore's number again, but Willie the Wisp met his match in Erich Barnes. The former Bear, always eager to stick it to Halas, spun Galimore around and threw him down hard after just a one-yard gain. If the Giants got the better of that play the Bears got the better of the next one. Wade resorted to a long count with a stut-tered cadence and drew linebacker Sam Huff, intent on blitzing, offsides.

Thanks to Jim Dooley, Wade knew what keys to look for that gave away Huff's intentions—his posture and the placement of his feet—and sniffed the play out perfectly, moving the ball to the 29. "Dooley discovered that Huff would go to his right on a passing situation. That's why I called a quarterback draw."[9] But on the next play defensive end Andy Robustelli stopped Joe Marconi cold at the 29 for no gain. On third and five, Wade went back to pass, drew the Giants' line attention, and then once again took off up the middle. At the 40-yard line he was hit by defensive back Allan Webb, whose helmet caused a fumble. Erich Barnes recovered the drop and was immediately tackled by Ditka. The game's first miscue was by the Bears, giving the Giants an excellent chance early in the game.

Tittle took the field with his offense, and an air of apprehension came over the crowd. On the first play Tittle handed off to Joe Morrison, who only got one yard before Doug Atkins took him down. Tittle then dropped back on second and nine and hit Morrison with his patented screen pass, and Morrison got all the way to the 29 for a first down before Bennie McRae tackled him, with some very rough assistance from Bill George and Ed O'Bradovich. Halfback Phil King next went off the right side of the Giants' line and got to the 26. On second and seven at the 26, Tittle sent Morrison up the middle once more, and he got a healthy six yards before the Bears' Larry Morris put him down. Tempers flared after the play; Bill George and Darrell Dess got into a shoving match that was over as quickly as it started. Tittle sensed his line's superiority at this point, and he called another running play, sending Morrison over the left guard (the fired-up Dess). Morrison got to the 16 for another first down. In the huddle Gifford told Tittle, "I can beat him [McRae] easy on a zig-out."[10] Tittle then called the same play for Morrison, and he got two more yards. It was time to take Gifford at his word. Tittle had him line up uncharacteristically wide on the right side, to give him room for the slant-and-out (zig-out) pattern, which would end in the icy right corner of the south end zone. With McRae's poor footing and Gifford's longer route giving him a chance to generate more speed, Gifford got a good two steps ahead of McRae and caught Tittle's perfect pass for a touchdown. Tittle's pocket collapsed just as he threw, and Morris, blitzing, made hard contact with Tittle's lead leg as he was throwing. Tittle later said he felt a twinge behind his knee after Morris' hit and his knee began to stiffen.[11] This occurred a split second too late for the Bears; after Chandler kicked the extra point out of reserve quarterback Glynn Griffing's hold, it was 7–0, Giants.

Once again Chandler kicked off, north to south, while Martin and Bull were deep. Bull took the kick at the four and was tackled by Lynch at the 19. Wade immediately went to Galimore, who was buried after gaining a yard by Jim Katcavage and Dick Modzelewski. On second and nine Wade passed to Bo Farrington, but it was broken up beautifully by Lynch, his third major contribution in the game's early moments. One of the reasons running plays were not working against the Giants was because they were in a 6–1 defense, going to a 4–3 on passing downs. Facing a third and long situation Wade sensed a blitz coming, so he threw a flare pass in the flat to Marconi, who made a good cut and got to the 30 before Jim Patton took him down. The Bears now had some breathing room with a first down, and Wade handed off to Galimore, who bobbled the handoff but got loose off tackle and made it up to the 33, where Tom Scott tackled him. Wade came up to the line, chanted a long count once again, and drew the Giants offside, making it second and two, but Wade next went to the well once too often. He handed off to Galimore, who was immediately thrown for a loss by linebacker Jerry Hillebrand and almost decapitated by Katcavage. Wade next threw to Johnny Morris, but the play was broken up by Barnes. With 4:32 left in the first quarter Green came in to punt with Dove and McElhenny deep. Green's booming kick was taken at the 25 by by Dove, who was put down with a hard tackle at the 27 by the Bears' Ted Karras.

Tittle opened the Giants' offensive foray sending Phil King through the middle, a play worth four yards. Next Morrison broke away from two Bears' tacklers and was taken down by Joe Fortunato at the 34. Even though it was third and short yardage Tittle thought he would cross up the Bears with a pass play. Morris, using Atkins as a screen, rushed in hard and hit Tittle low around the ankles. He took his time getting up and belittled him before he left, patting Tittle on his helmet; none of the Giants retaliated and Chandler came in to punt it away. Chandler boomed the kick, which went 52 yards and was caught by Johnny Morris at the 20. He got to the 25 where he ran into his own man, Joe Fortunato, and went down. The Bears took over on the 24.

On the first play from scrimmage Wade handed off to Galimore once more, hoping that the scatback could spring one, and indeed Willie had something going, which ended abruptly when he was hit in close order by Barnes, Sam Huff, and Jim Patton. He fumbled at the 30 and Barnes pounced on the ball. This was Galimore's second miscue handling the ball in the bitter cold and Halas had seen enough. It was the last play Galimore had in the title game, and unbeknownst to everyone at the time, tragically the last play of his career.

Tittle quickly lined up and decided to strike fast. Starting at the Bears' 31 he dropped back seven yards to pass. Feeling a heavy rush from O'Bradovich, who dove and got a hand on Tittle's leg, Tittle moved up in the pocket and threw on the run toward the middle of the end zone. Just as he released the ball, Atkins, diving at him from behind, hit him hard in the back of his knees, causing the pass to be a little higher than Tittle wanted.

In that instant it did not seem to matter. Del Shofner had Dave Whitsell beaten by three paces and put his arms up two yards deep in the end zone. Shofner was about 14 feet from a snowbank at the back of the end zone and only about 18 feet away from the four-foot brick wall, running full speed. He put his hands up to make the grab and the ball skipped off his extended fingers, out of his grasp. There are several accounts of how this happened.

Mike Ditka claimed that like many receivers in Wrigley Field's south end zone, Shofner got spooked about the brick wall, looked down and lost his concentration, and hence failed to make the catch.[12] Others claim that Whitsell resorted to one of his tricks that he used when he was beaten in pass protection—issuing the receiver fake warning. "The WALL, the WALL, LOOK OUT FOR THE WALL!" he supposedly yelled at Shofner, alarming him enough to make him break his concentration. Shofner's account was that the incompletion was completely on him. "It was a good pass. I just dropped it. It was just a miserable attempt."[13] The Bears dodged a bullet, as one of Halas' worst fears almost came to fruition. A touchdown at that point would have put the Giants ahead by two touchdowns, a deficit the Bears might find impossible to overcome on such a treacherous field against a defense like the Giants had.

Undaunted, Tittle immediately dropped back again on second down. He threw a screen pass in the left flat toward Phil King. He rushed the throw because Atkins had completely pancaked offensive tackle Roosevelt Brown and was ready to clobber him. The throw was wide of King, and Bears defensive tackle Fred Williams, who had sniffed out the screen pass perfectly, was waiting back with linebacker Larry Morris. Morris charged up, caught the ball in stride, evaded the Giants' Darrell Dess, picked up O'Bradovich and Atkins to block for him, and streaked down all the way to the Giants' five-yard line, where he was tackled by Dess and center Greg Larson. "The first 30 yards I wondered if they'd catch me; the last 30 yards I was afraid they wouldn't," was Morris' famous description of the tremendous play.[14] Morris played a fair amount of fullback at Georgia Tech and also gained some yards from the backfield when he was with the Rams; he looked more competent than he gave himself credit for on this particular run.

Bull came in the backfield for Galimore, and Wade immediately sent him off tackle, where he was tackled by Huff at the two. On second and goal Wade called a quarterback sneak; thanks to road-grading blocks by Jim Cadile, Ted Karras, and Mike Pyle, he had one of the easiest touchdowns of the year, as the three Bears forced LoVetere, Huff, and Modzelewski three yards back into the end zone. Bob Jencks kicked the extra point out of Whitsell's hold to tie the game, 7–7.

Leclerc lined up his special teams unit for the Bears' first kickoff of the day. Charlie Killett and Eddie Dove were deep for the Giants. Killett, a rookie halfback out of Memphis, had returned 14 kickoffs during the 1963 season, but none of them occurred in such horrible conditions. Gazing south, he lost the ball in the blinding sun, and the ball hit him in the shin and bounced forward, causing a mad scramble. The Bears' Charlie Bivins recovered the fumble on the Giants' five-yard line. The crowd went wild, but their ecstatic enthusiasm quickly ended when the Bears were called offside. This game-changing disappointment was the last play of the first quarter: Giants 7, Bears 7.

Knowing that this game was much too important to give young players second chances, Giants head coach Allie Sherman replaced Killett with the great veteran Hugh McElhenny for the kickoff. Leclerc's kick this time went to Dove, who caught it at the 14 and immediately headed for the east sideline. He got all the way up to the Giants' 37 where he was tackled by Jim Cadile.

On first down Tittle was unceremoniously dumped, unnecessarily hard, the Bears' Williams, who was called for roughing. After the penalty and replacement of the ball, Tittle handed off to Morrison, who gained only one yard before he was met by Bill George and Stan Jones. On the next play Tittle called Morrison's number again, and this time the hard-charging fullback got all the way to the 49, brought down by Morris and George. Suddenly the Giants had a fresh set of downs at midfield. Tittle dropped back to pass. He was hit hard by Bob Kilcullen, who was in for Williams at defensive tackle, but managed to release the ball in Aaron Thomas' direction, 15 yards down the field. Petitbon was covering Thomas and made a move to intercept; the ball was just out of his reach and Thomas made the grab, balancing down the sideline all the way to the Bears' 14-yard line, where he slipped out of bounds as he skidded along a retaining rope. Once again the Giants were knocking on the door, in the Bears' red zone.

Tittle handed to off to King, who managed six yards, brought down by Morris and George at the eight-yard line. Tittle called King's number again and he went straight up the middle to the four. Sensing how dominant his blockers were during this drive, Sherman sent the Giants' usual starting tight end Joe Walton into the game for Shofner. Even with Walton in as an additional blocker on the line, when Tittle handed off to Morrison he could only gain one yard. What happened on the next two plays typified the Bears' play all season.

With his team nine feet away from another score and his running plays up the middle so successful, Tittle thought it was time to cross the Bears up. The Giants tried their first end sweep of the day. Tittle handed off to Morrison, who cut upfield to sweep around the right end, O'Bradovich.

O'Bradovich held his ground but Morrison did not change his path. To his great surprise Morrison suddenly felt himself being taken down from behind. Atkins, in a display of uncanny athleticism, turned on the speed and caught him from behind after starting from his left end position on the other side of the line. The Giants looked at each other in disbelief as Tittle called the huddle. Pat Summerall on the NBC radio broadcast mentioned that at times during the season "from the ten-yard line in the Giants can have trouble scoring." He also added that Sherman liked to call sweeps in short yardage situations. Since the play did not work around right end, and the sun's angle would make the catch on a short, crisp pass play very difficult, Tittle called the same sweep, this time around left end, on Atkins' side of the field. The Bears played it as though they knew it was coming. Morrison took Tittle's handoff and veered left, waiting for some blocking to set up, when he was tackled hard by O'Bradovich for a three-yard loss. Like Atkins had done on the play before, O'Bradovich raced through the backfield from his end position to make the play on the other side of the line. If for some reason he would not have been able to make the tackle, it was doubtful that Morrison would have gotten any further, since Whitsell was in a perfect position to clean up. Two Giants sweeps completely foiled by some amazing athleticism by two Bears' linemen; the Giants would not try another sweep the entire afternoon. On third and goal from the six, Tittle tried a swing pass in the right flat to King. He threw it too hard and the pass fell harmlessly to the turf. If he had caught it, the chances were that he would get nowhere, since Fortunato was virtually on top of him. Don Chandler came in to kick a field goal out of Griffing's hold, and although the kick was almost blocked by Whitsell, racing in from Chandler's left side, the kick was good, and the Giants led, 10–7, with 9:49 left in the second quarter.

The Giants had the lead, but many sensed that fortunes had changed. The Bears' defense was impenetrable for three plays, two of them from only three yards out. The Bears started at their own 21 but did nothing on this possession. Wade hit Morris with a good pass after he had successfully faked out Pesonen, but Morris could not hang on to the ball as he hit the turf. Coia beat Lynch on a deep pattern on the next play, but Wade overthrew him. To confuse Wade the Giants were playing a zone pass defense on Ditka's and Morris' side and man to man on the other side. Green punted after Pesonen broke up a third and 10 pass to Ditka. Green's kick from the Bears' five seemed like the kick of the year. McElhenny fielded it at the Giants' 33 and was tackled 10 yards up field at the 43.

With the running plays and a short pass completely foiled by the Bears in his last possession, Tittle was ready to go back deep in the air. Shofner was back in at his split end position and on first down Tittle threw long for

Thomas. The play was defended perfectly by Petitbon, who got his hands on the pass but could not hold on for an interception. Tittle then called two draw plays; both worked, thanks to Phil King's efforts, and the Giants were now on the 32-yard line of the Bears. King departed the backfield and was replaced by McElhenny. From the 32, Tittle went back to throw and saw Gifford open well down field. Larry Morris, blitzing on the play, was ignored by Giants defensive tackle Roosevelt Brown, who was preoccupied with keeping Atkins off Tittle's back. Tittle wound up and threw long, and just as he released the ball Morris dove into his legs at full speed. Gifford made the catch just past McRae, who drove him out of bounds at the 35 and into the rolled-up tarp. Gifford was shaken up, but everyone's attention was back at the Giants' 40, where Tittle, badly slumped over, tried to kneel but was unable to get up. McElhenny helped him to his feet and held him up by his left arm, but as they went to the Giants sideline, it was obvious that the Tittle could not walk on his left leg. Glynn Griffing came in to replace Tittle, hardly a reassuring sight for Giants fans. Both Gibbons and Summerall thought it was Tittle's ankle and expressed doubt that he would be back at any point in the game. In the locker room Tittle, in great pain, told team physician Robert Sweeny and the orthopedist Anthony Pisani that he could not even bend his knee.[15]

With the green rookie Griffing in the game, the Giants game plan went out the window. On the first play McElhenny dove up the middle just inside the Bears' 30. On second down Griffing attempted to pass but was immediately smothered by Atkins just as he got the ball off for an incompletion. On fourth down Chandler came in and set up at the 37 to try a field goal. J.C. Caroline, racing in from the right side, got his hand on the ball enough to deflect the kick, which bounced harmlessly at the four-yard line.

With 5:38 left in the half the Bears took over. Lynch could not keep up with Coia's speed, and the Bears got up to the Giants' 42 on his catch of Wade's pass. Wade also hit Ditka, who put a great move on Pesonen, with a pin-point throw. The Bears could get nothing else going, however. Morris got open after putting two beautiful moves on Hillebrand and Barnes but dropped the pass. On the play the Giants' defensive tackle John LoVetere practically buried Wade in the ground just as he released the ball. Green punted, making another great kick that went out at the three-yard line. As the linesman ran over to mark the placement he fell, hard, on the icy field. Everyone at Wrigley Field saw firsthand how dangerous the playing conditions were on this afternoon.

With Griffing in at quarterback the Bears lined up against the run exclusively, and after two running plays, the Giants were faced with third and seven at the five-yard line. Sherman decided to punt on third down.

The logic behind this move was that if they waited until fourth down to kick and there was some snafu, the Bears could easily score on a safety or field goal or, at best, take over deep in Giant territory. If there was a foul-up on a third-down punt, Chandler could pass it away for an incompletion and they could try the kick again on fourth down. The Giants flubbed the snap, which Chandler almost dropped in the end zone, but he did manage to get the kick away, and it was fielded at the Bears' 38, by Roosevelt Taylor who was tackled hard by Barnes at the 46.

Tittle was not the only major Giants casualty in first half. Linebacker Tom Scott was victimized by a brutal block by an undetected Bear lineman and was out with a broken arm. Scott was replaced by rookie Al Gursky, a 12th-round pick out of Penn State and whose presence was duly noted by Dooley and Wade. In spite of this change the Bears could do nothing with the ball and punted back to the Giants as the half ended. The score was Giants 10, Bears 7, with a momentum change sensed by everyone but not reflected on the scoreboard.

At halftime the Tennessee State College Marching Band performed, while on the NBC radio broadcast Gibbons and Summerall speculated about Tittle's injury and drew some comparisons between this game and other recent Bears-Giants affairs. Gibbons remembered that the Bears knocked Sammy Baugh out with a concussion and went on to win 1943 championship game at Wrigley Field. Assuming Tittle did not come back and something happened to Griffing, Summerall worriedly mentioned that Frank Gifford would be the Giants' quarterback. He pointed out that in the Bears-Giants preseason game at Ithaca, the Giants were leading at halftime and the Bears went on to dominate the second half, in a game in which Don Chandler missed four field goals. Yet Chandler was instrumental in the Giants' huge win at Wrigley Field a year ago, when he *made* four field goals to give the Giants the Eastern Conference title. Giant halfback Phil King would be out of the game for the second half with an injured leg and badly sprained ankle. It was never proven that this was Ed O'Bradovich's payback from 13 months ago.

At the end of the half Gibbons and Summerall, along with everyone else in the country following the game, were stunned to see Tittle warming up, throwing passes on the sideline.

His badly swollen left knee was wrapped from hip to ankle, and his leg was numbed with two Novocain shots.[16] If the Giants' kickoff return was any evidence, his mere presence on the sideline gave the Giants a lift. McElhenny took Leclerc's kick at the eight-yard line in the middle of the field and immediately gave a good number of the Wrigley Field crowd a heart attack. The shifty old halfback still had moves and showed the Bears three of them, resulting in him not being touched until the Bears safety,

Roosevelt Taylor, took him down at the Giants' 46. Taylor was all that was between McElhenny and a touchdown, and the fearless little All-Pro made a textbook tackle to bring him down. Taylor, slow to get up after the jarring impact of his hit on a much larger foe, just made the biggest play of his career. McElhenny stayed in the game and carried the ball on the Giants' first two plays, moving the ball to the Bears' 42. On third and six Tittle fired a screen pass to Morrison and was hit hard when Atkins drove his shoulder into his hip. Morrison made the catch and rambled down to the Bears' 41, when a rough tackle by O'Bradovich and McRae caused him to fumble. George landed on the ball, but referee Norm Schachter incorrectly ruled that Morrison was down, no fumble; O'Bradovich went into a rage after the call. Sensing a good time to catch the Bears off-guard, Tittle called for a pass play and noticed that once again Gifford had badly beaten McRae. He called a pass play to Gifford, but with his injured leg Tittle could not throw with his usual authority. The ball was underthrown, McRae knocked it down, and Tittle was once again hit hard, this time by Jones. On second and 10, on yet another pass play, Tittle noticed that there were several yards between Shofner and Whitsell and threw in Shofner's direction. Whitsell was intentionally giving Shofner what Tittle thought was too much room, but Whitsell immediately broke for the ball, timed it perfectly, and made an interception. Shofner managed to get him down but took a tremendous hit from Bill George in the process.

Wade came out throwing for the Bears' first possession of the second half. A screen pass to Marconi moved the ball from the Bears' 26 to the 45. Two plays later Wade had Marconi go medium deep down the middle. The play worked so well that he got all the way to the Giants' 21. It had become obvious to Wade, Dooley, and everybody else that mattered that none of the Giant linebackers could keep up with the swift Marconi, let alone the even quicker Bull. Plays that could get either of them past the line of scrimmage were bound to be successful. Wade next spotted Coia open in the end zone but his pass was tipped away at the last second by a desperate Jim Patton, who knocked it out of Coia's hands. A drop by Morris followed, when he could not handle Wade's pass. Roger Leclerc came in to kick a field goal from the 28, but the kick was wide left. On the sideline Halas flung his chewing gum, sidearm, in disgust.

Tittle came out to lead the Giants' offense on five consecutive running plays, but their success ran out at midfield when Stan Jones put a brilliant stop on Morrison. While the Giants stayed on the ground during that drive, the Bears were throwing the ball more. Wade hit Ditka at the 35; when Ditka got to the 37 he was hit very aggressively and late by Erich Barnes. The play cost the Giants 15 yards for unnecessary roughing, as Ditka filed Barnes' transgression away; he was never one to let a bad deed go unpunished. On the following down the Bears lost yardage on a screen pass to Bull, but Wade connected successfully to Johnny Morris on the next play, before he was dropped to the frozen turf very roughly by Barnes. Erich Barnes was playing like his hair was on fire, disrupting the Bears every chance he got, and Ditka decided to take matters into his own hands. A few plays later Wade saw Morris again and threw his way, since Barnes was several yards behind him. Barnes came rushing up to make the tackle and was completely blind-sided on a crack-back block by Ditka, which knocked the rangy cornerback to the turf in pain. Barnes, trying to get up, repeatedly kicked the turf in anger. He calmed down when he saw the ref's flag as Ditka was called for offensive interference. The penalty cooled the Bears drive—Robustelli flattened Wade on a sack afterward—but a message had been sent. The Giants, such as Barnes, who had a tendency to get a little too truculent, were now on notice. Green punted the ball away, which was taken by McElhenny at the 25. He got to the 35 where he was gang tackled by several Bears.

The teams traded punts and Tittle came out with 4:43 left in the third quarter and opened his offensive series at the Giants' 35-yard line. He dropped back, looked downfield, and then immediately looked to his right where Morrison was waiting in the flat. Joe Fortunato had sniffed out the screen pass perfectly and tipped off O'Bradovich before the snap. O'Bradovich stuck his left arm out and made an interception, with Morrison and Jack Stroud desperately chasing him and finally bringing him down near the sideline at the 12-yard line. A very partisan security guard who happened to be right there helped O'Bradovich up and clapped him on the back repeatedly. George Allen had figured out the keys to the Giants' pass plays, schooled defensive captain Joe Fortunato in them thoroughly, and, just as Morris sensed Tittle's screen pass to the right in the first half, Fortunato sensed correctly and tipped off O'Bradovich on the screen pass to the left. "When Jack Stroud, at right tackle, dropped back without a push back, I sensed it was coming," explained O'Bradovich.[17]

Wade got a little too pass-happy on the Bears' first play, throwing toward Marconi in the end zone, when the ball was almost intercepted by Jerry Hillebrand, the young Giant linebacker who had five interceptions in his last six games. Halas went absolutely crazy with rage on the sidelines after the play. Wade then sent Bull around right end next, a play good for three yards, stopped by Barnes' very crisp tackle. On a play sent in by Luke Johnsos, who called plays from the pressbox, Wade had Ditka split out slightly wide to the right and had him do a slant pattern toward the goal posts. He dropped back only two steps and fired a laser right into Ditka's breadbasket. Ditka did a great job getting past the linebacker Hillebrand and caught the ball while taking a hard hit at the waist from safety

Dick Pesonen. Pesonen's great play got Ditka down at the two yard line; Ditka claimed he could have scored if he could have got his shoulder down to drive Pesonen back those last two yards. From the two Wade gave a silent count to Pyle, took the snap, and scored, while once again the Bears' interior line drove Huff and company back two yards into the end zone. Jencks' kick was good, and the Bears had their first lead of the day, 14–10.

Eddie Dove took Leclerc's kick at the five and was still on his feet at the Bears' 30, where he was hit hard, simultaneously, by Larry Glueck and McRae. Tittle set up shop at his own 31 and opened with an off-tackle running play by McElhenny which got about a yard. On second and almost 10 he handed off to McElhenny again, this time on a quick opener, and the future Hall of Famer took off, virtually untouched, suddenly in the clear. Just like on the kickoff that started the second half McElhenny seemed to have a game-changing sprint in front of him, but once again the diminutive, dauntless Roosevelt Taylor got in his way and made a beautiful open-field tackle at the 49, saving a touchdown. For McElhenny, who first teamed up with Tittle in 1952 in San Francisco, this game meant everything. He would be 35 years old in two days, had never been in a championship game before, and sensed this was his last hurrah. Tittle then went for it all, throwing long into the end zone for Thomas, and the ball was almost picked off by Petitbon. The crippled quarterback had no torque on the ball, and Thomas was also struggling with the sun. Pass attempts to Gifford and Shofner followed, and they were unsuccessful. On the national radio broadcast Pat Summerall marveled at Shofner being shut out all game by Dave Whitsell.

With three seconds left in the third quarter Chandler's kick was taken by Johnny Morris at the 18, and he could only advance one yard. On the play the Giants' Bookie Bolin was hit so hard by an unidentified Bear that he required emergency medical treatment after swallowing his tongue. The third quarter ended; it was the Bears' ball as the final quarter began.

The Bears started at their own 19. On first down Wade's pass to Coia was almost intercepted by Jim Patton, who could only get one hand on it; on the Bears' sideline Halas threw his hands in the air in disgust. It was uncharacteristic of Wade to take such risks so deep in his own territory with only a four-point lead. The Bears could not move the ball and Green punted from the five, with the Giants' Dove and McElhenny deep. It was not a particularly good punt but the ball took a Bear bounce and the Giants started at their own 39.

Big Johnny Johnson came in to replace Fred Williams at tackle. Morrison started the Giants out with a successful run up to the 45 where he was belted hard by Roosevelt Taylor. Morrison, woozy after the hit, ran on the next play also and fumbled. His drop was recovered by Richie Petitbon, giving the Bears the ball with great field position on the Giants' 40-yard line with 12:59 left.

Wade wisely kept the ball on the ground on the first play, and Bull fought his way up to the 45 where Sam Huff made the tackle. Bull ran again on second down and lost two yards when he was tackled by Modzelewski. Two completions to Morris followed, setting up a chance for Wade to drop back and then take off through the middle. His run put the Bears on the Giants' 33; Wade's planned running plays were proving hugely successful. Bull ran off tackle on the next play and got a first down at the 28. It took two from the Giants' secondary, Pesonen and Barnes, to bring him down; the Bears' offensive line was now dominating the Giants. Bull next fought his way to the 25 before Robustelli took him down. Wade called Bull's number a third consecutive time, but he was stopped at the line of scrimmage by Gursky and Robustelli. Remembering how successful the look-in slant pattern pass to Ditka was on the touchdown drive, Wade called the play again. This time, however, Ditka was hit hard by Pesonen and could not hang on. Leclerc came in for a field goal attempt, which had enough height and depth but was wide to the right.

Apprehension set in with the crowd at this point; with 8:22 remaining, the Giants had the ball on their own 25, down only four points when it could have been 10. Morrison took Tittle's handoff on first down and got up to the 37. Johnson and Morris made the tackle and made him pay for those yards; Morrison was slow getting to his feet and was replaced by Webster. Tittle then wanted to throw. Shofner went long and got behind both Taylor and Whitsell, but Tittle put too much on the ball, which sailed harmlessly over all of them. Tittle next fumbled the snap but recovered his drop before any damage was done. Webster quickly exited the backfield on the next play, caught Tittle's pass over the defensive line and got all the way to midfield. Johnny Johnson, who seemed to know the play was coming, caught Webster from behind to make the tackle. On the first down play that followed, Tittle's injury and suffering became apparent.

He dropped back to pass when his pass blocking broke down, allowing O'Bradovich and Morris to come at him full speed. He ran with a noticeable limp to avoid them and hastily got rid of the ball, which fluttered to the turf, near nobody. If there was any measure of sympathy with any of the Bears on this frigid December 29 it occurred on this play. O'Bradovich and Morris were both in a position to annihilate Tittle, but they held up and left him untouched. On third down Tittle found Gifford open in front of McRae, and the Giants suddenly found themselves at the Bears' 36 with 4:59 left on the clock. On the next play he overthrew Thomas but followed that up with a completion to Morrison, who was dropped at the line of scrimmage. At this point Tittle decided to go for it all; Gifford seemed to be having his way with McRae, so Tittle had Gifford go long into the end zone. Just as he released the ball he was hit, hard and low again by his day-long nemesis Larry Morris, who hurdled more than four feet in the air to avoid McElhenny's pass block. This contact changed the ball's trajectory, Gifford slipped on the icy five-yard line, and McRae, with his feet still under him, made the interception.

Another clutch performance by the Bears' defense had given the Bears' offense the ball at the 20. On the first play Bull was brought down by Katcavage after a two-yard gain; it was second and nine, 3:47 left on the clock. The Bears took their time in the huddle, and Wade called out a delayed snap count; Bull then executed one of his best runs of the year, fighting off a bevy of menacing Giants and getting up to the 33-yard line. Time out was called by the officials, now with 3:25 remaining. Wade called on Bull yet a third time, and he got to the 35 before Huff and Modzelewski stopped him, going for the ball as much as for Bull. Wade sensed that Bull was really feeling it; he ran a quick opener and gained four more, out to the 39, where Barnes and Katcavage ended his progress. The clock stopped with the two-minute warning.

The next play would be huge for both teams. The Bears had the ball, on third and three, at their own 40-yard line. A first down would virtually assure their victory. The Giants' defensive line was gassed, which explains at least some of Bull's most recent success, but Bull was pretty gassed himself. The timeout gave him a short breather, but logic would dictate that Marconi would be called upon. The Bears crossed the Giants up by having Bull run it once more. He went straight ahead, and it looked like he got the precious first down, but the refs called for a measurement. Maddeningly, to Bears fans, the clock was stopped again. According to the yardstick measurement Bull was two feet short; the Bears had to punt. The Giants called time out—they now had only one left—and Green came in to punt.

Dove and McElhenny went deep for the Giants. As if every Bears fan did not have enough dread already, Pyle's snap to Green was high; Green had to jump to catch it but still managed to get the punt off without any difficulty. The kick bounced down at the 30, with Dove and McElhenny not going anywhere near it. Luckily for the Bears the ball took a Chicago bounce and died at the Giants' 17. There was 1:40 remaining in the game, the Giants had a fresh set of downs, and they had one time out remaining. The Bears trotted out with their five defensive back formation. Tittle had to move his team 83 yards in 100 seconds against the best NFL defense in the last two decades.

On first down Tittle threw quickly to Thomas at the 28; he made the catch but the officials debated about the ball's placement. The crowd booed vociferously when the clock was stopped again for a measurement; the Giants were given a first down. Tittle then completed a short pass to McElhenny at the 34, but he could not get out of bounds. The clock kept ticking, so the Giants called their last time out. Tittle threw to McElhenny once more, and this time he was tackled at the 45, on one of the most vicious hits of the day, administered by Fortunato. Fortunato laid on top of him longer than necessary, and the Bears took their sweet time setting up at the line of scrimmage, as the Giants started another fresh set of downs. There was only 47 seconds left; time was becoming more of an enemy for the Giants than field position, the Bears' five defensive backs, or Mother Nature.

Tittle decided to throw long on first down. He was unable to complete the pass to Morrison, and on the play he was belted extremely hard by Atkins. The clock stopped with the incompletion with only 39 seconds left. Tittle next completed a sideline pass to Gifford, in a route that resembled his touchdown in the first quarter, but Gifford was ruled out of bounds when he caught it. Gifford, one of the most clutch receivers of his era, was Tittle's target on the next play as well. He made the catch, took a tremendous hit from McRae but somehow did not go down; Petitbon was right there to finish him off. The Giants were now at the 40-yard line of the Bears with only 17 seconds remaining. They lined up in a makeshift formation, receivers running deep and to the sidelines, and Tittle intentionally threw the ball out of bounds.

That nothing play cost the Giants seven seconds, but it also stopped the clock. Second and 10 at the Bears' 40, 10 seconds left, and the noise in Wrigley Field was enough to split its concrete foundation. The biggest play of the year was coming and both teams knew it. The Bears had three defensive backs—Whitsell, Caroline, and Petitbon—on Shofner's side of the field and two—McRae and Taylor—on Gifford's side. Tittle dropped back as Stroud desperately tried to keep O'Bradovich away from him, while on the other side of the line Brown was fighting a losing battle with Atkins. Tittle threw his last pass of the season toward the left side of the end zone. Four players were near the ball's destination: Caroline, Petitbon, Whitsell, and Tittle's hoped-for target Shofner, who trailed behind the three defenders by three yards. Petitbon positioned himself as though he were making a fair catch, standing two yards deep in the end zone, while Shofner was at the three, not even in the end zone, in no position to do anything. The Bears' fifth interception of the day ended the brutal battle; an exasperated Y.A. Tittle kneeled on the turf 40 yards away, banging his helmet on the frozen turf until it fractured. There were two seconds left as the Bear defenders triumphantly trotted off the field. Wade came in for the most insignificant quarterback sneak of his career as the gun went off. When Petitbon reached the Bears' sideline he bear-hugged assistant coach Phil Handler and lifted him into the air. Everyone surrounded Halas, while his favorite son, Sid Luckman, clad in an overstuffed orange ski jacket, escorted him down to the Bears locker room down the sideline with his arm around him. O'Bradovich acknowledged the roar of the adoring throng by throwing his helmet as far as he could into the stands. Twenty years later the fan who caught it returned it to him.[18]

The partisan Bears crowd went wild, with everyone standing and hailing their champions. The best defense in football proved its superiority over the best offense. On the NBC radio broadcast George Connor interviewed the victors in the Bears' locker room. Connor, a Hall of Fame inductee, was one of the best linemen in team history. He first talked with Doug Atkins. "Larry Morris played a hell of a game, but we decided to give the game ball to George Allen." In the background the microphones picked up the whole team singing, "Hooray for George! Hooray at last! Hooray for George! He's a horse's ass!"[19] The radio producers were not able to blank out the offending noun in time, so it was heard across the country. In his biography Halas claimed the players were singing to him, but in reality he knew better.[20] Allen acknowledged his players; thanked Halas for having confidence in him; and also thanked his defensive line coach, Jumbo Joe Stydahar, another Bears legend. Ed O'Bradovich summed up the defensive unit's feelings about Allen: "George Allen called us 'men.' Men. And call you by your first name and always give you respect. Instead of cussing at you constantly and doing everything to bring you down, his philosophy was just the opposite."[21]

Connor got ahold of Dave Whitsell next, who said, "Tittle had time to do nothing [*sic*] due to our front seven. I saw the interception coming." Whitsell also added that Shofner was the best receiver he ever played against.[22] Petitbon followed up his teammate's comments by calling the game his greatest thrill and saying that the team wanted the game real bad. He also mentioned that he did not feel the cold. "The Giants are the best passing team we faced all year ... our defense has got to be the greatest."[23] Larry Morris, coming to Connor's microphone next, reiterated that this was the greatest thrill of his life. He added that jumping around was part of their defensive plan, Tittle ws a great competitor, and the Bears were lucky to win. Regarding his game-changing interception, Morris added, "I kind of smelled it coming. I'm no halfback. I was scared, I was running out of fright."[24]

Connor followed the Morris interview with one with Wade; Wade thanked Connor for the opportunity. Wade started by saying the Bears used the same game plan they had been using and the defense deserved a world of credit. The cold did not bother his footing (Wade played with Chuck Taylor high-top basketball shoes), but it did bother his hands and was one of the reasons for his fumble in the first quarter. Wade also added that his first two runs were planned, and they worked well, like the Bears thought they would. Offensive line coach Phil Handler said the team never quit, it was always a team effort, and the tougher the game got, the tougher the players got. He also expressed his happiness for Halas, who stood by him 11 months earlier when his name surfaced in the early phase of the NFL's gambling investigation and who valued Handler's services for 10 years. Later on Handler admitted to some real apprehensions about the game. He felt that if Tittle had continue to throw to Gifford the Bears would have lost: "Gifford beat Bennie McRae easily, but Shofner was Tittle's favorite target."[25] Connor finally got Halas up to the mic. The owner/coach called it a great thrill, reminded everyone that the Bears were the number one defensive team, and said the game was a great team effort. He also added that it was a pleasure to bring the championship back to the great city of Chicago. Interestingly, Halas gave no credit to any individual player or his assistants.[26]

When Connor was through with Halas, he sent the radio feed up to Gibbons and Summerall in the broadcast booth. Summerall singled out Whitsell for doing such a great job on Shofner, mispronouncing the Bear cornerback's name in the process. This gaffe was another example of how he was more familiar with the Giants than the Bears throughout the broadcast. He had fond memories of playing with the Giants; his last game with them was two years earlier at the end of the 1961 NFL season. Earlier in the broadcast he singled out Lynch for having the most interceptions in the season—without mentioning Roosevelt Taylor having the same number—and referred to several Giants by their nicknames. Perhaps Summerall still had some hard feelings toward the Bears from his previous bad experiences with them when he played with the Chicago Cardinals.[27]

Over on the first base side of Wrigley Field a morgue-like atmosphere hung over the Giants locker room.[28] As Giants trudged up the open metal staircase from the field they were subjected to merciless hoots, insults and taunts from the rabid Bears fans standing below. Roosevelt Brown had tears streaming down his cheeks, as did Tittle, limping badly up the stairs.[29] McElhenny kept silent with his head down, but offensive tackle Jack Stroud, in a violent pas-de-deux all day with the much younger O'Bradovich, gave it back to the crowd. He turned to face the throng below him, gesturing, as columnist Robert Markus described, "like a wrestler inciting a crowd to synthetic fury."[30]

Tittle talked freely, but in a whisper, to the press from the small cubicle he shared with Gifford and Griffing. Gifford was trembling with tears in his eyes.[31] The cramped, impossible conditions in Wrigley Field's antiquated and inadequate visitors' locker room just made things worse. "Yes, it [the knee] hurt," Tittle explained, "but please don't take this as an alibi. The Bears played a good game. The knee was hurt the first time on the touchdown to Gifford. I got hit just as I threw. Then on the play when I had to go out I got hit from the side just as I threw the ball. The first time didn't hurt too much, but the second time it really hurt. I felt it pop. The Bears are a hell of a team to play when you can't run too well."[32]

He blamed himself for the two interceptions, saying, "I just was not doing a good job acting out the screens." Asked if some of the other brutal hits he sustained meant that the Bears inflicted more than the usual physical punishment, Tittle finished up with "No, they didn't hurt me much. They played a good clean game."[33]

Allie Sherman patiently answered questions for almost an hour, at one point warning the press, "Let's get this straight right off, I am not alibiing. Anyone who says I am is misquoting me. But anybody who says Tittle can't come up for the big games should be ashamed of himself. He's played more big games for me than anyone else in the league because we've been in more big games. I don't know of any other quarterback who would have gone out there in his condition and done the job he did. And the rest of our guys could have broken down between halves after Y.A. got hurt. But they didn't."[34] He also would not use injuries as an excuse: "I can't even discuss the injuries, because it would sound too much like an alibi and I wouldn't want to take anything away from the Bears. We could have had it, but they got it."[35]

Shofner offered his feelings about the difficult, disappointing afternoon as well. He praised Whitsell and Taylor, who were so effective that he did not have one pass reception. "I can't remember when that's happened before."[36] He refused to compare Whitsell to Green Bay's Jesse Whittenton, who covered him in the two championship games for the Packers. "Dave [Whitsell] played a mighty good game today," was all he would say. He also demurred when asked to compare this game to the Giant victory in Wrigley Field 13 months ago: "Anything would have been better," adding when asked about the pass he could not catch in the end zone after Galimore's fumble, "It was a good pass, I just dropped it. It was a miserable attempt."[37] Nobody corrected him that he had not dropped it, that it skipped out of his outstretched hands.

An unidentified Giant begged to differ. "It was not a good pass, but I've seen Del catch a hundred like it because he's a marvel at making tough catches. If he had hauled it in, we would have had a 14–0 lead and we'd have beaten the Bears by 30 points."[38]

After the rough preseason game between the two teams in Ithaca five months earlier, Dr. Sweeney, their team physician, marveled the Giants were remarkably unscathed and free of injuries. The New Yorkers had no such luck in this frigid championship game. Tittle's diagnosis was two torn ligaments in his knee.[39] Linebacker Tom Scott got a broken left forearm. Halfback Phil King's knee and ankle were sprained so badly he never played after the second quarter. Bookie Bolin swallowed his tongue after suffering a severe concussion.[40] Through it all, the hometown favoritism so evident before the game continued even after the result was in. *New York Times* columnist Arthur Daley was still not convinced that the best team won.[41]

The Giants finally vacated the cramped locker room and boarded the bus for O'Hare Airport. The 18 players who flew back to New York City got a pleasant surprise when they de-planed to the greeting of 500 cheering fans at John F. Kennedy Airport, bearing signs that said "Welcome Giants, First in the hearts of New York Fans" and "Y.A. Tittle, Please Come Back for Another Season."[42]

The *Chicago Daily Defender* pointed out that the Bears won the championship because of their thorough pre-game preparations. The Bears scouted the last two Giant games of the season with a cadre of analysts with different duties.[43] Thanks to Jim Dooley, Wade and his offense were comprehensively briefed about the Giants' defensive keys, and George Allen's film studies gave the defense reliable keys throughout the game. While Dooley's and Allen's studiousness all through the season were huge factors in the Bears' success, the *Defender* seemingly overlooked that the Giants lost key players aside from Tittle and that Tittle's injury may have stifled their offense as much as the Bears did.

Chicago, with two major league baseball teams, two NFL teams through 1959, and a third pro football team—the Chicago Rockets/Hornets in the AAFC—for four seasons, had very little in its trophy case in the post-war era up to this point.[44] The Cubs were perennial doormats after losing a seven-game World Series in 1945. The White Sox broke a 40-year dry spell, winning the American League pennant in 1959, only to be disappointingly defeated by the Los Angeles Dodgers. The Cardinals won the NFL title in Comiskey Park in 1947 and lost the NFL championship game in 1948. The Bears got to the NFL championship in 1956 but performed so poorly in Yankee Stadium against the Giants that many chose to forget it. As everyone knew their last championship was in 1946. The Rockets managed a record of 7–32–3 from 1946 to 1948. They changed their name in an effort to change their luck in 1949 and went 4–8.

Lean years, indeed, for Chicago fans. Since the end of the war, five professional teams, over 80 seasons, had appearances in only six championships, only two championship victories, and a 17-year championship drought (ending in 1963). While everyone knew the 1963 Bears were an older bunch, the feeling was the team could easily repeat. Everyone in the city "felt good" about these Bears. How quickly those good feelings disappeared took everyone by surprise.

Afterword

Trouble, Sadness, and Fleeting Success

Sport Magazine was a national publication that awarded a highly coveted Chevrolet Corvette to the most valuable player in the NFL championship game. Three members of the defense—Larry Morris, Bill George, and Fred Williams—made a pact that if any of them won, they would share the car.[1] Earlier in the week Morris' wife took it upon herself to say that it was not fair for defensemen to be ignored so much and not get the recognition they deserve. All that was forgotten when the magazine announced that Morris' brilliant play on defense against the Giants earned him the car. He joked that it would be taken apart and that Williams and George would get key components from the vehicle. Instead, he gave each of them $1,000 and kept it himself.[2] This was the last piece of good news the '63 Bears would get in a good, long while.

The Chicago City Council decided to honor the Bears, and Mayor Richard J. Daley invited them to City Hall for a ceremony. Daley presented a five-foot trophy that he named in honor of the late President Kennedy to Halas and had a certificate of merit and Chicago Medal of Honor for each player and coach.[3] The Armand F. Hand Band—which had been entertaining Bears fans with its mellifluous renditions from its perch near the north end zone of Wrigley Field for years—was there, along with the 60-voice Chicago Fire Department Glee Club. All of Halas' coaches except Luke Johnsos were at the ceremony. While the entire roster was expected, the small fraction that appeared was an embarrassment to Daley and Halas. Rudy Bukich, J.C. Caroline, Billy Martin, Benny McRae, Johnny Morris, and Bill Wade were the only players to attend the ceremony.[4] The rest of the players got their swag in the mail.

Instead of any recognition from the city, the players were eagerly awaiting more materialistic and tangible rewards from Halas himself. Their appetites were whetted by the gifts Lombardi bestowed on his Packers after their championships. In 1961 Packer wives and fiancées got mink coats; unmarried or uncommitted players also got one to give to their mothers. In 1962 each player received a color television console.[5] The Bears players were much more focused on Halas matching Lombardi's championship largesse than on civic recognition.

George Halas rang in the new year at the Happy Patch Farm estate in Lake Forest, Illinois, owned by department store heir Joel Goldblatt. Also at the gathering were his daughter Virginia McCaskey and son-in-law Ed; his son Mugs Halas and his wife Terry; and longtime Halas acquaintance and *Chicago Tribune* publisher Don Maxwell, accompanied by his wife Marj.[6] They enjoyed a quiet festivity mentioned only in the social columns, with no newsworthy developments. It was also quite a contrast to a new year's party many of the players attended 34 miles southwest in Willowbrook, Illinois. Unfortunately, this would be a New Year's Eve that would not be forgotten for a while.

The venue for the players' soiree was Mike Ditka's Willowbrook Lanes, a new bowling establishment in Willowbrook in which Ditka had an ownership stake entitling him an eighth of the net profits.[7] The cost was $25 per couple.[8] At least four players came with their wives: Mike Ditka, Bill George, Joe Marconi; and Bennie McRae. Ed O'Bradovich was there with his fiancée, Arlene Gala, and J.C. Caroline came alone. A *Chicago Sun-Times* reader covered the event for Dick Hackenburg's sports column and noted: "Time—11:45. Place—Ditka's. Atmosphere—swinging. Bill George and his good looking wife sitting at a table talking to Joe Marconi's wife.... J.C. Caroline sings ... great Ed O'Bradovich starts twisting and J.C. outdoes him.... Ditka twists, really great, with his pretty brunet wife. Then Bennie McRae ... the Michigan mash ... undoubtedly the greatest dancer.... Everybody goes wild.... Nobody loaded.... Good time.... Bar closed 1:00 AM.... Real pros, every one."[9] This account was filed at 11:45 p.m., an hour and 15 minutes before the bar closed. The police reports and the front sections of every major Chicago newspaper covered what happened after that.

Two other party attendees were Tony and Nancy Parrilli. Parrilli was a teammate of O'Bradovich's at nearby Proviso High School and also the University of Illinois. His gridiron skills were good enough to earn him the Illini's Most Valuable Player Award in 1961. After Parrilli graduated, he was picked in the 11th round of the 1961 NFL draft by San Francisco, did not make the team, and then tried out with Washington but was cut after injuring his shoulder.[10] After his release from the Redskins he became a member of the Bears' taxi squad.

The gathering lasted well into the night. After 1:00 a.m. on January 1, another patron of the establishment, Raymond Messmaker, felt ill and went to the washroom. He told DuPage state's attorney William J. Bauer that he made an attempt to clean it when he was finished and left. Later he returned to the washroom, and while he was inside, Parrilli came in while Messmaker was still there. Parrilli complained about the condition of the room, Messmaker said. After that "he held me upright and began to pummel me and knock me against the wall. I couldn't fight back. Then someone came in and the fight got worse. I was shoved against the wall. Then someone else came in and I heard someone say, 'He's been shot.'"[11] Joe Marconi came in to break it up, and Marconi mistakenly got hit in the head with a handgun belonging to one of the guards after he had successfully gotten between Parrilli and Messmaker. The guard was holding the gun by the barrel to use it as a club or a blackjack. He swung the gun and hit Marconi in the head with the handle. When this occurred, a single shot went off and hit Parrilli in the forehead, instantly killing him. Marconi's head wound from the blow required eight stitches. The death was ruled an accident. The security guard whose gun went off got probation, and Nancy Parrilli sued for the loss of her husband. Several years later she collected $14,000, about half the wrongful death payment allowed by Illinois law at the time.[12]

Even with all of Halas' clout the story was front page news on January 3.[13] This was not the kind of publicity the team needed, was just the type of episode Halas always dreaded, and was also why he instituted such draconian rules on the players regarding off-field conduct. But by the middle of the month the players were more antsy about a championship gift, salary raises, and testimonials and endorsements. They would learn that more troubles were on the way.

Soon after the championship game Rick Casares, who had to watch the game from the bench in street clothes thanks to the broken ankle he got from Ray Nitschke, plotted his revenge. He told his good friend, the still-suspended Paul Hornung, that he would get even, and Hornung claimed he knew Casares was not kidding.[14] He got his chance at Fuzzy Thurston's Left Guard Restaurant in Appleton, Wisconsin. Thurston was hosting an event and Casares, Hornung, and Nitschke would all be there. Casares told Hornung that all Nitschke had to say was one thing and he would get him. Nitschke walked up to Casares and said, "Hey, Rick, congratulations. I heard you married that rich broad from Tampa." Casares asked Nitschke to repeat himself and then said, "You are a real asshole and I want you to come outside with me because I'm going to teach you a lesson."[15] Hornung knew it would be bad news for Nitschke if they fought, so once everyone was outside he stopped it before it started, while Casares launched a stream of taunts and insults at Nitschke, who simply stood there, soaking up the insults. Casares, according to Hornung, "hurt him as badly with his mouth as he would have with his fists. He humiliated

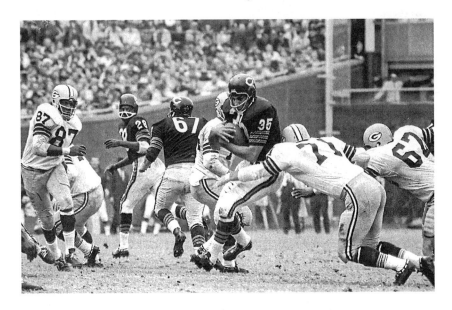

The great fullback Rick Casares, one of the most feared and intimidating players of his time, breaks a tackle attempt by Bill Forrester (71) while Willie Davis (87) rushes in. Willie Galimore (28) and Ted Karras (67) seal off the right side.

Nitschke, who took it without a peep."[16] Hornung later told Nitschke, "What you don't understand is that I saved your life."[17]

As a team captain, Joe Fortunato took it upon himself to poll the team members as to what they wanted as a memento for the championship. The choices he offered were a color television console, a mink coat, or a silver service. If Fortunato ever took the results of his poll to Halas, the consideration fell on deaf ears.[18] Months later every player got a small package in the mail from their owner/coach. Inside was a ring with gold carving of Wrigley Field and a diamond in the middle, personalized on the sides. Players' wives got the top of the ring in the form of a necklace. Unmarried or uncommitted players did not get the necklaces, so fiancées and mothers were shut out. Mike Pyle, single at the time, confronted Mugs Halas about the necklace handouts, and was told, "We don't want to see any of those pendants on any Rush Street floozies or Playboy Bunnies."[19] Many players were not happy about the situation. "It was the worst I've seen," said Doug Atkins, "a lot of them didn't even want to play." Larry Morris added, "He [Halas] was more interested in money than in the players."[20]

Another valuable source of spoils for champions at that time were endorsements and testimonials offered by businesses in the private sector that were eager to have their services or wares identified with successful athletes. To all the Bears' bitter amazement, Halas forbid his players from accepting either after winning the 1963 NFL championship. "You get paid to play football," was the reason he gave.[21] A good number of players ignored him. Ditka and Marconi had been spokesmen for a housing subdivision in the western suburbs. After the championship game Dave Whitsell and Doug Atkins signed national television endorsements for Mennen Speed Stick deodorant in spite of Halas' edict; no discipline came of it. Chet LaRoche, a college friend from Yale of Mike Pyle, arranged for Pyle to do a Chap Stick ad, and Johnny Morris started working for CBS's Chicago TV outlet, WBBM-TV.[22] The fact that Halas brought up the prohibition influenced the decision of many players to avoid making any contacts and missing out on lucrative opportunities.

At the end of January, the NFL announced the playoff payouts and receipts to the public. The league enjoyed a 4 percent growth in attendance, drawing 4,163,643 fans for 98 games, an average of 42,486 paying customers per contest. Cleveland drew the largest attendance, 487,430, an average of 69,632 per game; New York was next, 441,017, an average of 63,002 per game. In spite of their poor showing Philadelphia was third, 418,963, a paid attendance averaging 59,851, while St. Louis did the worst, drawing only 164,823, averaging only 23,546 per game.[23]

The revenue from the championship game was the most profitable in history, with gross receipts of $1,493,954. The Bears' players were extremely generous with their share of the championship pool. They included every member of the organization involved in the field operation of the club, voting 51.5 shares. Halas and quarterback coach Sid Luckman returned their shares to the pool, declining to participate in the split. The result was an award of $5,899 for each individual getting a full share, while the Giants each got $4,218. Members of the Green Bay Packers and Cleveland Browns each got $521 for finishing second, while the Packers received an additional $600 for winning the Runner Up bowl game and the Browns were awarded $400 as the losers of that contest.[24] The owners were tickled beyond pink with this news about the championship game revenue. Halas and Pittsburgh owner Art Rooney mentioned that they were going to church; "Such success just has to be indecent. Imagine $6,000 to one ball player for one game."[25] Yes, Halas thought to himself; just imagine that, and it just happened. His imagination got ahold of him, and it may have cost him his players.

Halas and Rooney's cooing about players making $6,000 for one game was tempered in the court of public opinion after City of Chicago Controller Alvin L. Weber publicized a report regarding Chicago's amusement tax receipts for 1963. By law Chicago collected 3 percent of every pro baseball and pro football ticket sold. Weber extrapolated the amusement tax paid by the White Sox, Cubs, and Bears to disclose what each team's gross revenue from paid attendance was. The Cubs, perennial doormats in base-ball's National League, generated the least, in spite of finishing above .500 for the first time in 17 years and flirting with first place in June. They drew 979,551 fans for a total gate of $1,613,333, averaging about $1.65 per fan in attendance. The Sox, who finished 26 games over .500 but were never in first place after June 28, drew 1,158,848 fans; they provided a much larger sum of $2,504,900, averaging $2.16 per fan, almost 31 percent more than the Cubs. The biggest surprise in Weber's figures, however, concerned the Bears. In their eight home games in Wrigley Field the Bears grossed $1,919,000 from a total attendance of 380,351, $5.05 per fan. The Cubs took in approximately $19,917 per game; the White Sox, $30,924; and the Bears, a whopping $237,500.[26]

Also at this time Pete Rozelle announced that the new NFL television contract for the 1964 season was $28 million, meaning each team would get two million just from the national broadcast rights. Local radio coverage was still taken independently by each team.[27] The days in which Halas had to scamper over to the American National Bank for a bridge loan until his season ticket orders came in were a distant, distant memory with this kind of revenue. He was certainly in a great position to reward his players for their championship season. If only his penurious nature had not gotten in the way.

George Halas spoke to Larry Morris before the season-opening Packer game in Green Bay and promised Morris a salary bump if the Bears won the championship. After Morris had been named Most Valuable Player in the victory over the Giants he went to talk pay with the Papa Bear. Halas reneged on the offer. Incredibly, he said Morris could not get more money, saying, "Well, you know, kid, we should have won it by more."[28] "He was more interested in money than in players," Morris later said.[29]

Ed O'Bradovich's salary issues were even more troubling.[30] O'Bra-dovich, a second-year man, made approximately $11,000 for the 1963 season. After his heroics in the title game he asked Halas for a $5,000 raise. Halas tersely said "no." "What do you mean, 'no'?" O'Bradovich said, reminding Halas that he had intercepted the Tittle pass to set up the winning touchdown. Then, in a comment more stinging that the salary refusal, Halas had the temerity to tell O'Bradovich, "Anybody could've done that." Infuriated, O'Bradovich responded, "Nobody did it but me and that pass led to the winning touchdown. I want my $5,000 raise or get rid of me." Halas responded, "You're not getting the $5,000 and we're not getting rid of you." To rub salt into the wound, and to get in a final word regarding O'Bradovich not showing up, Halas added, "Normally when a player leaves camp, it's $100 a day. But for you, I'll make it $200. Have a nice night, kid."[31]

O'Bradovich, a local boy who grew up so poor his family put water on their breakfast cereal instead of milk, had suffered a broken neck in his youth and still rose to football stardom.[32] He sometimes needed six shots a week to play in the Sunday games.[33] Halas' stance toward him, and all the other players, was unswaying. Perhaps he felt the record playoff award was compensation enough, that somehow the NFL's championship payout let him off the hook. The Packers got mink stoles, color televisions, salary raises fit for champions, unlimited endorsements. The Bears got a ring or a necklace, were forbidden endorsements and testimonials, and had their pay frozen. Halas collected fines for his coffers and whimsically threatened even higher financial penalties for some players. Lombardi's fines levied on players were set financial penalties, and everyone knew fines collected went to the team's end of the year party.[34] Johnny Morris' wife summed it up as follows: "when he didn't reward them, and in fact, treated them with contempt, they collapsed as a team and lost respect for him [Halas]. That team never again was going to play for him."[35]

When training camp opened six months later in Rensselaer things were no better. Mike Pyle pointed out, "There was a feeling that Halas didn't appreciate the championship team coming back. We just didn't feel we were any different from the way we were in the summer of 1963."[36] Tragedy struck in late July. Sunday, July 26, was an off day, and Willie Galimore and Bo Farrington decided to play some golf at a nearby country club, meeting some players for a pizza afterward. They left to return to camp at St. Joseph College at 10:30 in Galimore's Volkswagen. An L-shaped turn, marked with a CURVE sign, was on the route. The sign had been knocked down and not reposted, and when the Volkswagen reached the turn it left the road and rolled. Galimore and Farrington were thrown through the open sunroof and found 60 feet apart from each other. They both had skull fractures and Galimore had a crushed ribcage. Farrington was pronounced dead at the scene and Galimore's death was disclosed at the hospital.[37]

Bears trainer Ed Rozy asked Doug Atkins to come with him to identify the bodies.[38] Bill Wade packed each player's belongings to spare their relatives from the task.[39] "The tragedy haunted us all season," said tackle Bob Wetoska. "We kept looking at last year's game movies and there would be Willie and Bo doing so well and that gives you an awful feeling." Richie Petitbon added a similar perspective: "It was terrible. That killed the whole year. Took a lot out of us."[40] Halas declared that calling their wives was the hardest thing he had ever done.[41] Years later sportswriter Bill Jauss revealed that Halas told him that he paid for the educations of all of their offspring and he did not want any publicity for it.[42]

After defeating the College All-Stars 28–17 on August 7, 1964 proved to be one of the most disappointing seasons in the Bears' history. They opened the season with a loss in Green Bay and proceeded to lose six of their next eight games. By November 8 the Bears were 2–7, tied for last place in their division with San Francisco. They would win three of their last five games but ended the season with a humiliating 41–14 pantsing in snowy Wrigley Field at the hands of the Minnesota Vikings. In a game in which the Bears got only nine first downs, Fran Tarkenton had a near-perfect 130.6 quarterback rating. In some ways this last game was even worse than the humiliation they experienced in week three, when they lost to Baltimore in a record-setting 52–0 debacle; the Vikings held a 31–0 lead at halftime.

The team offered no excuses at the end of the season for their poor showing. Bob Wetoska said the deaths of Galimore and Farrington, along with the team's inability to succeed in third-down situations on both sides of the ball, ruined the year.[43] Dave Whitsell blamed it on a bad start and injuries. Atkins said, "Too many factors were responsible for our showing this year to put your finger on any one."[44] Other players cited injuries, the two deaths, and avoidable mistakes. Halas told the press, "This was the seventh season in 45 years when we have lost more games than we have won. It was hard to take, but no harder than any other losing season."[45]

Of course, a major issue was the apathy some players had toward their owner/coach over the fact that he did not see fit to treat them like champions in the first place. Halas seemed to have forgotten one of Amos Alonzo Stagg's early lessons on being a good coach, that nobody cares what you know, until you know they care. Perhaps his age was to blame. Life expectancy for a man born in 1895 in the United States was approximately 47 years, and he was 68. His "you haven't given me enough" attitude toward the players also extended to his staff, and he was about to lose somebody more valuable to the team than any player was for practically the same reason.

George Allen's wife said that Halas told Allen that he wanted Allen to be the head coach when he retired. The problem was he never gave him a timetable. Allen, distinguishing himself as perhaps the chief architect of the 1963 championship, outdid himself in his role as general-manager-without-title in the 1965 NFL draft. With the signing war between the NFL and the AFL heated past a boil, the NFL scheduled their draft extremely early, on November 28, 1964. Allen picked Dick Butkus, Gale Sayers, tackle Steve DeLong, fullback Jim Nance, Dick Gordon, tackle Frank Cornish, fullback Ralph Kurek, and halfback Brian Piccolo. Everyone except DeLong and Nance signed with the team. Those that did sign made a difference in the 1965 season, when the Bears went 9–5 and challenged Baltimore for the division title. Allen's defense came back to shine as well, and at the end of the season Allen was eager to become a head coach, frustrated that Halas still felt the need to be in charge. He told the Rams he was interested in their head coach opening, and Halas initially granted him permission to talk to them. When Halas learned that Rams owner Dan Reeves was very serious about signing Allen, and that Allen reached out to the Rams, he changed his tune, denying permission to Reeves and accusing the Rams of tampering. At the time Allen was making $19,000 a year with the Bears; the Rams offered him $44,000 per season with a two-year contract, complete control over coaching and personnel, and a training facility for the team in Long Beach, California. Allen signed Reeves' contract on January 4, 1966.[46]

The reality of cold, modern NFL economics had finally hit Halas, and he did not like it. The most important individual in his organization was offered a job with a salary commensurate with other NFL executives, and he was about to lose him. Halas bitterly filed suit against Allen, charging him with breach of contract. Public opinion was very much on Allen's side; NFL protocol was that a team would not stand in an employee's way when an opportunity to improve one's lot in life occurred. The judge said that Halas' contract with Allen was binding, but after the ruling, Halas, not wanting to look any worse than he already did and knowing how selfish and small his actions appeared, told the judge that he wanted to withdraw the case, and he let Allen go.

Halas lost his general manager, personnel guru, and defensive mastermind when Allen departed. Assistant coach Chuck Mather, one of the pioneers in the application of closed-circuit television and IBM computers on the sidelines, also left, dedicating himself exclusively to his off-season insurance business. The Allen-led Rams went 8–6 and the Halas-led Bears, 5–7–2; the Rams beat the Bears in the Coliseum and the Bears beat the Rams in Wrigley Field. In 1967 Allen's Rams finished first in the newly-aligned Coastal Division but lost the playoff game to the Packers, 28–7. Halas' dream of catching Lombardi's legacy was shattered. He would be lost trying to navigate the treacherous waters of the modern NFL without Allen to captain the ship.

Much of the core of the '63 championship team was gone by this time. The Bears lost Atkins and Whitsell in the expansion draft when they were taken by the New Orleans Saints. Atkins signed with the Saints for $50,000, twice as much as Halas ever paid him. Rick Casares was on the Miami Dolphins, and Ted Karras joined his brother Alex in Detroit. Angie Coia now played for Washington, as did defensive tackles Fred Williams and Stan Jones. Maury Youmans was in Dallas, and Larry Morris in Atlanta. With Dick Butkus joining the Bears in 1965, Bill George joined Allen in Los Angeles. Larry Glueck and Billy Martin were out of football.

After a dismal 24–0 loss to the Cleveland Browns on October 22, 1967, a game in which Bear quarterbacks were sacked five times, the offense gained a paltry 20 yards on the ground and amassed an offense of only 136 yards, nationally syndicated columnist Mike Royko, the most respected journalist in Chicago at the time, wrote a stinging diatribe against Halas in *The Chicago Daily News*. He said that Halas was "a tight-fisted, stubborn, mean old man ... there isn't a famous Chicagoan in or out of jail who generates such intense dislike." Royko also added, "George Allen has taken a rabble in L.A. and built it into a possible champion, and since Allen has left, Halas has taken a champion and turned it into a rabble." He also described a meeting he had with Halas after a loss. "He was sitting in his long underwear, on a bench in front of his locker sipping from a pint of whiskey."[47]

Halas finally gave up coaching, naming Jim Dooley head coach, in 1968. He offered the job to Bill Wade, whom he had grown to greatly admire, but Wade reluctantly said no and returned to Nashville, his hometown. Dooley was 7–7 in 1968 but only 13–29 in his three following seasons. During the 1969 NFL draft the Bears were so disorganized that they passed when it was their turn in the first round. Dooley complained that he had no scouts and no personnel organization whatsoever while he coached.[48] When Halas fired him at the end of 1971 he put in another loyalist, Abe Gibron, who coached for three seasons with an 11–30–1 record. It had been nine years since Allen left, nine years without any competent individual performing key functions. After his departure, their record in those nine seasons was 41–79–6. Allen's record over the same nine seasons was 89–32–5. No team in the NFL matched Allen's success between 1966 and 1973; only one NFL team did worse than the Bears during the same stretch, the expansion New Orleans Saints, at 30–77–5 over eight seasons (1967–1974). Players wanted out of Chicago; it had become the Siberia of the NFL and where the bad boys on other teams were threatened with banishment.[49] St. Louis Cardinals center Wayne Mulligan got fed up with how the team was treating him physically and asked for a trade to any team but the Bears. The Cardinals promptly dispatched him to Chicago.[50] The Bears—a proud, historically successful, charter member of the NFL—had become the league's laughingstock.

In September 1974 Halas finally turned over the reins of his organization to a modern, successful NFL executive, hiring Jim Finks away from the Minnesota Vikings to become the Bears' executive vice president and general manager. Finks, a proven expert at evaluating NFL talent, slowly changed the organization's direction and built the foundation for the 1985 Super Bowl champions.

One theory about Halas' self-destructive reluctance to turn his team over to younger, more innovative minds was his obsession with his legacy and how Vince Lombardi threatened it. By the mid–1960s Lombardi was the face of the NFL, and the Bears' championship 1963 season was seen as a brief interruption of Lombardi's supremacy, an interruption not of Halas' doing but Allen's, especially in light of Allen's success after he left the Bears. David Maraniss expands on this idea in his biography of Lombardi: "Halas hated to lose to Lombardi. As soon as Babe Parilli was cut by the Packers in 1959, his first call came from Halas, who was less interested in his quarterbacking abilities than in debriefing him on whatever he had picked up during training camp with Lombardi. In the privacy of his film room in Chicago, Halas was heard more than once snarling, 'Look at that sonofabitch' at the sight of Lombardi stalking the sidelines."[51] It was Lombardi's offense at Yankee Stadium in December 1956 that scored 47 points against Halas' defense. It was Lombardi who got the phone calls from the White House and the Kennedys following his early success in Green Bay. It was Lombardi who in four short years rose to national prominence as the model American executive, earning thousands for each personal appearance. One would think the championship in 1963 might be reason enough for Halas to end his legendary career in a blaze of glory, but it paled in comparison to the Lombardi legend. Blind envy seemed to overcome Halas' rational thinking, and for more than a decade his beloved team would pay the price.

Epilogue
The Price They Paid

The world champion 1963 Chicago Bears, like so many members of their guild in that era, played a big price as the years went by for their football immortality. In early 2013 the members of the team were approached with an offer of a 50th year reunion gala.[1] Eighteen players out of a total roster of 42 were needed to make it happen. Attendees would be paid $3,000 to travel to Chicago, sign memorabilia, and appear at an autograph show. Halfback Ronnie Bull volunteered to help gather his teammates. Only 15 players were healthy enough to commit, so the event never occurred. "It was the most depressing thing I've ever been through," Bull explained.[2]

As of October 2022, 10 players on the 1963 championship team were still alive. Johnny Johnson was 81. Ronnie Bull, Jim Cadile, Mike Ditka, Larry Glueck, and Ed O'Bradovich were 82. Roger Davis and Richie Petitbon were 84, Bob Wetoska 85, and Johnny Morris 87.

DOUG ATKINS died in 2015 at age 85. The middle 12 years of his 17-year career were with the Bears, from 1955 through 1966. Halas left Atkins unprotected in the expansion draft in 1966 and he was taken by the New Orleans Saints, where he had three stellar seasons to end his career. Atkins is number eight in the *Chicago Sun-Times'* "100 Greatest Bears"[3] list and was inducted into the Pro Football Hall of Fame in 1982. Injuries from his NFL career left him with difficulties with his hip, collarbone and toes as well as broken leg, a torn groin muscle, and a torn bicep. He kept up a lifelong friendship with fellow Tennessean Bill Wade after their playing careers were over.[4]

STEVE BARNETT passed away in 2015 at age 85. After playing with the Bears in 1963 he went to the Washington Redskins in 1964, his last year in football. Barnett was a first team All-American at Oregon and also an Academic All-American, and he was voted into the Oregon Sports Hall of Fame in 1980.[5]

Tom Bettis died in 2015 at the age of 82. Bettis' last season as a player was 1963 and he coached in the NFL from 1966 through 1994 for six different franchises: Kansas City, St. Louis, Cleveland, Houston, Philadelphia, and Los Angeles.[6]

Charlie Bivins left the Bears in 1966 and then played for Pittsburgh and Buffalo. Bivins died at 56 in 1994.

Rudy Bukich died in 2016 at the age of 86. Bukich ended his NFL career in 1968, playing for the Bears. He led the NFL in completion percentage in 1964 and passing in 1965. Bukich was enshrined in the USC Hall of Fame and the Pasadena Rose Bowl Hall of Fame after his playing career. He worked in real estate development in Southern California and suffered from Chronic Traumatic Encephalopathy (CTE) before he passed away.[7]

Ronnie Bull played with the Bears through 1970; his last year in the NFL was 1971, with Philadelphia. A two-year All-American at Baylor, he was one of the most reliable running backs in Bears history and deserves a high rank in the "100 Greatest Bears" list. Bull resides in Chicago's western suburbs, has been active in educational administration, and has worked in specialty advertising.[8]

Jim Cadile played with the Bears in 1972 and also with the Honolulu Hawaiians in the World Football League in 1974 and 1975. He resides in Medford, Oregon.[9]

J.C. Caroline died in 2017 at the age of 84. Caroline's distinguished 10-year career with the Bears ended in 1965, when he retired from pro football. Caroline, number 65 on the "100 Greatest Bears" list, was inducted into the College Football Hall of Fame for his stellar career at the University of Illinois. He returned to the campus area after his Bears career, coaching the football team at Urbana High School. Caroline is one of the rare NFL athletes physically unscathed by his career. At age 80 he weighed 205 pounds, 15 pounds less than his playing weight, and had not needed any surgical interventions.[10]

Rick Casares, who died in 2013 at age 82, played for Washington in 1965 and Miami in 1966 after leaving the Bears after the 1964 season. Casares is in the Florida-Georgia Athletic Hall of Fame and the University of Florida Hall of Fame, is on the Honorary Florida All-Century Team and the Tampa (Florida) All-Century Team, and is number 24 in the "One Hundred Greatest Bears" list. He held many Bears rushing records that were eventually broken by Gale Sayers or Walter Payton, and he remains the number-three rusher in Bears history. After his career was over Casares had both knees, an ankle, and a shoulder replaced, as well as surgeries on his wrist and ribs.[11] Casares belongs in Pro Football's Hall of Fame.

ANGELO COIA died in 2013, age 74. Coia joined the Redskins in 1964 and started in the Atlanta Falcons' inaugural game in 1966. Coia was involved in horse racing after his football career and also scouted for the Oakland Raiders. Coia had a longstanding relationship with Raiders owner Al Davis. Davis was Coia's running backs coach at the Citadel, and when he left to coach at USC, Coia went west and joined him.[12]

ROGER DAVIS was the first guard drafted in the first round in Bears history. He was traded to Los Angeles for Jon Arnett, as a result of Willie Galimore's untimely death. He played for the Rams in 1964 and then two more seasons for the New York Giants, ending his NFL career after 1966. Davis worked for Nationwide Insurance in his native Cleveland and is now retired.[13]

MIKE DITKA has been the most recognizable player from the 1963 team for decades. He left the Bears when Halas traded him to Philadelphia for quarterback Jack Concannon and played through 1968 for the Eagles. From 1969 to 1972 he was on the Dallas Cowboys, where he stayed as an assistant coach. Ditka is number nine in the "100 Greatest Bears" list and was inducted into the Pro Football Hall of Fame in 1988. He buried the hatchet with Halas in 1982 and led the Bears to their only Super Bowl victory in 1985. Ditka has been a national spokesman for private corporations, an NFL television analyst, and a restauranteur.

JOHN FARRINGTON died in July 1964, at the age of 28, in an automobile crash in Rensselaer, Indiana.

JOE FORTUNATO, who died in 2017 at the age of 87, spent his entire NFL career with the Bears, retiring after the 1966 season, and then coaching as an assistant with the Bears through 1968. Fortunato was named to the Pro Football Hall of Fame's All Decade Team for the 1950s, is number 25 in the "100 Greatest Bears" list, and was inducted into both the Mississippi State Hall of Fame and the Italian American Hall of Fame. Fortunato was involved in his community and had an ownership stake in the Big Joe Oil Company prior to his passing.[14] Fortunato deserves to be fully enshrined in the Pro Football Hall of Fame.

WILLIE GALIMORE died in 1964 at the age of 29 in an automobile crash in Rensselaer, Indiana. His uniform number, 28, was retired by the Bears, and he is number 47 on the "100 Greatest Bears" list. Galimore's son Ron became an Olympic gymnast. Like his running mate Rick Casares, Galimore belongs in the Pro Football Hall of Fame.

BILL GEORGE died in 1982 at age 52, in an automobile wreck near Rockford, Illinois. George was inducted into the Pro Football Hall of Fame in 1974; like Galimore, his uniform number, 61, has been retired by the Bears. George is number six in the "100 Greatest Bears" list and was working as a manufacturer's representative at the time of his passing.[15]

LARRY GLUECK played with the Bears through 1966 and went into college coaching. He coached at Harvard, Penn, Villanova, and Lehigh before becoming the head coach at Fordham, a position he held for eight years.[16]

BOBBY JOE GREEN died in 1993 at age 57. His last season with the Bears was 1973, later than any of his championship teammates. Green is number 97 on the "100 Greatest Bears" list. He went into advertising and served as the kicking coach for the University of Florida, his alma mater.[17]

BOB JENCKS died in 2010, age 69. He kicked for the Bears through 1964, retiring after the 1965 season when he played for Washington. Jencks got a Ph.D. in geography from Indiana State after his playing days and was a professor at St. Anselm College in New Hampshire.[18]

JOHN JOHNSON played with the Bears through 1968 and ended his career the following season with the New York Giants. The Gary, Indiana, native returned to the Chicago area and has worked in sales management, recruitment, and outplacement.[19]

STAN JONES died in 2010, at the age of 78. He was with the Bears through 1965 and closed out his career the following year in Washington. Jones is number 15 on the "100 Greatest Bears" list and was inducted into the Pro Football Hall of Fame in 1991. After his playing days, Jones coached as an assistant at Denver, Buffalo, Cleveland, and New England.[20]

TED KARRAS died in 2016 at age 81 after suffering from Alzheimer's disease. Karras, one of Bill Wade's favorite bodyguards, played with his brother Alex in Detroit in 1965 and ended his career the following year, joining George Allen in Los Angeles. Karras' football legacy was perhaps unmatched by any Bear in history. His two brothers, Alex and Lou, both played in the NFL as did his son, Ted II. His grandson, Ted III, currently plays for the Cincinnati Bengals.[21]

BOB KILCULLEN died in 2019 at age 83 after having declining health and memory issues. Kilcullen spent his entire career with the Bears, retiring after the 1966 season. He sold real estate in his native Texas and was instrumental in establishing the Dallas Arts Center; Kilcullen himself was skilled painter and sculpturer.[22]

ROGER LECLERC died in 2021 at 84, with neurological issues and memory loss. He was the second-leading scorer in history when he left the Bears in 1966 to play one more season in Denver. Leclerc taught high school math for 39 years after his playing career was over.

HERMAN LEE died in 1991, age 59. Lee ended his 10-year NFL career with the Bears in 1966; in his rookie year Lee was with Pittsburgh.[23]

EARL LEGGETT died in 2008 at age 75. Leggett ended his successful Bears career in 1966, when he joined George Allen in Los Angeles. Leggett joined Atkins and Whitsell in New Orleans for the last two years of his career, which ended in 1968, and coached the Los Angeles Raiders as an assistant. Hall of Famer Howie Long credited Leggett for shaping his career. Leggett's son Brad played with the New Orleans Saints in 1991.[24]

JOE MARCONI died in 1992 at age 58 of a heart attack. Marconi ended his 11-year NFL career with the Bears in 1966, working as an executive in the steel industry until his death.[25]

BILLY MARTIN died in 1976 at the age of 38. He played with the Bears for three years, through the 1964 season.[26]

BENNIE MCRAE died in 2012 at the age of 72. Nine of his 10 years in the NFL were with the Bears; he played for the New York Giants in 1971, his final season. He is number 68 on the "100 Greatest Bears" list. McRae founded the successful McRae Construction Company in Newport News, Virginia, after his playing career was over.[27]

JOHNNY MORRIS played his entire NFL career with the Bears and still holds the team record for career receiving yards. Morris' last year with the team was 1967; he is number 46 on the "100 Greatest Bears" list. After his playing career Morris became a fixture on Chicago-area television with his sports broadcasting.[28]

LARRY MORRIS died at the age of 79 in 2012 after suffering from dementia. Morris played 11 years in the NFL, seven of them for the Bears. He left the Bears after the 1965 season and spent his last year in Atlanta. Morris is number 89 on the "100 Greatest Bears" list and deserves to be ranked much higher. After his playing days Morris was involved in real estate development in his native Georgia. His family donated his brain to Boston University after his death for research on Chronic Traumatic Encephalopathy.[29]

ED O'BRADOVICH spent his entire 10-year career with the Bears, retiring after the 1971 season. He is number 52 on the "100 Greatest Bears" list. After his playing career O'Bradovich became one of the principals of the Bear Oil company and started to cover pro football on his radio shows in this Chicago area. O'Bradovich's candid commentaries with the late Doug Buffone, and currently with fellow Hall of Famer Dan Hampton, are appointment radio spots for all Bears fans.[30]

RICHIE PETITBON spent 10 years of his 14-year career with the Bears. Coveted by George Allen, he finally rejoined Allen in 1969 in Los Angeles. He also played for Los Angeles in 1970 and then followed Allen to the Washington Redskins, finishing his playing career there in 1971 and 1972. Petitbon ranks 42nd on the NFL's all-time interception leader list with 48. He became the defensive coordinator for Washington in 1981, a position he held until 1992, and was their head coach in 1993. The Redskins won three Super Bowls with Petitbon coaching their defense. His 38 interceptions was the best in Bears history for many years, and Petitbon is number 39 on the "100 Greatest Bears" list.[31]

MIKE PYLE died at age 76 in 2015 suffering from neurological issues and dementia. His entire nine-year NFL career was with the Bears, his last year being 1969. Pyle is number 88 on the "100 Greatest Bears" list. After his playing days he worked for a telecommunications company and spent more than 20 years on Chicago radio. Like Ted Karras, Pyle's football lineage runs deep. His brother Palmer Pyle played for Baltimore, Minnesota, and Oakland, and his nephew Eric Kumerow played for Miami. Three of his great-nephews are current NFL players: Jake Kumerow, Jr., in Buffalo, Joey Bosa in Los Angeles for the Chargers, and Nick Bosa in San Francisco.[32]

ROOSEVELT TAYLOR died at age 82 in 2020. Taylor never missed a game in the nine years he played with the Bears, starting in 1961. In mid-season 1969 he was traded to San Francisco, playing there until 1972, when he joined George Allen's Washington Redskins. Taylor is number 37 on the "100 Greatest Bears" list; arguments can be made for this peerless pass defender and diminutive but ferocious tackler being a Hall of Fame. After his playing career Taylor was successfully involved in 17 different businesses in his native New Orleans.[33] His son Brian played for the Bears in 1989 and the Buffalo Bills in 1991.

BILLY WADE died at age 85 in 2016. Wade played for the Bears in the last six of his 13 years in the NFL. Wade led the NFL in passer rating in 1961 and pass completions in 1962, and he was as skilled at running the ball as he was with passing it. His game management and mastery of conservative offensive game planning was instrumental in the 1963 Bears championship. Wade is number 82 on the "100 Greatest Bears" list and deserves a much higher ranking. After his playing career Wade turned down Halas' offer to coach the team, opting instead to return to his native Nashville,

Tennessee, where he was a civic leader and bank executive. Wade was also instrumental in establishing the significance of the Fellowship of Christian Athletes, becoming a positive influence on thousands of young people through his work with that organization. Wade went blind in 2004 and spent his last years suffering from severe dementia. His family donated his brain for CTE research after his death.[34]

BOB WETOSKA spent his entire 10-year NFL career with the Bears, retiring from pro football in 1969. He was one of the most consistent offensive lineman in Bears history and deserves to be on the "100 Greatest Bears" list. Wetoska got involved in a packaging corporation in the Chicago area after his playing days and eventually took over the company.[35]

DAVE WHITSELL died in 1999 at age 63. Whitsell's middle six years of his 12-year NFL career were with the Bears, from 1961 through 1966. Left unprotected in the expansion draft, Whitsell spent his last three years in New Orleans, and much to Halas' chagrin he led the NFL in interceptions in 1967 with 10, winning the UPI "Comeback Player of the Year" award. Whitsell finished his career with a remarkable 46 interceptions, 19 of them in the last three years of his career. He ranks 52nd in the NFL's career interception totals. The cagey cornerback is number 98 on the "100 Greatest Bears" list.[36] After his playing days he owned a trailer park in Louisiana.[37]

FRED WILLIAMS died in 2000 at age 71. A 14-year NFL defensive lineman, Williams was with the Bears for 13 seasons, finishing his career in 1965 with Washington. He is number 67 on the "100 Greatest Bears" list and was involved in liquor sales after his football career.[38]

Chapter Notes

Chapter 1

1. "Investigate Rumors of Pro Scandal," *Chicago Tribune*, January 4, 1963, B1, and "NFL Sifts Scandal Rumors," *Chicago Sun-Times*, January 5, 1963, 64.

2. "Reveal Details of Football Probes," *Chicago Tribune*, January 5, 1963, B1, and "Passed Lie Tests, Says Rick Casares," *Chicago Tribune*, January 6, 1963, B1.

3. "Passed Lie Tests, Says Rick Casares," *Chicago Tribune*, January 6, 1963, B1, and "Senate Probes Pro Grid," *Chicago Sun-Times*, January 6, 1963, 95.

4. Michael E. Lomax, "Detrimental to the League: Gambling and Governance of Professional Football, 1946–1963," *Journal of Sport History* 29, no. 2 (Summer 2002), 291, and Bernard P. Parrish, *They Call It a Game* (Lincoln, NE: Authors Choice Press, 1971), 206.

5. Lomax, 291, and Parrish, 206.

6. Parrish, 206, and Steven A. Riess, *City Games: The Evolution of American Urban Society and the Rise of Sports* (Urbana: University of Illinois Press, 1989), 154.

7. Parrish, 207.

8. Lomax, 294.

9. *Ibid.*

10. Parrish, 207.

11. *Ibid.*, and "One Tough Little Guy," *Sports Illustrated*, February 6, 1967.

12. Lomax, 295, and Parrish, 211–213.

13. Lomax, 296–299.

14. *Ibid.*, and Parrish, 195–196.

15. FBI Document #124-10207-10057 JFK Assassination Probe, "CIP, Gambling, Bahamas," Classified Information May 4, 1963–September 29, 1998, Unclassified September 30, 1998.

16. Parrish, 198.

17. *Ibid.*

18. *Ibid.*, 199–202. There are at least three sworn affidavits presented in Federal Court, Miami, Florida, on September 2, 1960, documenting Rosenbloom betting *for* the opponents of Baltimore Colts—the team he owns—to win.

19. W.C. Heinz, "Boss of the Behemoths," *Saturday Evening Post*, December 3, 1955, 72.

20. Lomax, 291.

21. *Ibid.*, 291–293, and Parrish, 213.

22. Lomax, 292.

23. *Ibid.*

24. *Ibid.*

25. "Undesirable Contacts Provoke a Pro Football Inquiry," *New York Times*, January 5, 1963, 14.

26. Paul Hornung, *Golden Boy: Girls, Games, and Gambling at Green Bay (and Notre Dame, Too)* (New York: Simon & Schuster, 2004), 150–151.

27. "Suspicions About Casares Linger," *Chicago Tribune*, October 25, 1960, and "Bears Lick a Few Wounds," *Chicago Tribune*, October 25, 1960, B1, and Jeff Davis, *Papa Bear: The Life and Legacy of George Halas* (New York: McGraw-Hill, 2005), 342.

28. Davis, 342.

29. "Bears Bench Casares!" *Chicago Tribune*, October 28, 1960, E1.

30. "Undesirable Contacts," *New York Times*, January 5, 1963, 14.

31. "Passed Lie Tests, Says Rick Casares," *Chicago Tribune*, January 6, 1963, B1.

32. *Ibid.*

33. *Ibid.*

34. *Ibid.*, and "Grid Gaming-Probe Figure Fumes," *Chicago Sun-Times*, January 7, 1963, 3.

35. "Passed Lie Tests, Says Rick Casares," *Chicago Tribune*, January 6, 1963, B1.

36. "Reveal Details of Football Probes," *Chicago Tribune*, January 5, 1963, B1.

37. "Off-Field Jobs Add to NFL Woes," *Chicago Sun-Times*, January 8, 1963, 72.

38. "Handler's Outside Job OK, Bear Owner Says," *Chicago Sun-Times*, January 11, 1963, 60.

39. "Reveal Details of Football Probes," *Chicago Tribune*, January 5, 1963, B1.

40. "Grid Gaming-Probe Figure Fumes," *Chicago Sun-Times*, January 7, 1963, 3, and Hornung, 45.

41. "Reveal Details of Football Probes," *Chicago Tribune*, January 5, 1963, B1.

42. *Ibid.*

43. "Grid Gaming-Probe Figure Fumes," *Chicago Sun-Times*, January 7, 1963, 3.

44. "Casares Speaks Out," *Chicago Tribune*, January 7, 1963, C2.

45. "Casares Reveals Two Lie Tests," *Chicago Sun-Times*, January 6, 1963, 89.

46. "Quick, Boy, Bring Halas Biography of Comiskey," *Chicago Daily Defender*, January 7, 1963, 21.

47. Alex Karras, *Even Big Guys Cry* (New York: Signet, 1977), 157–158.

48. David Maraniss, *When Pride Still Mattered: A Life of Vince Lombardi* (New York: Simon & Schuster, 1999), 334–338.

49. *Ibid.*

50. *Ibid.*

51. Parrish, 199.

52. *Ibid.*

53. "Unaware of Probe, 49ers Say," *Chicago Sun-Times*, January 7, 1963, 63.

54. *Ibid.*

55. *Ibid.*

56. "NFL Keeps Steady Vigil on Gamblers," *Chicago Sun-Times*, January 7, 1963, 69.

57. *Ibid.*

58. "Lions Linked with 'Known Hoodlums,'" *Chicago Sun-Times*, January 9, 1963, 60.

59. Karras, 157–158.

60. *Ibid.*, 13.

61. *Ibid.*, 53–55.

62. Alex Karras, https://www.pro-football-reference.com/.

63. Lomax, 301.

64. "Inquiry Widens in Pro Football," *New York Times*, January 8, 1963, 5.

65. "Lions Linked with 'Known Hoodlums,'" *Chicago Sun-Times*, January 9, 1963, 60.

66. Lomax, 302.

67. *Ibid.*

68. "G.S. Halas' Son to Wed Miss Martin," *Chicago Tribune*, January 17, 1963, A14.

69. "Bears Sign Barnett, No. 2 Pick," *Chicago Sun-Times*, January 25, 1963.

70. Michael Oriard, *Brand NFL: The Making and Selling of America's Favorite Sport* (Chapel Hill: University of North Carolina Press, 2007), 12.

71. *Ibid.*

72. Davis, 320.

73. "Rozelle Reports on NFL Probe," *Chicago Tribune*, January 29, 1963, B1.

Chapter 2

1. "McClellan to Continue Probe," *Chicago Sun-Times*, February 3, 1963, 78.

2. Karras, 167–168.

3. "Allen to Head Bear Defense," *Chicago Tribune*, February 13, 1963, B1.

4. *Ibid.*

5. *Ibid.*

6. George Allen, Class of 2002, Pro Football Hall of Fame, https://www.profootballhof.com/players/george-allen/.

7. *Ibid.*

8. Davis, 332.

9. *Ibid.*

10. *Ibid.*, 335.

11. *Ibid.*, 334–335.

12. *Ibid.*, 356.

13. *Ibid.*, 367–370.

14. Cleveland's Paul Brown drafted consecutive ROYs, Jim Brown and Bobby Mitchell, 1957–58; Detroit's GM Andrew Anderson drafted Nick Pietrosante and Gail Cogdill, consecutive ROYs, 1959–60.

15. Michael E. Lomax, "The African-American Experience in Professional Football," *Journal of Social History* 33, no. 1 (Autumn 1999), 165.

16. Davis, 361–362.

17. Mike Ditka, *Ditka: An Autobiography* (Chicago: Bonus Books, 1986), 72–73.

18. James W. Johnson, *The Wow Boys: A Coach, a Team, and a Turning Point in College Football* (Omaha: University of Nebraska Press, 2006), 97.

19. Davis, 135.

20. *Ibid.*

21. Johnson, 135.

22. Davis, 156.

23. *Ibid*, 165.

24. "Shaughnessy Accepts Post with Redskins," *Pittsburgh Post-Gazette*, March 15, 1944, 36.

25. Michael McCambridge, *America's Game: The Epic Story of How Pro Football Captured a Nation* (New York: Random House, 2005), 67.

26. Davis, 279.

27. *Ibid.*, 282.

28. *Ibid.*, 251.

29. *Ibid.*, 326.

30. *Ibid.*, 366–367.

31. *Ibid.*, 364.

32. *Ibid.*, 370.

33. "Bears Sign Stydahar as Defense Aide," *Chicago Tribune*, February 15, 1963, C1, and "Stydahar Rejoins Bears as Coach," *Chicago Sun-Times*, February 15, 1963, 68.

34. "Bears Sign Stydahar as Defense Aide," *Chicago Tribune*, February 15, 1963, C1.

35. Davis, 284.

36. "Bears Sign Stydahar as Defense Aide," *Chicago Tribune*, February 15, 1963, C1.

37. "Evolution of the Pastime Feud," *Chicago Sun-Times*, February 24, 1963, 73.

38. *Ibid.*, and "Has Baseball Really Lost Glamor?" *Chicago Sun-Times*, February 25, 1963, 49.

39. "Still Growing, Says Baseball in Debate Over National Pastime," *Chicago Sun-Times*, February 26, 1963, 72.

40. "Evolution of the Pastime Feud," *Chicago Sun-Times*, February 24, 1963, 73.

41. "14 Million to Majors in '63 Radio-TV Rights," *Chicago Sun-Times*, March 1, 1963, 68.

42. *Ibid.*

43. "Request Retraction of Scandal Story," *Chicago Sun-Times*, March 19, 1963, 70.

44. *Ibid.*

45. "Bryant Says Lie Detector Test Clears Him of Fixing Charges," *Chicago Sun-Times*, March 18, 1963, 60.

46. *Ibid.*

47. Butts and Bryant each sued the Curtis Publishing Company for $10 million. Bryant settled for $300,000, and Butts, whose case went to the Supreme Court, got $460,000. The settlement was a partial factor in the *Post* ceasing publication in 1969.

48. "George Plays First String on Ad Staff," *Chicago Tribune*, March 18, 1963, C6.

49. Lew Freedman, *Clouds Over the Goalpost* (New York: Sports Publishing/Skyhorse, 2013), 159.

50. "George's Bear Future Cloudy," *Chicago Sun-Times*, March 19, 1963, 70.

51. "Taking a Look in the Bears History Book: Bill George," https://www.windycitygridiron.com/2010/8/6/1608011/taking-a-look-in-the-bears-history.

52. George Vass, *George Halas and the Chicago Bears* (Chicago: Henry Regnery, 1971), 188.

53. Ditka, 27.

54. Davis, 314.

55. *Ibid.*, 320.

56. Freedman, 161.

57. Hornung, 101.

58. *Ibid.*, 115–116.

59. "Bears Draw Packers First as '63 Foe," *Chicago Tribune*, March 24, 1963, B3.

60. *Ibid.*

61. "Book Bears, Colts in Grid Twin Bill," *Chicago Sun-Times*, March 31, 1963.

62. "Dooley Signs to Coach Bears' Offensive Ends," *Chicago Tribune*, March 31, 1963, B3.

63. Davis, 149.

64. *Ibid.*, 368.

Chapter 3

1. "They Should Have Known Better," *Chicago Sun-Times*, April 18, 1963, 76.

2. "Guilty Stars Mist Earn NFL's OK," *Chicago Sun-Times*, April 19, 1963, 80.

3. "Resume," *Chicago Tribune*, April 18, 1963, E1.

4. Brad Schultz, *The NFL's Pivotal Years* (Jefferson, NC: McFarland, 2021), 139.

5. "Resume," *Chicago Tribune*, April 18, 1963, E1.

6. "Says Casares," *Chicago Tribune*, April 18, 1963.

7. "Halas Not Surprised," *Chicago Tribune*, April 18, 1963, E1.

8. "Tribune Scoop," *Chicago Tribune*, April 18, 1963, E2.

9. Davis, 74.

10. *Ibid.*, 37.

11. *Ibid.*, 142.

12. *Ibid.*
13. "Bet Habits Key Grid Ban," *Chicago Sun-Times*, April 19, 1963, 67.
14. Hornung, 45.
15. "Hood Many Skar Slain," *Chicago Tribune*, September 11, 1965.
16. Karras, 160, and "The Mafia Organization in the Detroit Area," Exhibit 18, Hearings Before the Permanent Subcommittee on Investigations of the Committee on Government Operations, United States Senate Part 1, 25 September–9 October 1963.
17. Karras, 160–161.
18. *Ibid.*
19. "Resume," *Chicago Tribune*, April 18, 1963, E1.
20. *Ibid.*
21. Thomas Henderson and Peter Knobler, *Out of Control: Confessions of an NFL Casualty* (New York: Pocket Books, 1987), 98.
22. Hornung, 45.
23. "Packers Support, Stand by Hornung," *Chicago Sun-Times*, April 19, 1963, 70.
24. "Vince, Players Shocked, Hurt," *Milwaukee Sentinel*, April 18, 1963, 3.
25. Hornung, 152.
26. Karras, 168–171.
27. "'Not Guilty' Karras Plans to Fight Ban," *Milwaukee Journal*, April 18, 1963, 3.
28. Karras, 174.
29. *Ibid.*, 173–175.
30. "NBC Awarded NFL Title Go for $926,000," *Chicago Sun-Times*, April 26, 1963, 75.
31. "Narcotics Cloud Liscomb Death," *Chicago Sun-Times*, May 11, 1963, 6.
32. "Heroin Caused Lipscomb Death," *Pittsburgh Press*, May 15, 1963, 1.
33. Freedman, 46.
34. *Ibid.*, 47.
35. *Ibid.*, 49–52.
36. "Bears Swap Adams for Rams' Draft Pick," *Chicago Tribune*, May 26, 1963, E3.
37. Emerson High School has produced 10 NFL players; Hobart has produced eight.
38. "Plastic Dome For Sox Park?" *Chicago Sun-Times*, May 17, 1963, 82.
39. *Ibid.*
40. *Ibid.*
41. In the 1940s Cleveland Browns owner Mickey McBride was owned the largest taxicab conglomerate in Ohio.

Players who did not make the Browns roster that the team wanted to hold in "reserve" were put on the payroll of his Zone/Yellow Taxicab Company and referred to as members of the "taxi squad."
42. "NFL Pension Plan OK'd by IRS," *Chicago Sun-Times*, May 24, 1963, 78.
43. www.census.gov, 1963.
44. "NFL Pension Plan OK'd by IRS," *Chicago Sun-Times*, May 24, 1963, 78.
45. "NFL Gets Full-Time Watchdog," *Chicago Sun-Times*, May 23, 1963, 112.
46. "Ex-Policeman Is Hired to Keep Players Out of Trouble," *New York Times*, May 23, 1963, 63.
47. *Ibid.*
48. https://americanfootballdatabase.fandom.com/wiki/1925_nfl_championship_controversy.
49. Ibid.

Chapter 4

1. "Paddy Driscoll Placed in New Post by Bears," *Chicago Tribune*, June 2, 1963, B4.
2. *Ibid.*
3. https://www.baseball-reference.com/players/d/driscpa01.shtml.
4. Davis, 44–45.
5. APFA is the American Professional Football Association, precursor to the NFL.
6. Davis, 68.
7. *Ibid.*, 315.
8. "Bears Give Draft Choice for Steeler Vet Tom Bettis," *Chicago Sun-Times*, June 12, 1963, 85.
9. Few high school conferences were represented in the NFL as much as the Chicago Catholic League. In 1955, the 19th year of the NFL draft, Bettis was the 47th Catholic League alumnus to be drafted into the pros.
10. "Bears Get Bettis from Steelers," *Chicago Tribune*, June 12, 1963, E3.
11. "Halas' Son Will Head Bears," *Chicago Tribune*, June 16, 1963, B1.
12. Davis, 104.
13. "Halas' Son Will Head Bears," *Chicago Tribune*, June 16, 1963, B1.
14. Davis, 459.
15. *Ibid.*
16. *Ibid.*, 147.
17. *Ibid.*

18. "Galimore Ready to Run Again for Bears," *Chicago Tribune*, June 9, 1963, B5.
19. *Ibid.*
20. https://www.cfbhall.com/about/inductees/inductee/willie-galimore-1999/.
21. Since Galimore was selected, 33 players from Florida A&M have been taken in the NFL draft.
22. Freedman, 87.
23. "Bears Sign Taylor," *Chicago Daily Defender*, June 26, 1963, 22, and "Karras, Davis Accept Pacts," *New York Times*, June 30, 1963, 125.
24. Davis, 308.
25. "Fruit of the River," *Chicago Tribune*, January 1, 1964, J32.
26. Richard Whittingham, *We Are the Bears* (Chicago: Triumph Books, 1991), 31.
27. *Ibid.*, 109.
28. *Ibid.*, 28–29.
29. *Ibid.*, 30.
30. *Ibid.*, 224.
31. Davis, 376.
32. Whittingham, 59.
33. "Halas Adopts 'Show Me' Plan at Bears Camp," *Chicago Tribune*, July 21, 1963, B3.
34. *Ibid.*
35. Davis, 381.
36. "Halas Adopts 'Show Me' Plan at Bears Camp," *Chicago Tribune*, July 21, 1963, B 3.
37. "Packers Discuss Bears," *Chicago Tribune*, July 21, 1963, B3.
38. *Ibid.* (all quotes).
39. "Bears Beat Stars on Blocked Kick!" *Chicago Tribune*, July 26, 1963, B1.
40. "Bears Outdo All-Stars 13-12," *Chicago Sun-Times,* July 26, 1963, 70.
41. "Bears Beat Stars on Blocked Kick!" *Chicago Tribune*, July 26, 1963, B1.
42. "Jencks Has Jumbo Frame and Memory," *Chicago Tribune*, June 4, 1963, C 1.

Chapter 5

1. "Slothful Bears Face 2nd Mile Test," *Chicago Sun-Times*, July 31, 1963, 54.
2. "Stars Digest Bears' Game Experiences," *Chicago Tribune*, July 27, 1963, A1.
3. *Ibid.* (all quotes).
4. "All-Stars Topple Green Bay, 20–17," *Chicago Sun-Times*, August 3, 1963, 60.
5. "All-Stars Must Start Fast," *Chicago Sun-Times*, July 31, 1963, 58.
6. "Collegians Shake Packer Dynasty,"

Christian Science Monitor, August 5, 1963, 12.
7. David Maraniss, *When Pride Mattered: A Life of Vince Lombardi* (New York: Simon & Schuster, 2000), 347.
8. *Ibid.*, 347–48.
9. *Ibid.*, 345.
10. "Mental Bet Might Have Fired Pack," *Chicago Sun-Times*, August 4, 1963, 80.
11. "Bears Lose Bettis for Seven Weeks," *Chicago Sun-Times*, August 6, 1963, 69.
12. "Halas Velvet Glove Missing: Gets Tough," *Chicago Tribune*, August 8, 1963, B6.
13. "Bettis Injury Not Severe," *Chicago Tribune*, August 7, 1963, C4.
14. "Sports of the Times, the O'Bradovich Affair," *New York Times*, August 8, 1963, 24.
15. *Ibid.* (all quotes).
16. "Giants Seek to Give Bears an Education," *Chicago Sun-Times*, August 7, 1963, 67.
17. "Bears K O Giants, 17–7 in '63 Opener," *Chicago Tribune*, August 11, 1963, B1.
18. *Ibid.*
19. "Bears' 2nd Half Rally Sends Giants to 17–7 Loss," *New York Times*, August 11, 1963, 45.
20. *Ibid.*
21. *Ibid.*
22. "Sports of the Times," *New York Times*, August 27, 1963, 40.
23. "Bears Rip Giants 17–7, *Chicago Sun-Times*, August 11, 1963, 84.
24. McMichael, 106.
25. "Bears Look Ahead to Redskin Game," *Chicago Sun-Times*, August 13, 1963, 62.
26. Dick Hackenberg column, *Chicago Sun-Times*, August 6, 1963, 70.
27. "Bears Tom Neck Out for Three Weeks," *Chicago Sun-Times*, August 18, 1963, 98.
28. "Willowbrook Head Facing Bribe Charge," *Chicago Tribune*, August 17, 1963, S3.
29. *Ibid.*
30. "Operate on Bears' End Youmans," *Chicago Tribune*, August 16, 1963, B1.
31. "McRae Fits Into Bear Picture," *Chicago Sun-Times*, August 22, 1963, 98.
32. *Ibid.*
33. "Football, Track Standout McRae

Passed Away," *University of Michigan Letter Winners Club,* January 24, 2013.

34. "Bears Battle Packers Tonight, *Chicago Tribune,* August 24, 1963, B1.

35. "Answer Night for Bear Fans," *Chicago Sun-Times,* August 24, 1963, 58.

36. "Brickhouse to Air Baseball and Football," *Chicago Tribune,* August 24, 1963, B4.

37. "Bears Battle Packers," *Chicago Tribune,* August 24, 1963, B1.

38. *Ibid.*

39. *Ibid.*

40. "Casares Vows Never to Stop Running Again," *Chicago Tribune,* August 29, 1963, D7.

41. "Work on Pass Defense," *Chicago Tribune,* August 27, 1963, B4.

42. "Bears' Defensive Line Overhauled by Stydahar," *Chicago Tribune,* August 28, 1963, B1.

43. *Ibid.*

44. "Wade Defends Bear Offense," *Chicago Tribune,* August 29, 1963, C2.

45. *Ibid.*

46. *Ibid.*

47. "Galimore Will Play Saturday," *Chicago Tribune,* August 26, 1963, C1.

48. Davis, 246–249.

49. *Ibid.,* 247.

50. "Ted Collins Dies at 64," *Daytona Beach Morning Journal,* May 28, 1964, 2.

51. "The Unhappiest Millionaire," *Sports Illustrated,* April 4, 1960, 38.

52. Karras, 144–145.

53. "Sox Beat KC 11–4 in Front of 410 Fans," *Chicago Sun-Times,* September 29, 1963, 86.

54. To make matters worse, the Cards played the home-state New York Giants, and the 21,923 in attendance were overwhelmingly Giants aficionados.

55. "The Unhappiest Millionaire," 38.

56. Davis, 246.

57. "Clothes Auction Brings $40,000," *Lawrence* [KS] *Journal-World,* November 21, 1963, 7.

58. "New Breed Restores Old Rivalry," *Chicago Sun-Times,* July 14, 1963, 81.

59. "Lemm Feels Success in Cards," *Chicago Tribune,* August 29, 1963, B3.

60. Don Schiffer, *1962 Pro Football Handbook* (New York: Pocket Books, 1962), 43.

61. Dick Hackenberg column, *Chicago Sun-Times,* August 6, 1963, 78.

62. The historic Edgewater Beach Resort, three miles north of Wrigley Field, was the home of many visiting teams playing the Cubs and Bears until the hotel's demolition in 1967. Halas lived in the Edgewater's Cooperative Apartments until his death.

63. "Cardinal Victory Puts Bears in Solitary," *Chicago Sun-Times,* September 1, 1963, 46.

64. *Ibid.*

65. *Ibid.*

66. "Bears, Cards Reach Final Drill for Battle," *Chicago Tribune,* August 30, 1963, B1.

Chapter 6

1. "Induct 17 in Pro Football Hall of Fame," *Chicago Tribune,* September 1, 1963, B1.

2. *Ibid.*

3. "Say Hey! Who's Gonna Play," *Chicago Sun Tines,* September 5, 1963, 104.

4. "Eagles' Jurgensen and Hill Walk Out," *Chicago Tribune,* September 5, 1963, B1.

5. *Ibid.*

6. "Two Eagles Sign; Rejoin Squad," *Chicago Tribune,* September 6, 1963, B1.

7. *Ibid.*

8. "Bears Plan: Chase Blues in Jazzland," *Chicago Tribune,* September 8, 1963, B1.

9. "Bears Storm to 14–7 Victory," *Chicago Tribune,* September 8, 1963, B3.

10. "News Is Good for Bears, Bad for Halas," *Chicago Tribune,* September 9, 1963, B2.

11. "Bears Trade Art Anderson," *Chicago Tribune,* September 11, 1963, B1.

12. "Pack Preps for Bears with Morning Drills," *Chicago Sun-Times,* September 19, 1963, 74.

13. *Ibid.*

14. "Jeralds Dropped; Bears May Deal," *Chicago Sun-Times,* September 13, 1963, 66.

15. *Ibid.*

16. Maury Youmans, *'63* (Syracuse: Syracuse University Press, 2004), 43.

17. Whittingham, 155.

18. Davis, 384.

19. "Packers Respectful of Bear Ambitions," *Chicago Sun-Times,* September 13, 1963, 66.

20. "Two Games Kick Off NFL Pro Card Tonight," *Chicago Tribune*, September 14, 1963, B2.

21. "Bears Underdogs for NFL Opener," *Chicago Sun-Times*, September 14, 1963, 61.

22. Maraniss, 348.

23. "Bears Jar Packers, 10–3," *Chicago Sun-Times*, September 16, 1963, 76.

24. Hornung, 168

25. Maraniss, 345.

26. *Ibid.*, 348.

27. "It's All Bedlam as Bears Cheer," *Chicago Tribune*, September 16, 1963, B1.

28. Davis, 385.

29. "It's All Bedlam as Bears Cheer," *Chicago Tribune*, September 16, 1963, B1.

30. Davis, 385.

31. "Week of Violence," *New York Times*, September 17, 1963, 58.

32. "Burroughs Suspended for One Game," *Chicago Tribune*, September 17, 1963, B1.

33. "NFL Opening Games Take Heavy Injury Toll," *Chicago Tribune*, September 17, 1963, B1.

34. "Wisconsin Governor Fights Braves' Move," *Chicago Sun-Times*, September 16, 1963, 66.

35. Peter Goldenbock, *Wrigleyville* (New York: St. Martin's Press, 1996), 310.

36. Davis, 385–386.

37. Youmans, 83–84.

38. Brad Schultz, *The NFL's Pivotal Years: Remaking Pro Football, 1957–1962* (Jefferson, NC: McFarland, 2021), 95–97.

39. *Ibid.*

40. "Bears Wary of Minnesota's Kids," *Chicago Sun-Times*, September 19, 1963, 112.

41. "Vikings Coach Hopes Bears on Cloud 9,"*Chicago Tribune*, September 18, 1963,B1.

42. "Mum's the Word for Bears," *Chicago Tribune*, September 19, 1963, E1.

43. "Rough Stuff? Finesse, Says Shocked Halas," *Chicago Tribune*, September 21, 1963, B3.

44. "Halas Glad That's Over!" *Chicago Tribune*, September 23, 1963, B1.

45. *Ibid.*

46. "Williams Hurt," *Chicago Tribune*, September 23, 1963, B2.

47. "Operate on Shoulder of Bears' Williams," *Chicago Tribune*, September 24, 1963, B1.

48. "Bears Add Big Tackle to Squad," *Chicago Sun-Times*, September 26, 1963, 110.

49. "NFL Investigator Queries Conerly," *Chicago Sun-Times*, September 22, 1963, and "NFL Clears Conerly in Check Probe," *Chicago Tribune*, September 25, 1963. B3.

50. "Lions' Coach Predicts 5-Team Race in West," *Chicago Tribune*, September 25, 1963, B1.

51. *Ibid.*

52. "Bears Find Movies Are More Violent," *Chicago Tribune*, September 26, 1963, B1.

53. "Three TD's Off Bears in Four Games," *Chicago Sun-Times*, September 24, 1963, 72.

54. "Bears Enter Lions' Den," *Chicago Sun-Times*, September 29, 1963, 91.

55. "Bears Humble Lions, *Chicago Sun-Times*, September 30, 1963, 72.

56. "McRae's Steal Hurt Us Most— Lions' Coach," *Chicago Sun-Times*, September 30, 1963, 71.

57. "Bears Humble Lions," *Chicago Sun-Times*, September 30, 1963, 72.

Chapter 7

1. "Bears Off to Best Start in 15 Years," *Chicago Tribune*, October 1, 1963, C1.

2. *Ibid.*

3. "Show Us Soon So We Won't Forget," *Chicago Sun-Times*, October 1, 1963, 67.

4. *Ibid.*

5. "Lowe Sidelined," *Chicago Tribune*, October 1, 1963, C3.

6. "Bears Come Home, Future Bright," *Chicago Sun-Times*, October 1, 1963, 67.

7. Stuart Shea, *Wrigley Field: The Unauthorized Biography* (Washington, D.C.: Brassey's, 2004), 157–158.

8. *Ibid.*

9. *Ibid.*, 236.

10. *Ibid.*, 138.

11. Davis, 64.

12. Shea, 235–236.

13. "Chicago Bears vs. Detroit Lions, December 15, 1963 * Wrigley Field," *National Football League Illustrated*, p. 47. A game-day program, formatted identically for all NFL home games.

14. Shea, 241.

15. *Ibid.*, 238.

16. "Pellington in Final Season with

Baltimore," *Reading Eagle*, October 7, 1964, 68.

17. "48,000 to Watch Undefeated Bears Meet Colts Sunday," *Chicago Sun-Times*, October 5, 1963, 57.

18. *Ibid.*

19. From the game film, *1963 Chicago Bears* (Naperville, IL: Rare Sports Films, 2003).

20. "Bears Make It 4 in a Row," *Chicago Tribune*, October 7, 1963, B1.

21. "Buddy Young Calls Colts' HB's Lethargic," *Chicago Daily Defender*, October 10, 1963, 34.

22. "Bears Spin with Help from 'Spare Part' Bukich," *Chicago Tribune*, October 8, 1963, C1.

23. "Defensive Stats Tell Tale of Bears' Rise," *Chicago Tribune*, October 10, 1963, B1.

24. "Ex-Rams Doing All Right," *Christian Science Monitor*, October 10, 1963, 6.

25. "Old Man Halas Wants Last Laugh," *Chicago Sun-Times*, October 11, 1963, 69.

26. *Ibid.*

27. "Bears' Five TD Passes Beat Rams, 52–14," *Chicago Tribune*, October 14, 1963, C1.

28. *Ibid.*

29. "Bears Scoring Passes Jar Rams," *Chicago Tribune*, October 14, 1963, C1.

30. *Ibid.*

31. "Bill Wade Dies," *The Tennessean*, March 10, 2016, 15.

32. Dan Pompei, "Bill Wade Spread Joy," https://theathletic.com/2364998/2021/02/10/chicago-bears-bill-wade-nfl/, February 10, 2021.

33. *Ibid.*

34. *Ibid.*

35. Davis, 355.

36. Youmans, 8.

37. *Ibid.*, 114.

38. Karras, 145.

39. "Lombardi's '63 Packers His Best," *Christian Science Monitor*, October 11, 1963, 9.

40. Schiffer, 102.

41. "Bears Practice in the Rain," *Chicago Sun-Times*, October 16, 1963, 67.

42. "Stagg Feared Purdue; Halas Fears 49ers," *Chicago Daily Defender*, October 15, 1963, 22.

43. "Into 36 Lives, Showers Fall," *Chicago Tribune*, October 16, 1963, D1.

44. "Oh No, 49ers 20, Bears 14,"

Chicago Daily Defender, October 21, 1963, 24.

45. "49ers Shatter Bears' Five Win Streak, 20–14," *Chicago Sun-Times*, October 21, 1963, 76.

46. "Halas Sees Defeat as Bears Stimulant," *Chicago Sun-Times*, October 22, 1963, 76.

47. *Ibid.*

48. "Pack's Starr Suffers Broken Hand," *Chicago Sun-Times*, October 22, 1963, 76.

49. "Lombardi Calls Lemm 'Unstable Man,'" *Chicago Sun-Times*, October 24, 1963, 114.

50. "Bears Hold Private Pep Rally—Sort Of," *Chicago Sun-Times*, October 23, 1963, 84.

51. *Ibid.*

52. "Eagles Sign Ex-Giant Guglielmi," *Chicago Sun-Times*, October 25, 1963, 75.

53. *Ibid.*

54. "Bears Don't Underrate Eagles' Hill," *Chicago Sun-Times*, October 24, 1963, 106.

55. "Bears in a Snarling Mood for Underdog Eagles Here," *Chicago Sun-Times*, October 25, 1963, 66.

56. *Ibid.*

57. "Bears Lousy & Lucky: Ditka," *Chicago Tribune*, October 28, 1963, C2.

58. *Ibid.*

59. "Bears, Packers Stand Alone, *Chicago Sun-Times*, October 29, 1963, 72.

60. "Arrest Eight for Scalping Bears Tickets," *Chicago Tribune*, October 29, 1963, C3.

Chapter 8

1. "Packers Get Bratkowski from Rams as Insurance," *Chicago Tribune*, October 30, 1963, C1.

2. "Green Bay Packers Find That Man Again," *Chicago Daily Defender*, October 29, 1963, A22.

3. "Bears Capture #7, Throttle Colts," *Chicago Sun-Times*, November 4, 1963, 80.

4. "Upset Fears Nag Halas," *Chicago Sun-Times*, November 10, 1963, 99.

5. "Rams Better, Svare Insists," *Chicago Sun-Times*, November 8, 1963, 78.

6. "O'Bradovich Joins Bears," *Chicago Sun-Times*, November 7, 1963, 136.

7. *Ibid.*

8. Davis, 382.

9. *Ibid.*, 388, and Freedman, 138.
10. "Want to See the Big Game?" *Chicago Tribune*, November 13, 1963, C1.
11. *Ibid.*, and Davis, 388.
12. "WGN Special Adds Mills and Holcomb," *Chicago Tribune*, November 16, 1963, B2.
13. "Want to See the Big Game?" *Chicago Tribune*, November 13, 1963, C1.
14. *Ibid.*
15. "Fans Line Up for Bears Tickets," *Chicago Tribune*, November 12, 1963, B1.
16. "Halas Comes to Defense of Offense," *Chicago Tribune*, November 12, 1963, B1.
17. Youmans, 175.
18. *Ibid.*, 87–88.
19. *Ibid.*, 174.
20. Davis, 388.
21. "Bears Keep Their Guard Up," *Chicago Tribune*, November 13, 1963, C1.
22. *Ibid.*
23. "Lombardi Sees Victory Over Bears," *Chicago Tribune*, November 13, 1963, C1.
24. "Packers Close Practices to Public & Press," *Chicago Tribune*, November 14, 1963, D1.
25. "Figures Point Up Packer & Bear Class," *Chicago Tribune*, November 14, 1963, D2.
26. *Ibid.*
27. "Lombardi Gives Roach Shot at Bears," *Chicago Tribune*, November 15, 1963, C1.
28. Youmans, 173.
29. Maraniss, 348–349.
30. *Ibid.*
31. Hornung, 129.
32. Maraniss, 349.
33. Hornung, 129.
34. Maraniss, 349.
35. "It's All Over but the Shouting," *Chicago Tribune*, November 16, 1963, B1.
36. Maraniss, 350.
37. "Halas Writes a Simple Plan for Big Job," *Chicago Tribune*, November 18, 1963, B2.
38. Davis, 389.
39. Maraniss, 350.
40. Davis, 327.
41. "We Can Beat Bears, Says Parker," *Chicago Tribune*, November 20, 1963, B1.
42. "Ball Control Won Says Wade; Vince Glum," *Chicago Sun-Times*, November 18, 1963, 71.
43. Maraniss, 350.
44. *Ibid.*, 350–351.
45. Davis, 389, and Hornung, 167.
46. "Rick Casares Dies," *New York Times*, September 17, 2013, 87.
47. Davis, 371–372.
48. Hornung, 167.
49. Maraniss, 316.
50. Davis, 382.
51. Edward Gruver, *Nitschke* (New York: Taylor Trade, 2002), 37.
52. *Ibid.*, 44.
53. Hornung, 166.
54. *Ibid.*, 91.
55. *Ibid.*, 86.
56. *Ibid.*
57. Hornung, 166–167.
58. "Sid Luckman Wins Court Suit," *New York Times*, November 19, 1963, 67.
59. "Bears Task: Getting Up Again," *Chicago Tribune*, November 22, 1963, C1.
60. *Ibid.*
61. *Ibid.*
62. "Brown's Day of Reckoning Approaches," *Chicago Tribune*, November 21, 1963, F1.
63. Davis, 327.
64. "We Can Beat Bears," *Christian Science Monitor*, November 20, 1963, 37.
65. *Ibid.*
66. "Martin to Take Casares' Spot on Bears Roster," *Chicago Tribune*, November 23, 1963, C1.
67. "Pittsburgh Hides to Set a Bear Trap," *Chicago Sun-Times*, November 21, 1963, C3.
68. *Ibid.*
69. Schultz, 140.
70. *Ibid.*
71. *Ibid.*, 141.
72. Weber was the most dominant high school team in the Chicago area in the early '60 s, winning city championships in 1961 and 1964.
73. "Bear Field Goal Ties Steelers, 17–17," *New York Times*, November 25, 1963, 35.
74. Davis, 392.
75. *Ibid.*
76. "We'll Settle for Tie," *Chicago Tribune*, November 25, 1963, C1 (all quotes).
77. Davis, 393.
78. "Lions Tie Packers," *New York Times*, November 29, 1963, 53.

Chapter 9

1. Wilson, drafted by the Milwaukee Braves as a catcher, is one of the few NFL players in this era who did not go to college, playing football in the U.S. Army instead.
2. "Halas Tells How Fans Help Bears Act," *Chicago Tribune*, November 30, 1963, C1.
3. *Ibid.*
4. "Bears Battle Troublesome Vikings Today," *Chicago Tribune*, December 1, 1963, D1.
5. Youmans, 203.
6. *Ibid.*
7. "Vander Kelen Not Awed," *Chicago Tribune*, December 2, 1963, E1.
8. *Ibid.*
9. Freedman, 213.
10. *Ibid.*, 212.
11. Vander Kelen Not Awed," *Chicago Tribune*, December 2, 1963, E1.
12. *Ibid.*
13. "Bears Veto Transfer of Playoff Site," *Chicago Tribune*, December 4, 1963, C1.
14. *Ibid.*
15. *Ibid.*
16. *Ibid.*
17. "No Orders from Bears Yet," *Chicago Tribune*, December 7, 1963, C1.
18. "Former Illinois NFL Star Woodson Dies," *Chicago Tribune*, February 16, 2014, B3.
19. "Bears Lose Earl Leggett," *Chicago Tribune*, December 8, 1963, D1.
20. "Packers Route Rams, 31–14," *Chicago Tribune*, December 8, 1963, D1.
21. "Packers Cling to Hope," *Chicago Tribune*, December 9, 1963, B1.
22. *Ibid.*
23. *Ibid.*
24. "Packer Vet Tells Why Bears Lead," *Chicago Tribune*, December 11, 1963, C1.
25. *Ibid.*
26. "Bear Fact: They Can't Afford to Lose," *Chicago Tribune*, December 10, 1963, B1.
27. "Bears Move Indoors for Three Vigorous Workouts," *Chicago Tribune*, December 11, 1963, C1.
28. *Ibid.*
29. "Have Edge on Bears, Says Lions Star," *Chicago Tribune*, December 12, 1963, B1.
30. *Ibid.*

31. David Maraniss, *Once in a Great City* (New York: Simon & Schuster, 2015), 297–299.
32. *Ibid.*
33. *Ibid.*
34. *Ibid.*
35. "Bears Received Lift Enclosed in Sorrow," *Chicago Daily Defender*, December 17, 1963, 46.
36. "Lions Hall Still Looking for Morris," *Chicago Tribune*, December 16, 1963, C2.
37. *Ibid.*
38. *Ibid.*
39. *Ibid.*
40. *Ibid.*
41. *Ibid.*
42. Post-game radio interview on WGN Radio, 720 AM Chicago, December 15, 1963.

Chapter 10

1. "Sabbath Ritual Will End Today for Giants' Fans," *New York Times*, December 15, 1963, 83.
2. "Green Bay Packers Find That Man Again," *Chicago Daily Defender*, October 29, 1963, A 22
3. "Everyone Agrees Gifford Held Victory in Palm of Right Hand," *New York Times*, December 16, 1963, 48.
4. "If Only 49ers Made Playoff," *Chicago Tribune*, July 19, 1963, C8.
5. "In the Wake of the News," *Chicago Tribune*, December 17, 1963, C1.
6. *Ibid.*
7. Davis, 387.
8. *Ibid.*, 395.
9. "Open Ticket Sales at 9 Monday," *Chicago Tribune*, December 17, 1963, C1.
10. *Ibid.*
11. "NFL Sets Up Theatre TV for Title Game," *Chicago Tribune*, December 19, 1963, G1.
12. *Ibid.*
13. "Five Bears Selected on All-Pro Team," *Chicago Tribune*, December 18, 1963, C1.
14. "Feature Bout: Atkins-Brown," *New York Times*, December 23, 1963, 42.
15. *Ibid.*
16. "Doug Atkins Highlights," https://youtube.com/results?search_query_=Doug+Atkins, NFL Productions, 2005.

17. "Feature Bout: Atkins-Brown," *New York Times*, December 23, 1963, 42.
18. *Ibid.*
19. McMichael, 110.
20. "Shofner's Christmas Wish: An Eager Defender," *New York Times*, December 23, 1963, 40.
21. *Ibid.*
22. *Ibid.*
23. "Bears in Bowl," *Chicago Tribune*, December 19, 1963, G2.
24. "The Tower Ticker," *Chicago Tribune*, December 19, 1963, B20.
25. "Giants Hear of Bears," *Chicago Tribune*, December 20, 1963, C3.
26. *Ibid.*
27. "Bears' Galimore at Wieboldt's," *Chicago Daily Defender*, December 19, 1963, 34.
28. Official NFL Program, Lions at Bears, December 15, 1963, 40.
29. Official NFL Programs for the Chicago Bears, 1962 and 1963 seasons.
30. Davis, 409–410.
31. "No Cold Relief in Sight," *Chicago Tribune*, December 20, 1963, 1.
32. "Bears Get Ready for NFL Playoff," *Christian Science Monitor*, December 24, 1963, 7.
33. The minimum wage in 1963 was $1.25, and the hay workers received about $3.65 per hour.
34. "Bears Get Ready for NFL Playoff," *Christian Science Monitor*, December 24, 1963, 7.
35. "Few December 29 Seats for Public Sales," *Christian Science Monitor*, December 21, 1963, 11.
36. "Gold Rush On: Title Game Tickets Go Fast," *Chicago Tribune*, December 24, 1963, B1.
37. *Ibid.*
38. "Big Wind Blows in from the East," *Chicago Tribune*, December 21, 1963, B1.
39. "*Ibid.*
40. *Ibid.*
41. "Everybody Happy?" *Chicago Daily Defender*, December 26, 1963, 36.
42. "Giants' Offense Tests Bears' Defense," *Christian Science Monitor*, December 26, 1963, 37.
43. *Ibid.*
44. "Giants Better Look Out for Jones Boy," *Chicago Tribune*, December 23, 1963, B1.
45. *Ibid.*

46. "Shofner, Huff, and Webster of Giants Say They Are in Shape for Title Game," *New York Times*, December 24, 1963, 12.
47. "Santa Halas Gives Bears Gifts: Sleds," *Chicago Tribune*, December 25, 1963, E1.
48. "Bears Try to Shake Off Holiday Mood," *Chicago Tribune*, December 27, 1963, C1.
49. *Ibid.*
50. *Ibid.*
51. "Santa Halas Gives Bears Gifts: Sleds," *Chicago Tribune*, December 25, 1963, E1.
52. *Ibid.*
53. "Sherman Names Thomas to Start," *New York Times*, December 28, 1963, 8.
54. *Ibid.*
55. *Ibid.*
56. "Bears Hold Private Drill in Lakefront," *Chicago Tribune*, December 28, 1963, B1.
57. *Ibid.*
58. *Ibid.*
59. "Giants and Bears in Money Game," *New York Times*, December 28, 1963, 18.
60. *Ibid.*
61. "Dry Field Likely," *New York Times*, December 29, 1963, 36.
62. "Giants Find Footing Okay for Cleats," *Chicago Tribune*, December 29, 1963, B1.
63. "Bears Battle Giants for Title Today," *Chicago Tribune*, December 29, 1963.
64. Davis, 395–396.

Chapter 11

1. "Dry Field Likely," *New York Times*, December 28, 1963, 38.
2. "Bears Battle Giants for Title Today," *Chicago Tribune*, December 29, 1963, B1.
3. *Ibid.*
4. "Profile of a Pro," *Chicago Tribune*, December 27, 1963, C1.
5. No hot water was mentioned by Frank Gifford, October 23, 1972, during an ABC-TV *Monday Night Football* broadcast, and repeated by Gifford, October 15, 2005, at the Rosemont Horizon Sports Card Show in Rosemont, Illinois.
6. Y.A. Tittle, *Nothing Comes Easy* (Chicago: Triumph Books, 2009), 184.

7. "Sports of the Times," *New York Times*, December 29, 1963, 110.

8. Play by play description taken from the Miley Collection's compact disc recording of the national NBC-Radio broadcast of the game, announced by Jim Gibbons and Pat Summerall.

9. Davis, 397.

10. Tittle, 196.

11. *Ibid.*

12. Davis, 397–398.

13. "Frustration Grips Giants," *Chicago Tribune*, December 30, 1963, B1.

14. From the official NFL Films narration of the game.

15. Tittle, 197.

16. Davis, 398.

17. *Ibid.*, 399.

18. *Ibid.*

19. "Sports of the Times," *New York Times*, December 31, 1963, 14.

20. Davis, 400.

21. *Ibid.*

22. *Ibid.*

23. "Chicago Interceptors Studied Game Film," *Christian Science Monitor*, December 31, 1963, 10.

24. *Ibid.*

25. *Ibid.*

26. Davis, 399.

27. Summerall played for the Chicago Cardinals from 1953 to 1957, and many Bear-Cardinal games were particularly brutal and intense. See Joe Ziemba, *Bears vs. Cardinals: The NFL's Oldest Rivalry* (Jefferson, NC: McFarland, 2022) for a comprehensive description of the rivalry and ill will.

28. "Frustration Grips Giants," *Chicago Tribune*, December 30, 1963, B2.

29. *Ibid.*

30. *Ibid.*

31. Tittle, 197.

32. *Ibid.*

33. *Ibid.*

34. *Ibid.*

35. "Sports of the Times," *New York Times*, December 31, 1963, 14.

36. "Frustration Grips Giants," *Chicago Tribune*, December 30, 1963, B2.

37. *Ibid.*

38. "Sports of the Times," *New York Times,* December 31,1963, 14.

39. "Tittle Out of Pro Bowl," *Chicago Tribune*, January 1, 1964, B1.

40. "Sports of the Times," *New York Times*, December 31, 1963, 14.

41. *Ibid.*

42. "Giants Welcomed Home," *Chicago Tribune*, December 30, 1963, B4.

43. "Bears Had Every Play of Giants Down Pat," *Chicago Daily Defender*, December 31, 1963, 21.

44. See Charles Billington, *Wrigley Field's Last World Series* (Chicago: Lake Claremont Press, 2005), and also Charles Billington, *Comiskey Park's Last World Series* (Jefferson, NC: McFarland, 2019), for a detailed history of Chicago's post-war professional sports history.

Afterword

1. Freedman, 295.

2. *Ibid.*

3. "Saluted by City Council," *Chicago Tribune*, December 31, 1963, B1.

4. *Ibid.*

5. Color television consoles were luxury items until the late 1960s and cost over $400, when the minimum wage in 1963 was $1.25.

6. Kup's column, *Chicago Sun-Times*, December 31, 1963, 24.

7. Davis, 404.

8. "Story of Grid Star's Killing Corroborated," *Chicago Tribune*, January 4, 1964, 6.

9. "Two Guns Affected the Illini Scene," *Chicago Sun-Times*, January 3, 1964, 65.

10. "Tells of Brawl with Parrilli," *Chicago Tribune*, January 3, 1964, 1.

11. *Ibid.*

12. Davis, 405–407.

13. "Tells of Brawl with Parrilli," *Chicago Tribune*, January 3, 1964, 1.

14. Hornung, 158–159.

15. *Ibid.*, 166–167.

16. *Ibid.*

17. *Ibid.*

18. Davis, 406–407.

19. *Ibid.*, 408.

20. *Ibid.*, 407.

21. *Ibid.*, 410.

22. *Ibid.*

23. "Bears Set Generosity Mark," *Chicago Tribune*, January 29, 1964, B1.

24. *Ibid.*

25. *Ibid.*

26. "Bears Gross $1.9 Mil for Season," *Chicago Tribune*, January 22, 1964, B1.
27. "Bears Set Generosity Mark," *Chicago Tribune*, January 29, 1964, B1.
28. "Championship Did Not Bring Riches," *Chicago Tribune*, September 3, 2013, B1.
29. Davis, 407.
30. McMichael, 131–132.
31. *Ibid.*
32. Dan Pompei, "I Don't Tiptoe Through the Tulips," *The Athletic*, October 23, 2019, https://theathletic.com/1308630/2019/10/23/i-dont-tiptoe-through-the-tulips-bears-legend-ed-obradovich-doesnt-yell-he-speaks-from-the-heart/.
33. Youmans, 239.
34. Maraniss, *When Pride Still Mattered*, 378.
35. Davis, 408.
36. *Ibid.*, 410.
37. Freedman, 300–301.
38. Davis, 412.
39. Freedman, 300–301.
40. *Ibid* (both quotes).
41. *Ibid.*
42. Davis, 412.
43. "After the Fall, Bears Tell Why," *Chicago Tribune*, December 14, 1964, C1.
44. *Ibid.*
45. *Ibid.*
46. *Ibid.*, 429.
47. "Mike Royko," *Chicago Daily News*, October 3, 1967, 3. The whiskey description was a bit of hyperbole. Trainer Ed Rozy, a Halas confidant since 1948, used to pour some whiskey into a Coca-Cola bottle for Halas at halftime. The players distrusted Rozy and considered him one of Halas' spies.
48. Davis, 444.
49. "Presidential Pardon for Abe Gibron?" *Chicago Tribune*, September 12, 1974, B3.
50. "Mulligan in a Stew About Being Sent to Bears," *St. Louis Post Dispatch*, August 23, 1974.
51. Maraniss, *When Pride Still Mattered*, 298.

Epilogue

1. "Chicago's Overlooked Champions," *Chicago Tribune*, September 3, 2013, B1.
2. *Ibid.*
3. "Bears100: A Celebration & Look Ahead," *Chicago Sun-Times*, September 1, 2019, Sunday edition magazine insert. All mentions of "100 Greatest Bears" are from this reference.
4. "Atkins a Study in Pride and Pain," *Chicago Sun-Times*, January 2, 2007, 68.
5. https://oregonsportshall.org/time line/steve-barnett-football/.
6. "Former Packers' #1 Pick Tom Bettis Passes Away at 82," NBCSports.com, December 19, 2016.
7. "EX USC QB Rudy Bukich Dies," USC Trojans Athletics, March 1, 2016, https://usctrojans.com/news/2016/3/1/Ex_USC_Quarterback_Rudy_Bukich_1953_Rose_Bowl_MVP_Dies.
8. "1963 Bears Where Are They Now," *Chicago Tribune*, September 3, 2013, B1.
9. *Ibid.*
10. https://sportingchancepress.com/j-c-caroline.
11. "Casares Ought to Count for More," *Chicago Sun-Times*, September 18, 2013, and "1963 Bears Where Are They Now."
12. "Angelo Coia Dies, Ex-NFL Player and Philadelphia High School Star," *The Philadelpia Inquirer*, January 4, 2013.
13. "1963 Bears Where Are They Now."
14. *Ibid.*
15. "Bill George, Bears Linebacker," *New York Times*, October 1, 1982, 47.
16. "1963 Bears Where Are They Now."
17. *Ibid.*
18. "William R. Jencks," *New Hampshire Union Leader*, September 8, 2010, 14.
19. "1963 Bears Where Are They Now."
20. "Stan Jones, 78, Lineman for Bears In '50s & '60s," *New York Times*, May 24, 2010, 46.
21. "Chicago's Forgotten Champions," *Chicago Tribune*, September 1, 2013, Section 3.
22. "Robert Kilcullen," *Dallas Morning News*, August 24, 2019.
23. "Roger Leclerc, Who Kicked for Bears Title Team in 1963, Dies," *Chicago Sun-Times*, December 2, 2021, 57
24. "Earl Leggett Remembered as Life-Changer," *Vicksburg Post*, May 20, 2008.
25. "Joe Marconi, Football Player," *New York Times*, August 25, 1992.
26. "1963 Bears Where Are They Now."
27. "Football, Track Stand Out Bennie

McRae Passed Away," University of Michigan Letter Winners M Club, December 4, 2013.
28. "1963 Bears Where Are They Now."
29. https://Wikipedia.orgwiki/larry_morris.
30. "1963 Bears Where Are They Now."
31. *Ibid.*
32. Mike Pyle Dies At 76," *New York Times,* July 31, 2015, 46.

33. "1963 Bears Where Are They Now."
34. *Ibid.*
35. Ex-Bear Wetoska Still Does His Job Quietly, *Chicago Tribune,* August 9, 1994.
36. Muskegan Area Sports Hall of Fame, https://www.mashf.com/1989 inductees.htm/whitsell.
37. "1963 Bears Where Are They Now."
38. Arkansas Sports Hall of Fame, Class of 1978, "Fred Williams."

Bibliography

Books

Berkow, Ira. *Giants Among Men*. Chicago: Triumph, 2015.

Billington, Charles N. *Comiskey Park's Last World Series*. Jefferson, NC: McFarland, 2019.

Billington, Charles N. *Wrigley Field's Last World Series*. Chicago: Lake Claremont Press, 2005.

Davis, Jeff. *Papa Bear: The Life and Legacy of George Halas*. New York: McGraw-Hill, 2005.

Ditka, Mike. *Ditka: An Autobiography*. Chicago: Bonus Books, 1986.

Freedman, Lew. *Clouds Over the Goalpost*. New York: Sports Publishing/Skyhorse, 2013.

Goldenbock, Peter. *Wrigleyville*. New York: St. Martin's, 1996.

Gruver, Edward. *Nitschke*. New York: Taylor Trade, 2002.

Henderson, Thomas, and Peter Knobler. *Out of Control: Confessions of an NFL Casualty*. New York: Pocket Books, 1987.

Hornung, Paul. *Golden Boy: Girls, Games and Gambling at Green Bay (and Notre Dame)*. New York: Simon & Schuster, 2004.

Johnson, James W. *The Wow Boys: A Coach, a Team, and a Turning Point in College Football*. Lincoln: University of Nebraska Press, 2006.

Karras, Alex. *Even Big Guys Cry*. New York: Signet, 1977.

Maraniss, David. *Once in a Great City*. New York: Simon & Schuster, 2015.

Maraniss, David. *When Pride Still Mattered: A Life of Vince Lombardi*. New York: Simon & Schuster, 1999.

McCambridge, Michael. *America's Game: The Epic Story of How Pro Football Captured a Nation*. New York: Random House, 2005.

McMichael, Steve. *Amazing Tales from the Chicago Bears Sideline*. Chicago: Sports Publishing, 2017.

Oriard, Michael. *Brand NFL: The Making and Selling of America's Favorite Sport*. Chapel Hill: University of North Carolina Press, 2005

Parrish, Bernard P. *They Call It a Game*. Lincoln, NE: Authors Choice Press, 1971.

Riess, Steven A. *City Games: The Evolution of American Urban Society and the Rise of Sports*. Urbana: University of Illinois Press, 1989.

Rollow, Cooper. *Cooper Rollow's Bears Football Book*. Ottawa, IL: Jameson Books, 1977.

Schiffer, Don. *1962 Pro Football Handbook*. New York: Pocket Books, 1962.

Schultz, Brad. *The NFL's Pivotal Years*. Jefferson, NC: McFarland, 2021.

Shea, Stuart. *Wrigley Field: The Unauthorized Biography*. Washington, D.C.: Brassey's, 2004.

Tittle, Y.A. *Nothing Comes Easy*. Chicago: Triumph, 2009.

Vass, George. *George Halas and the Chicago Bears*. Chicago: Henry Regnery, 1971.

Whittingham, Richard. *We Are the Bears*. Chicago: Triumph, 1991.

Youmans, Maury. *'63: A Great NFL Team Time Has Forgotten*. Syracuse: Syracuse University Press, 2004.

Periodicals

"Boss of the Behemoths." *Saturday Evening Post*, December 3, 1955.
"Chicago Bears vs. Detroit Lions, December 15, 1963." *National Football League Illustrated*, Official NFL game-day program.
"Football, Track Standout McRae Passed Away." *University of Michigan letter Winners Club*, January 24, 2013.
Lomax, Michael E. "The African-American Experience in Professional Football." *Journal of Social History* 33, no. 1 (Autumn 1999).
_____. "'Detrimental to the League': Gambling and Governance of Professional Football, 1946–1963." *Journal of Sports History* 29, no. 2 (Summer 2002).
"One Tough Little Guy." *Sports Illustrated*, February 6, 1967.
"The Unhappiest Millionaire." *Sports Illustrated*, April 4, 1960, 38.

Websites

https://americanfootballdatabase.fandom.com1925_NFL_Chapionship_controversy.
https://ashof.com/class-of-1978-fred-williams (Arkansas Sports Hall of Fame).
https://basball-reference.com.
https://CollegeFootballHallofFame.com.
https://NBCSports.com.
https://oregonsportshalloffame.org/timeline/steve-barnett-football.
https://sportingchancepress.com/j-c-caroline.
https://theathletic.com./2364998/2021/02/10/chicago-bears-bill-wade-nfl/.
https://theathletic.com.1308630/2019/10/23/bears-legend-ed-o'bradovich-doesn't-yell-he-speaks.
https://Wikipedia.orgwiki/larry_morris.
https://www.mashf.com/1989inductees.htm/whitsell (Muskegon Area Sports Hall of Fame).
https://www.nfl.com.
https://www.profootball-reference.com.
www.census.gov.
www.profootballhof.com.

Newspapers

Chicago Daily Defender
Chicago Sun-Times
Chicago Tribune
Christian Science Monitor
Dallas Morning News
Daytona Beach Morning Journal
Lawrence [KS] Journal-World
Milwaukee Journal
Milwaukee Sentinel
New Hampshire Union Leader
New York Times
Philadelphia Inquirer
Pittsburgh Post-Gazette
Reading [PA] Eagle
Vicksburg [MI] Post

Other

Audio Compact Disc. *11963 NFL Title Game: Giants vs. Bears*. The Miley Collection.
Audiotape. WGN 720 AM Radio broadcast of December 15, 1963, 3:30 PM, CST.

FBI Document #124-10207-10057. JFK Assassination Probe. "CIP, Gambling, Bahamas." Unclassified by the U.S. Federal Government, September 1998.

"The Mafia Organization in the Detroit Area." Exhibit 18, *Hearings Before the Permanent Subcommittee on Investigations of the Committee on Government Operations*. United States Senate. Part 1, 25 September–9 October 1963.

1963 Chicago Bears Season. DVD recording. Naperville, IL: Rare Sports Films, 2003.

Index